Belabored

Thea Williams

ISBN-13: 9798325000812

Cover design by: Art Painter

Library of Congress Control Number: 2018675309

Printed in the United States of America

To my blind friend, Tina, who has more vision than most sighted people I know.

Contents

Introduction

"And you know that you fight for the lost causes harder than for any other. Yes, you even die for them." – Mr. Smith Goes to Washington. Directed by Frank Capra. By Lewis R. Foster. Screenplay by Sidney Buchman. Columbia Pictures, 1939. VHS.

Many believe the goal of reversing the runaway train of abortion in this country is a lost cause. Perhaps it is, but I want to do my part to shed light on how the institutionalization of this practice has affected the generations of children who have been raised in the post-Roe v. Wade culture.

As both the pro-life and pro-choice camps scramble to make their voices heard in the wake of the Supreme Court's 2022 decision returning abortion laws to the states (Dobbs v. Jackson Women's Health Organization), it is more important than ever that books like *Belabored* contribute to public discourse. This novel does not attempt to answer any and every question about what our society calls a woman's right to choose; rather, the story invites thoughtful readers to question the values they may have osmosed over the past 50 years since Roe v. Wade was enacted. My main goal is to show the confusion that occurs when young minds, having grown up in a pro-choice culture with ever-widening abortion parameters, face an unexpected pregnancy. Secondarily, I highlight the ambivalence that even pro-life women may experience when confronted with an unwanted or difficult pregnancy.

I also want to draw attention to crisis pregnancy centers, which provide resources and referrals to parents who are not prepared to raise a child. There are between 2,500 and 4,000 underfunded and unsung pregnancy centers across our country, many of which have come under violent attack since the majority opinion in the Dobbs case was leaked (the aforementioned attacks have largely gone unprosecuted). In *Belabored*, the main character's mother runs a fictitious pregnancy center (and is herself a former client); through this story line, the book demonstrates the compassionate care and respect these vital organizations give to both unborn children and their parents.

Finally, *Belabored* explores two options that people confronting undesired pregnancy often consider: adoption and abortion. The current adoption process in the United States is often staggeringly expensive and typically supports the rights of biological parents much more than those of prospective adopters. I believe our society should make this a fairer and more affordable option for average Americans. I also feel compelled to offer support and help to individuals who chose to abort pregnancies. Many experience intense remorse after this decision, so I want to shed light on groups and ministries that offer hope and healing to those struggling with guilt in the aftermath of abortion.

I invite my audience into the lives of Tanya, an unwed teen, and Emma, an overwhelmed mother of two, both of whom find themselves unexpectedly pregnant. Quite simply, these characters must decide whether to accept or reject the child within. My prayer is that readers will become engrossed in the worlds of these women and, more broadly, find themselves viewing pre-born life through the humane lens of the Creator who fashioned it in the first place.

Prologue

"Love is a fruit in season at all times, and within reach of every hand."– *Mother Teresa*

I sit frozen on a hard chair while I wait for my visitor. My eyes are practically swollen shut from the barrels of tears I've cried over the past few – what? Hours? Days? Months? I don't even know what day it is, let alone how long this has been going on. My chest and belly ache from racking sobs. Though my stomach's empty, I fight against perpetual nausea. It even hurts when I go to the bathroom. I wonder if this is the start of a UTI. He comes in. His dark, wavy hair is tamed back in its usual unfashionable way. My grief fog lifts for a minute, and I think for the thousandth time how someone needs to take him aside and bring him up to date on current trends. He's gained weight since I last saw him. His head looks precarious, topping off that pear-shaped build, like somehow it might just topple off those skinny shoulders and land on the floor next to those gargantuan, smelly feet of his. His clothes, as always, reflect a tight budget and even narrower fashion sense. At times, I've been embarrassed by his lack of style. Yet today he carries with him a strong presence that somehow, I never noticed before.

He sits down across from me and leans forward. I don't look at him, but instead keep my eyes on the paint-chipped floor. Slowly, he raises my face and offers me his handkerchief. *Who carries a handkerchief these days?* I find myself thinking ironically, followed by, *What am I, crazy? Who worries about nonsense like that at a time like this?*

4

"How ya doin'?" he asks.

"What do you want?" I choke out.

I pick at a piece of loose skin around what used to be one of my fingernails. It's gnawed and swollen and starts to bleed. I hear Mom's voice in my head.

Oh, Tanya, honey, you've bitten it down to the quick again! Oh, Sweetheart, you have such pretty hands, if only you wouldn't bite your poor little nails!

Without thinking, I wrap his clean, white hankie around my bleeding finger. I wonder if he'll recoil or say something cute like, "Just keep it." But if he noticed, he doesn't let on.

"I came to talk to you," he replies softly.

I sneer, "There's nothing to talk about. My life's ruined."

His voice doesn't waver as he responds, "Oh, no. Your life's just beginning. And I still want to be a part of it."

"Yeah, right!" I smirk. "Well, that's not funny. That's, like, totally lame!"

"Tanya, don't you get it? I know what you've done, and I still want you in my life."

He pauses, then adds, "Whaddaya say?"

Chapter 1 Tanya

"It's not time to worry yet." – Atticus Finch in Harper Lee's <u>To Kill a Mockingbird</u>

"Tanya, Honey, are you sure you need more potatoes?" Mom asks with emphasis on "more" and an eye on my protruding gut.

Since I loathe being reminded about my weight, I answer with a resounding, "No, I probably don't need more, but I did want more, and thanks for embarrassing me in front of the whole family."

With that, I haul myself up from the table and stomp out of the room, ignoring her apologies and pleas for me to stay. I thump up the stairs into my room and slam the door. I flounce onto my bed and swing my size 10 feet onto the comforter, taking great pleasure in not removing my shoes because that would annoy Mom.

I refuse to let tears come.

My shirt is high-waisted and when I lie on my back, I can see how flabby my stomach is. It literally ripples like grape jelly. We read an article in my ecology class about how whale blubber can be boiled down to make oil. I don't know about whale blubber, but I bet my belly fat could power a whole village for about six months. Mom's advice about the potatoes has brought all that up, so I do what I always do when I get to feeling awful about my body – I mentally compare myself to some of the massive girls I go to school with. Lucy Draper must weigh 250 pounds and carries herself like an orangutan. Somehow it makes me feel better to envision her in the dress she wore last year to the junior prom – a flowery nightmare that accentuated every bulge.

"Tanya!" Mom's apologetic voice interrupts my mental image of Lucy swinging her tree trunk arms over the dance floor.

I start to respond, then remember how much it bugs her when I play deaf.

"Tanya, please answer me!" she begs, her footsteps getting closer to my door.

Why should I make things easy on her, when she causes a lot of my appearance problems to begin with? She's always trying to save money by taking me to the thrift shop. What 17-year-old girl in 2017 America wants to shop in secondhand stores? I have a hard time finding clothes that look right anyway because my scrawny shoulders are out of proportion to my mega-hips.

Mom loves to tell the story of how my Aunt Fran almost died having my cousin, Sam, because her hips are narrower than the gate Christians are supposed to aim for if we want to make it to heaven. That'll definitely never be said of my hips! When I see myself in the mirror, my body looks like a lightbulb (the old-fashioned kind my stepfather hoards, not those corkscrew shaped deals). I'm only about 30 pounds overweight according to the doctor, but the BMI charts the gym teachers keep shoving at us every year say I'm obese. *Obese!* It's a little disheartening when you're not even out of your teens and the powers that be declare you a whale just because you're too short for your weight.

Mom tries the knob on my bedroom door. I smile, thinking of her irritation when she jiggles it without success.

"Alright, Tanya, that's enough. Please open the door!"

Jess screams from the kitchen, "Mommy, do I hafta eat my peas?"

Mom thinks she's good at multitasking, but she gets distracted easily. Even though David answers my sister's whining with, "It's OK, Hon, I'll take care of her," Mom can't leave it alone.

"Yes, Jessica, you have to eat two spoonfuls, just like always! You know the rule!" she bellows, instead of letting David handle it.

She lowers her voice but continues speaking frantically through the door.

"Tanya, I don't wanna play this game with you. I know you can hear me, and I need you to open this door!"

"Fine!" I bark. I rise from the bed and turn the knob to detach the lock with as much defiance as I can muster.

Chapter 2 Mary

"Life is not easy for any of us. But what of that? We must have perseverance and above all confidence in ourselves. We must believe we are gifted for something and that this thing must be attained." – Marie Curie

Dave flashes me a disapproving look when I comment about Tanya having a second helping of potatoes. He doesn't have to bother. I know it's a mistake even as the words leave my lips. I see the hurt Tanya plays off as anger, and realize I've messed up again.

"Was I that out of line?" I ask, hoping he'll tell me what I want to hear. I wince at the sound of Tanya clomping loudly up the stairs, followed by the hinges on her flimsy bedroom door rattling when she smacks it shut.

My darling husband equivocates.

"I don't know if I'd say, 'out of line,'" he begins. Dave better never go into politics. His mouth tries to be diplomatic, but his face just can't lie. "Maybe a little, uh –"

"I know, I know. Out of line."

"Well, you meant well, Hon. Yo, Jess, put that fork in your mouth before those peas go all over the floor!"

Our three-year-old smiles impishly before allowing said veggies to cascade onto the linoleum.

"Alright, Jess, now you're gonna have to pick all those up right this –. Hey, Ralph, no! That's not for you! You know you're not supposed to have table food!"

Dave is fighting a losing battle. Our salt and pepper beagle may be getting old, but he's still awfully quick on the draw. Ralph's every bit a hound, and he has the whole lot sucked up, scarfed down, and probably digested before Dave can even finish his sentence.

I offer some backup.

"Jessica Rose, your father's right. No more playing with your food."

She says, "OK, Mommy," giggles, and plunges her hand into the mashed potatoes. I start to say something, but Dave intervenes.

"Now, listen up, Girlie, you heard me, and you heard your mother," he says, trying to sound stern as he cleans her fingers with the tablecloth. Honestly, sometimes I don't know which one is worse.

"Dave!" I moan, to which he replies, "Well, you said it had to go into the wash anyway!"

Realizing getting proper nourishment into Jessica is a lost cause, I revert back to fretting about Tanya.

"Do you think I should try to talk to her?" I ask Dave.

"Couldn't hurt," he answers in his usual non-committal way. I know he's trying not to get between Tanya and me, but I wish he would be a bit more decisive sometimes.

I push in my chair and head for the stairs. When I reach the top, I call to her from the landing, but she ignores me.

I try again. "Tanya, please answer me!"

No reply.

Standing outside her room, I realize she's locked the door again. I have to insist she open it, which isn't how I want this to go. I want to make things better, but I can't have her shutting me out like that.

I hate the tight rope I'm always walking these days.

"What, Mother?" she harrumphs when I enter.

Why can't I keep my mouth shut? I'm one of the only women I know who has a close relationship with her teenager, but if I'm not careful, I'll lose her. Why do I have to pick at her about little things that don't matter? When I think of the problems some of my friends are facing with their kids, and things that are going on with some of the people who walk into the pregnancy center, I realize how blessed I am to have a daughter like Tanya. Somehow, though, I just can't seem to stay quiet when I see her making self-destructive decisions.

That's what's going through my mind, but I can't think of a way to say any of it. Instead, I do what I always do. I go into default parenting mode, correct her tone of voice, and watch more miles of wall go up between us with every word.

I want to remind her how darling she was as a child, with that flowing blonde hair and those sky-blue eyes. I want to say that she's still lovely, but her lack of self-confidence makes her appear awkward. That it hurts my heart to see her going around in baggy sweats to disguise her bulky dimensions. That her ruddy cheeks wouldn't be dotted with so much acne if she would lay off the junk food and sweets. But I don't know how to say any of that without making her more defensive.

I think she must realize on some level that I can't really understand her eating problem or what drives it, because I've always had the opposite trouble. I used to have to double up on skirts just to make it appear I had any figure at all!

I try to start over.

"Tanya, Honey, how 'bout a truce? I don't want to argue with you, and I don't think you want to argue with me. Am I right?"

After a minute, she mutters, "Yeah, I guess."

"Good. Then how 'bout we start over? Listen, I'm sorry about the potato comment. You're almost 18. You don't need me counting your calories. Forgive me?"

"Fine," she groans without much conviction. "I mean, I hate when you do it anytime, but especially in front of Jess and David. Why can't you understand that?"

Good question, I concede mentally. *I'd love to know the answer to that myself.*

"I'm sorry, Sweetheart. You're right. I would hate that, too. I guess the only thing I can say is, my concern for you sometimes gets the better of me, and I forget that we're not alone. I'll try not to embarrass you again. Now, will you come back down to dinner?"

She isn't going to go that far. She begs off, saying she isn't hungry, but I know better. Tanya's always hungry.

I try a different tack.

"How 'bout joining me when I put Jessica to bed? She loves being with you so much!"

Tanya's always been a godsend with her little sister. My marriage to Dave upset her, I know it did, because it was just the two of us for such a long time. She had barely adjusted to the idea of having a stepfather when we sprang the news on her that a baby was on the way. Still, she's adapted, and I think really loves Jessica, despite the crowdedness of our small twin house and having to share me with two other people.

The look on her face answers before her mouth does. She makes an excuse about having a lot of homework, but it's not convincing. I guess she hasn't quite forgiven me yet.

My face must show disappointment because she makes a counteroffer.

"Maybe Chuck and I can take her to the playground after school tomorrow instead," she begins, then gives herself an out by adding, "if I'm not too busy."

I brighten at the thought of Tanya and her sweet boyfriend pushing Jess on the swings. He comes from a big family and doesn't mind having my little one around. That would actually be a better deal for me anyway, because afternoons are when Jess has all that boundless energy and I'm exhausted from work. I may even get a chance to decompress!

I pretend to believe Tanya's story about the homework, then casually try to coax her into making good on the playground offer.

"Oh, Sweetheart, that sounds great. Your sister would love that. Thanks so much!"

With that, I kiss her on the head and say goodnight.

Chapter 3 David

"Fatherhood requires love, not DNA." – Unknown

My body may be in 2017, but my head's back in the early '90's.

"Lenny, lemme help!" I begged my 20-year-old brother, who, along with our other brother, Al, had been trying hard to fill the hole left by my father's sudden death. Together, they started a business and were determined to provide for our family so my mom could focus her attention on raising our other brother, Jack, and me. At the moment, I wasn't making their job easy.

"Listen, Davey, I know you wanna help, but these tools could hurt you," Len cautioned me, prying the drill out of my nine-year-old fingers. I was about ready to start fourth grade, and tired of being the baby of the family. I wanted people to praise me the way they did Lenny and Al. I wanted to do my part.

We were in the basement, where Lenny and Al had set up shop. Len was trying to construct a model for a trade show, and I was underfoot. He'd been patiently answering my unending stream of questions and steering me away from the power tools for the better part of an hour. I guess he'd about had it. Just when I thought he was ready to shoo me out of there once and for all, he had a stroke of genius. Guiding me over to a piece of scrap wood, he scooped up a handful of nails and thrust a hammer into my grasping hands. I guess he figured my thumbs could better recover from a hammer whack than whatever mischief I could get into when his back was turned.

"Alright, Davey, this is your last chance," he solemnly warned me. "Now, here's what I need you to do. I need you to make sure at least 30 nails end up perpendicular to this piece of wood. Do you know what 'perpendicular' means?"

"Uh uh," I said, shaking my head.

He demonstrated how he wanted me to drive the nails in straight, forming an upside down "T" with the base of the wood. I tried to grab the hammer from him, but he was having none of it.

"Hold on, Dave. I haven't finished giving you your instructions. You gotta learn to listen. Here's the deal. Angled nails aren't good enough."

He showed me what he meant.

"See, if that happens, if they go in at an angle, you're gonna have to pull them out with the claw end of the hammer and start over. Like this, see? Here, now you try it."

I went to work with gusto and, when all was said and done, Lenny's model was complete, and I knew how to wield a hammer. I even had a blue half-moon on my thumb to prove it.

Recalling that incident all these years later, I marvel. Now that I'm a father, it amazes me that Lenny knew instinctively how to get me out of his hair without crushing my pride. I hope I osmosed some of those parenting skills, because I'd sure like to use them with my two daughters.

Except only one of them is buying what I'm trying to sell. Jess laps it up, but Tanya keeps a polite distance, calling me "David" instead of "Dave," and basically keeping me at arm's length.

I can't really blame her. Growing up with three brothers whose idea of closeness involved bathroom humor and knuckle cracking contests didn't exactly prepare me for living with all this estrogen. I knew when I married Mary that there would be sort of a learning curve for Tanya and me, an adjustment period, but I figured we'd have most of that worked out by now. But if anything, life's only gotten more confusing.

These thoughts tumble through my mind in no particular order, as I watch my wife interact with my older daughter tonight at the dinner table. Wait, make that "stepdaughter." I offered to change that status shortly after Mary and I got married, but Tanya turned down my offer to adopt her. I stupidly assumed she'd be as welcoming of me as I was of Al and Len when they stepped into my dad's shoes. Plus, I figured, what with the new baby on the way, it would make her feel like she was just as much my kid as the one coming along.

Clearly, I was wrong. Either I spoke too soon, or Tanya just wasn't interested.

"Uh, I, uh, I guess I just never thought about it," she stammered when I brought up adoption. She fiddled with a string hanging from her sweatpants and avoided looking at me. I sat there like an idiot, pretending to be fascinated by a fly caught between the screen and the windowpane behind Tanya's head.

"Well, uh, what *do* ya think about it?" I finally asked when it became clear she wasn't going to add anything to her previous statement. Instead of answering, she yanked on the thread she'd been playing with, making a pull in the fabric.

I'm no genius, but when a loose thread is more interesting than an invite to be someone's daughter, well, I have to figure I'm being shot down. I leaped into the embarrassing silence.

"Oh, listen, no worries," I spluttered. "I mean, no worries, no hurry. Just, whenever, I mean, *if* ever, I mean, *what*ever. Listen, I better go see if your mom needs help in the kitchen."

Real grace under pressure, I thought, slinking away. *Hemingway, you've got nothing to worry about.*

While watching the drama tonight over mashed potatoes, of all things, I feel just about as deficient as I did then. Thank God the games I'm inventing to get my three-year-old to choke down peas are having the desired effect, or I might be tempted to pack it in. Mary makes a veiled comment about Tanya's weight, which sends the kid away from the table in a huff and makes my wife feel awful. Next thing you know, Jess and I are sitting there alone while Mary tries to patch things up with Tanya.

I know she's worried about the kid's weight and social life, but if I could only get her to realize she needs to pick her battles. It's tough, though, as the stepdad. I have to keep my mouth shut most of the time, but still try to back Mary up when she needs it.

I flunked out of my first year of college because, as a geology major (a useless course of study if ever there was one), I couldn't handle the heavy-duty math and science. The dynamics between Mary and Tanya make about as much sense to me as Newtonian physics.

Chapter 4 Tanya

"First appearance deceives many." – Ovid

"Tonna, come snuggle with me and Mommy!" Jess begs when Mom brings her up for the night. This is just what I'm trying to avoid.

Yes, Mom apologized and I accepted, and yes, we can be friends again. She doesn't always get it right away, but often she gets it down the line, if you know what I mean, and that makes it worth hanging in there with her. But when she asks me to do the "family bed" thing when she's reading Jess a bedtime story, it gets to be a bit much. I have to lie and say I've got homework to finish. I won't say it's not cozy when the two of us squeeze into Jess's little twin bed with her in the middle; Jess loves it and says cute things like, "I am warm, and very, very toasty!" But it really is a little weird, and we have to wedge ourselves in the way I do the secondhand jeans Mom got me last spring. Then, when you factor in the safety rail that keeps my hyperactive sister from cracking her skull open when she gets out of bed (at least it slows her down) – well, it's too much.

Mom comes through like a champ.

"Jessica, Tanya has to study. She can't read with us tonight."

Jess starts to whine and fake cry, something Mom won't put up with.

"Now, that's enough, young lady," she scolds. "You come on in with me and we'll read *Winnie the Pooh*."

Jess wails louder and keeps pleading.

I do love the kid, so I commit to the playground.

"Listen, Dolly," (that's what I sometimes call her), "if you're a good girl and tuck in with just Mom tonight, maybe Chuck and I will take you to the playground tomorrow."

Mom tries to hide her smile, but I know she's thrilled at the idea of getting some time to herself after work.

"Yay!" Jess exclaims. "OK, Mommy, let's do Pooh!"

I find myself wishing it were that easy for me to forget my disappointments. I have a hard time letting go of things like that, especially things that really strike a nerve. Like, for example, I haven't gone back to my church youth group since the day Ryan Neeley texted just about everyone but me, inviting them over for a swim party. I didn't take a poll, but it seemed like just about everybody except me and this other girl, Caitlyn Briggs who, like me, isn't very attractive, got an invite. It was bad enough I was left out, and it didn't help that I had a wild crush on him, and still do, if you want to know the truth. He tested my commitment with that stunt, but if he texted me today, I bet I'd answer.

"That's my good girl," Mom says, then turns to me. "Thanks, Tanya, for our talk. I feel much better. I hope you do, too."

"Me, too," I lie. I mean, it's not that I'm sorry we made up, but sometimes she just wants to be more buddy-buddy than I can handle these days. Like she still wants to hold my hand once in a while, like when I was a little girl and it was just her and me. It's one thing when you're seven, but not at this age. I have enough social obstacles to overcome as it is.

19

The things that cause most of my appearance problems are my acne and my weirdly shaped body. I have very unpredictable skin, meaning one week, things will be fine, and the next week, my face looks like the surface of the moon. Mom says it's a blessing I'm a girl so I can use makeup to cover it up, but I envy girls like Susan Kilroy, whose alabaster skin with its rosy highlights makes her look like the porcelain doll Mom gave me the day she told me she and David were going to get married. But I digress.

Mom says I'm too hard on myself, but then she goes and says things like do I really want more potatoes, when clearly, I do or I wouldn't be reaching for the bowl, would I? She's also pretty quick to point out that I'm scarring my face when I pop my zits, but I can't help it. It's either that or go around looking like I have an unrelenting case of chicken pox. When my back started breaking out, she said, "Hallelujah! Maybe it'll limit itself to your back so you can cover it up!" She's all about covering up unsightly things, which I think is one of the reasons she married David. She won't admit it, but I'm pretty sure she was pregnant with Jess before the wedding – either that, or Jess was an awfully big preemie, which is what Mom wants me to believe.

The thing is, I don't understand why she doesn't just come clean and admit they were fooling around before the wedding. After all, she told me all about the circumstances of my birth, which were a lot more intriguing when you get right down to it. Apparently, there was this guy who looked a lot like Kirk Cameron, but according to Mom, he checked his honesty at the door most of the time. Mom says the final straw was when he stole a Phillies

Phanatic car magnet from another car while she waited for him to finish pilfering so they could go to dinner. She got one last meal out of him (I have to give the girl credit for getting her needs met), then told him to hit the road. Afterwards, she found out she was pregnant with me. She decided she would rather raise a kid alone than co-parent with a thief, so she just never told him about me. I guess it was just as well. She found out later that he died in a car wreck when I was about two, so I wouldn't have had a father either way.

I guess one of the reasons she won't tell me the truth is because she frames my whole birth story as a big error in judgment. Not that she makes me feel like a mistake – it's not that at all. She tells me all the time how glad she is that she kept me and that I'm a wonderful daughter even when I'm not. But I think she's probably mad at herself for doing the same dumb thing twice. That and the fact that she's the director of a pregnancy center where they help girls like her who get into these types of situations. They sort of rescued her when she was having me. They gave her clothes and other baby stuff, and she says they really helped her emotionally. They even gave her a job, and she eventually went back to school for her degree so she could do more for them. When their director left, they hit Mom up to take the job. I think she'd be mortified to admit that, after landing that position, she got herself into the same boat again 15 years later.

Then there's the fact that Mom adores Chuck. Don't get me wrong. Chuck's a nice guy, and he thinks the sun rises and sets on me, for some reason I can't figure out. He's been interested in me since the day we met at the burger place we both worked at before

21

he started his new job. I was working the register and he was prepping food, and he kept smiling at me over the fry pit and insisting I smile back before he would hand over the fries. It would have made me feel good if I hadn't kept noticing the way Steve McElroy was eyeing Megan Natale as she rang up customers. Steve looks like a Greek god and Megan, well, she's sort of an Italian princess – not someone I find beautiful, but apparently, she makes Steve's heart skip a beat. They've been going out for a couple weeks now, and since Chuck is friends with Steve, we're supposed to double date next Saturday if we can all get the night off. I'm going to see if I can get away with "forgetting" to ask for off, since I figure watching Steve drool all over Megan will be not quite as much fun as having a tooth pulled. It's one thing to be on a date with a guy who doesn't excite you, but it's another thing to be on that same date, wishing you could be the girl in the other couple. That's been the story of my life.

I don't think Mom gets that at all. I know her skin broke out when she was young, but she never had a problem attracting men, apparently. She still has pictures of herself with old boyfriends, which for some reason doesn't bother David at all. If I were him, I wouldn't want my wife keeping a photo record of the ones who got away, but he just smiles and says they don't know what they're missing. She even has some shots of herself on the beach looking like a model. I couldn't get my big toe into any of her swimsuits and would look ridiculous if I tried. Mom's one of those women who's not a classic beauty but knows how to really put together what she has.

Anyway, Mom thinks Chuck's the greatest thing since baby wipe warmers. That's right, there really is such a thing, to keep apple-sized butts from getting chilled while they're being, you know, *handled*. I never could figure out why, on the one hand, we spend big bucks on junk like that and cribs that look like four poster beds, but on the other hand, we stick our kids in day care practically the minute they exit the womb. Why not scale back on non-essentials and actually stay home and raise the kids? As a veteran of day care and all the living by the clock that goes with it, I would much rather have skipped those frantic mornings and been satisfied playing with pots and pans if it meant I got to bang them around with my own mother, rather than playing on a tablet with babysitters.

But that's another story. What I was trying to get at is that Mom can't see Chuck the way I do. I mean, some of the guys in her past were drop-dead gorgeous, which is something I'd like to have happen to me just once in my life. I went on a retreat with my church one time, and Ryan Neeley was hanging all over Debbie Friel the whole time. Debbie Friel, whose hair looks like it just barely escaped a close encounter with a bunch of geese, and who must get her clothes from the Salvation Army. I tried to pay attention to the "Rah Rah, let's be 'on fire' Christians!" pep talks the youth minister spouted, but I was miserable the whole weekend. I know Ryan has nothing upstairs, but oh, how I'd love to be bored with him for a few days.

Mom keeps telling me there's more to Chuck than his looks, which aren't terrible, but nothing to brag about, either. His hair's the color of mucky sand and would probably curl if he let it grow out a bit. He has dull, almost muddy brown eyes. I don't get so much as a shiver when I look into them. He's tall and lanky, which makes me look even pudgier when we're together.

I have to admit, though, what Chuck lacks in looks he makes up for in work ethic. Wouldn't give up his fast-food job till he was sure he'd landed one at the gas station near his house. He doesn't just pump gas, although he'd probably be quite content with that. He got the job because he was able to sell them on the fact that he changes his own oil and knows how to do repairs like brake pads and routine maintenance. He figured he could pick up some training and get paid for it, which sounded better to him than flipping burgers all through college. I know he's sweet and has a lot on the ball, but is that enough to build a relationship on? I mean, I felt affection towards the 70-something crossing guard who used to say, "Good morning, morning glory!" while helping me cross the street, but I wouldn't want to go to the prom with him, either.

Chapter 5 Mary and David

"Who, being loved, is poor?" – Oscar Wilde

Tanya and Chuck took the baby to the playground yesterday. That's another thing – I've got to stop calling her that. Poor child keeps reminding me she's not a baby, she's three *and a half* (that half really means a lot to her), goes to the potty all by herself, even picks out her own clothes.

I'll be 40 next month, and Jessica will almost certainly be my last child. It's hard to let go of the concept of my own fertility. Makes me feel old. When I moan about it to Dave, he smiles and says he loves every wrinkle, something no woman wants to hear.

The way Tanya tells it, Jess took off for the swings like a rocket the minute they unhooked the straps on her car seat. I guess that's when the diaper bag fell out of the car, spilling its contents all over the grass. Oh, that's right, I'm not supposed to call it a diaper bag. Jessica wants me to call it her "big girl bag" now that she's out of diapers. Whatever. It still comes in handy to carry snacks and juice and makes for a nice dumping ground to shove things in when I run out of room in my purse, which is most of the time.

Apparently, I neglected to remove the coin filled baby bottle Colleen Caspar gave me last Sunday for the pregnancy center's fundraising drive. I remember stuffing it into Jessica's bag after the church service, but then I forgot to take it out and add it to our growing pile of change to benefit the center. When Jessica knocked her bag off the seat, I guess the bottle rolled under the car or something, because when Tanya and Chuck repacked everything, they didn't see it.

Dave and I went back to the park to search for it, but no luck. Some undeserving kid probably has a nice chunk of change in his piggy bank now.

I'm so mad at myself. The pregnancy center works on a shoestring budget, and we could have used that cash, especially with Christmas just around the corner. Colleen had even stuffed some paper money in there.

Dave says I have to let it go, and he's right.

"Earth to Mar. You in there, Mar?" my husband jumps into my reverie. I look up from the onions I'm slicing for Thanksgiving tomorrow. Don't ask me why, but Dave loves creamed onions.

"Oh, yeah, I'm fine, Hon. Just thinking about the baby bottle again. I know, I know. It's over and done with, but still."

He smiles indulgently and starts cutting up the carrots I hand him. My husband's the first to admit to being a consumer rather than creator of meals, but he's more than willing to help out. We have some of our best conversations under the fluorescent light in our antiquated kitchen. It's on Dave's long to-do list to hang the new fixture I picked out, but given his level of handyman expertise, maybe I'm better off waiting.

Suddenly, I catch a distinct twinkle in his eye.

"Dave Gullickson, what's up with you?" I say with mock suspicion.

"Oh, nothing that a kiss from a ravishing woman can't get out of me," he teases.

"Oh, yeah? Well, if I see one, I'll send her right over."

"Now, that's enough of that, Mrs. Gullickson – oh, Lord, how I wish I could've given you a more normal name!"

I agree, but I'll never tell him that.

"Listen, I took you for better or worse, for richer or poorer. If I had wanted a guy named 'Smith,' that's who I'd have married. So, let's get off of the name subject and tell me what's up with that Cheshire cat grin?"

"Alright, alright, you wormed it out of me. It so happens that today was a banner day. I'm about to show you something that I have a feeling is gonna make you forget all about the pittance in that bottle. Now, all I need is that kiss so I can show you what I have in my pocket."

Every once in a while, I like to catch Dave off guard. I know he won't expect me to lunge at him with my eyes full of onion tears. So that's exactly what I do.

****

"Whoa, woman, give a guy a chance to protect himself!" I snort when she grabs for the letter. Actually, it's a "paid in full" hospital bill for a longstanding debt she incurred before we were married. When she reads it, she breaks down in tears – real tears, not from the onions – and hugs me so hard I almost lose my balance.

The bill goes back to when Tanya was a lot younger. The poor kid had broken her arm and needed surgery to have it set right. Mary's insurance has always been lousy, and she still owed almost two grand when I married her. I'm not Sir Galahad, but I try to do

27

what's right. Getting my wife out of debt comes under that category.

"Oh, Dave, what a great Thanksgiving present! I'm so glad this is where we were headed!" she squeals as I kiss the top of her head. That's something I do often, since I'm 6'2" to her 5'7".

She's referring, of course, to the unforgettable conversation we had the night she asked me to marry her. You heard that right. Mary's no shrinking violet, and she knows what she wants. Oh, my lips popped the question, but she brought it to the table.

She opened the subject by asking coyly, "Dave, where are we headed?"

Her attempt at subtlety amused me, so I decided to tease her.

"Why, home, of course," I responded with a rogue smile.

"Dave Gullickson, you know perfectly well what I'm talking about!" she grumped, mock hitting me on the shoulder as she did so. That's a mannerism I find endearing; I joke that she should find a support group to help her kick the habit.

I looked her right in the eye and said, "We're heading for the altar. We both know that."

She smiled, then frowned.

"What's the matter, Mar?" I put to her. "I just asked you to marry me. Why doesn't that make your day?"

"Oh, it does, Sweetie! Nothing's the matter. It's just, well, we're not exactly setting the world on fire with our salaries. Are we gonna be able to make it with kids and all?"

I pulled her close – well, as close as the bucket seats in my 2005 Honda Civic would allow. I bought it new when I got out of college and landed my first real job in graphic design. It's getting a little long in the tooth now.

"We're gonna be fine," I assured her. In the back of my mind, I was having a lot of the same reservations she was, but I knew we loved each other, and that would make penny pinching a little easier. I'm not one of those romantics who believe love conquers all, but neither do I think wealth makes for happiness. Too often, I've seen just the opposite. Look at Hollywood.

So, we tied the knot, and part of the package in my mind was Tanya's outstanding medical bill. I told Mary not to worry about it anymore and took over the monthly payments she had been struggling to make. I added a little extra whenever I could, and after three and a half years, the deed was done.

"Dave Gullickson, you are the sweetest, most wonderful man who ever walked the earth!" she crows as we continue prepping for Thanksgiving. As usual, I chop and she cooks. My idea of haute cuisine is my signature tuna salad, the secret ingredient being just the right amount of wine vinegar, but the girls don't want to have that every night, so I humor them by pretending to enjoy the amazing meals Mary turns out. My jobs are things I can't get into too much trouble with, like peeling potatoes and tearing up bread for stuffing.

"That's what they tell me," I say in response to her gushing. "So how was work today?"

"Oh, it was good. A little sad. A woman came in today with her husband. They're looking for hope 'cause they just found out their baby's gonna be born disabled. I mean, seriously disabled.

29

May never walk. They don't know where to turn, so they came to us."

"Man, that is sad. I can't imagine what we'd have done if that had happened with Jess."

"Or Tanya, for that matter," she reminds me.

"Oh, sure, of course, but I mean, I wasn't around then, so I'm just thinking of Jess."

"I know what you mean, Sweetie. Anyway, we referred them to some agencies that deal with their child's disability and gave them a few pamphlets. We told them we can help them out with diapers and things like that, clothes even, if they need it. I don't think they're gonna take us up on our offer of counseling, not that we have much to say that could cheer them up at this point, but we just hope we can steer them away from abortion."

"Y'know, Mar, I'd like to know what you could say to keep them from going that route. I mean, you know I'm not for it, but in all honesty, what a tough road."

"Well, the good thing is they have faith. They attend a Catholic church, and their priest actually sent them to us. Works out better when ministers don't try to tackle these sorts of problems long term. They can't be experts on everything, but this is all we do, day in and day out. We know who to connect them with, the mountains they're gonna have to climb. We don't just say, 'Don't abort; God doesn't like that.' We come alongside them and stick with them, before and even after they give birth."

Mary's passionate about her work, but for me, it's just part of our bread and butter. But I do know this: I meant what I said to

Mary. I wouldn't want to know how I'd react if something like this came my way. I consider myself a God-fearing man, but this is one trial I'm glad he didn't see fit to send me.

I guess my eyes are starting to glaze over because Mary changes the subject.

"Listen, let's not talk about work. We have so much to be thankful for. Two healthy kids, a nice home, one less medical bill, thanks to my wonderful husband, good jobs where we make a difference – oops, there I go again, talking about work!"

"You do good work, Hon," I reply, then turn my attention to hacking up celery for the stuffing.

"No, Sweetie, it's gotta be minced fine, like this. Remember how I showed you before?" Mary says, smiling indulgently and taking the knife from my clumsy hands.

If Thanksgiving dinner's a success, it won't be because of me.

Chapter 6 Tanya

"Who would ever think that so much went on in the soul of a young girl?" – Anne Frank

Pastor Kaplan texted me today. He and his wife, Vicki, run the youth group at my church.

If you're thinking that's a strange name for a Baptist minister, you're right. He was raised traditionally Jewish, but claims his belief that Jesus – "Yeshua," he calls him – is God's son only makes him more so. The way he tells it, Jesus and his first followers were Jewish, so why shouldn't he consider what they have to say?

I'm sure Mom hounded him to get in touch with me, and I don't appreciate it. She knows how I feel about church these days, and I told her what happened with Ryan. Why can't she respect my feelings? Let her and Dave drag Jess with them on Sundays, and leave me to sleep in.

He asked if he and Vicki could take me out for a Coke. They're such nice people that I didn't have the heart to tell them I'm not interested in that stuff anymore. It's gonna have to be a short visit, though, because I'm really busy with this debate project at school.

Senior year, everyone has to take a quarter class that drives us all crazy. We're paired up to research and present a slide show about a controversial topic. Then each partner writes a paper taking either the pro or con position. As if that's not enough, we then get the distinct privilege of debating the whole thing in front of the class. There isn't enough makeup in the world to disguise the breakout I'll be having that week.

In the meantime, I'm frantically trying to keep up with my other classes. I also have AP English and government, and ecology (yawn – I had to take a science, and that sounded like the least amount of work – I was wrong). Next semester I'll have creative writing, which will at least be fun. Hopefully, that'll take some of the sting out of calculus.

I don't know why I do this to myself. It's not like I plan to be a rocket scientist or anything like that. I guess I just like to show I can do things, and it seems to make Mom so happy. She could barely stay in her seat at my "graduation" from middle school when I picked up all those awards. Strange how everything has to be a big deal anymore. Whatever happened to just graduating from high school and college? Next thing you know, they'll be handing out awards when kids get their first tooth.

I text Pastor K, *lemme check my schedule and get back to u.* If I had a decent phone, I could send talk texts and not sound so illiterate, but with this ridiculous, antiquated slide phone, everything's an ordeal. I'm embarrassed to even pull it out around my friends. Mom won't see reason, though, and says I have to earn enough to buy what I want and pay the extra $50 a month for the upgraded plan. I don't know how she thinks I'm gonna be able to do that and save for college at the same time.

Wasn't she ever young?

Chapter 7 Mary

"You'll know I've stopped caring about you when I stop correcting you." – Thea Williams

I'm in trouble again. Tanya knows I asked Seth Kaplan to speak with her. I had hoped he'd think of it himself, what with her not being around for a few months, but I guess he's busy. Maybe the Catholics have a point about celibacy. Seth and Vicki sure have their hands full with those three kids and all their youth group responsibilities.

Tanya comes at me with both barrels.

"Mom, I know you put him up to it! He's never called me before, and now I have to take precious time from my schoolwork – the work you're so proud of when I bring home A's – to have a meeting I don't want and don't need! Admit it – you're behind this!"

I study my hands before responding. They're getting gnarly, just like my mother's. I would've hoped I'd at least be into my forties before arthritis started to rear its crippling head. Tanya lets loose with a few expletives, and I break my silence.

"Alright, Tanya, there's no need to speak to me that way. I won't have it. Yes, I'm not gonna deny it. But you have to understand, I'm worried about you. You're –"

"I'm fine, that's what I am! Mom, I'll be 18 in a week! I'm not your little baby! I'm not Jessica! I'm about to graduate, if I don't keep getting interrupted with ridiculous meetings to 'have a

Coke' that my hips don't need, at the top of my class! Why isn't that enough for you?"

"Oh, Sweetheart, I'm so sorry if I make you feel that way. You must know how proud I am of you. But, Honey, there's something so much more important than grades, your relationship with –"

"I know, I know. I've been hearing it my whole life. My relationship with God. Well, guess what, Mom? God gave me huge hips and thighs, and a face full of zits! Look, I'm not saying I don't believe in him, but why do I need to go to some building on Sunday morning when I need sleep so I can keep getting those A's you're so proud of? Why can't you just let me worship him in my own way?"

I don't know how to answer when she says things like that. I don't know why she's having such an awkward adolescence. I suspect she thinks I'm more attractive than she is, and no daughter wants to take a back seat to her mother. Besides, she won't take my advice when I try to give it. I've been where she is, I've done the growing up thing, and I could make some good suggestions so she could maximize what she's got until she grows into her best self.

I think all these things, but don't dare say any of them. Instead, I stare at the floor tiles, which are the one thing I love in our outdated kitchen. Their little blue cornflowers are so happy and carefree, like Tanya and I once were. Oh, we always had money problems, but that paled in comparison to the adhesive bond we used to have. When life became hard to handle, we got into the habit of crooning old songs about sticking it out together and making it against all odds.

I wish one of those ditties could fix things now.

Chapter 8 David

"Raising children is an uncertain thing; success is reached only after a life of battle and worry." – Democritus

"Come on, Tanya! We don't wanna be late for church," Mary calls, seemingly oblivious to the fact that late is exactly what Tanya wants to be. She must have convinced herself that our daughter is joining us out of interest, instead of the real reason, which is that she was tricked into it.

"Listen, I've gotta finish my hair, and I'm not even dressed yet!" Tanya bellows down the stairs. "Why don't you guys just go without me?"

"Oh, please, Honey, you don't wanna disappoint Pastor K., do you? I mean, didn't you promise to come hear him speak?"

That's how our day is starting. I hate to say it, but I think Mary was wrong to sic the youth minister on Tanya. The only reason she's agreeing to come to church after all these months is because Mary got after Seth Kaplan to get in touch with her. He's still in training and sometimes the senior pastor gives him a chance to preach. Today's one of those days, and I think he convinced Tanya to come cheer him on. A good strategy, but unfortunately, his last talk on seeking heavenly treasure in lieu of earthly things fell pretty flat. He seems like a decent guy, though, and my wife thinks he might be able to rekindle Tanya's interest in spirituality.

I think Mary and Seth may be putting the cart before the horse, though. I'm no expert, but it's always seemed to me that sitting in church doesn't make you a Christian any more than chilling at the beach makes you a seahorse. If I were them, I think I'd be putting more effort into conversations with the Almighty and less into arm twisting a teenager. Still, this comes under the vast category of things that aren't my business, so I say nothing unless I'm asked.

Anyway, Tanya comes down about as cheerful as a bear without honey. Mary manages to drag her out the door, but when we get to church, she sits stone-faced through Seth's mediocre sermon and reluctantly goes out with him and his wife, Vicki, after the service. Mary set it up that we would take the Kaplans' three kids out to lunch so Tanya can have time alone with the two of them. With coupons, the bill for the six of us only comes to $40, so Mary's a happy camper.

Jess has fun with the Kaplan twins, and it's kind of funny to watch their older kid mother the younger ones while they play in the ball pit. The kid's only seven, all of two years older than her twin sisters, but she calls them and Jess "Honey" and ushers them over to me and Mary whenever anyone gets a "boo boo". So, Mary and I are in pretty good moods when we meet up with Seth and Vicki at the church to swap kids at 3.

Tanya says almost nothing on the ride home.

When we get back to the house, she makes herself scarce by saying she has a lot of homework. I let Mary take a nap while Jess and I rake up a huge pile of leaves for her to jump in. We even manage to get a few of them out to the curb for pickup. I'd have bet money Jess would've strewn them all around, but she seems just as happy to do "grownup work" as she is to play.

38

That kid is so much fun. Everything makes her laugh. Sure, she's energetic, but what kid isn't at that age? I remember being outside from dawn till dusk when I was growing up, coming in exhausted and starving, wolfing down dinner, then running out again to play till the streetlights came on. Mom had to pry me away from my friends.

It's interesting that I'm getting such a kick out of a daughter. I have no experience with little girls, being from a family of all boys. My brother, Jack, and I darn near killed each other a couple of times, all in the name of male bonding. We used to play a game called "Tickers," which involved trying to make the other guy pass out by cutting off the circulation in his carotid. No one was more surprised than me when I woke up in the ER after "winning" the game when I was ten. Jack got Lenny and Al (who hustled me off to the hospital) to promise not to tell Mom, but when the bill came in – well, let's just say, Mom put the kibosh on that particular form of relationship building.

I guess I figured when Jess was born that she'd be breakable or something, but she loves doing the stuff I suggest, which are all the games I played as a kid – except Tickers, of course. Who'd have imagined life could be this good?

Tanya's seemed unhappy most of the time I've known her. I wonder if anyone ever taught her how to have fun.

Chapter 9 Emma

"It is not in the still calm of life, or the repose of a pacific station, that great characters are formed." – Abigail Adams

As Tom releases two-year-old Kevin from his car seat, the straps of which pin him in like two vinyl arms (rendered a bit less severe by the soft, dinosaur-clad covers Velcro-ed around them), my phone rings. The sweet, sing-song-y voice of my obstetrician fills my ears when I answer. In her usual endearing way, she identifies herself using her first name.

"Hi, Emma? Heidi Rivera."

"Oh, hi, Dr. R! How are you?" I begin, while attempting to wipe my four-year-old's runny nose with a napkin from last night's trip to the fast-food restaurant. "Kyle, stop. Mommy'll be done in a minute!" I chide my older son, who furiously resists my efforts to make him presentable.

"Sorry, Doc., I'll be right with you," I add, remembering my manners. "It's just, Kyle's fighting me on –"

"Take your time, Emma!" she chuckles on the other end of the phone. "I remember those days very well."

"Thanks, Doc," I say after laboriously winning the battle with Kyle. "Now, to what do I owe the pleasure of your call on a Saturday?"

"Well, I'm in the office tidying up some loose ends – you know me – and, lo and behold, I see that your lab results are back. I wanted to see if you and Tom could come in this week to discuss them."

I may not be Phi Beta Kappa, but I can detect when a doctor sounds too casual. Her seemingly innocuous statement sets alarm bells clanging in my head. First of all, why is she calling me on the weekend? Why can't this wait till the appointment I have scheduled next Thursday? Why does she want us both there? Something's not right.

"OK, Doc," I say with the familiarity I'm entitled to, if only because I allow Dr. R. to peer into crevices of my body where angels fear to tread. "What's going on?"

"Well, Em, I'd really rather speak with both of you, if at all possible. Is Tom able to talk, too, by any chance?"

"Well, yes, he is, but he's chasing after Kevin at the moment," I reply with growing suspicion. "We just got home from a foliage ride and they're raking up a big pile of leaves for the boys to jump in. Can you just give me the short version of what's up?"

"Sure, of course, Em. The fact is, there was an unusual finding in your AFP test. That's the blood you had drawn recently. Turns out the levels were higher than we like to see, which could indicate a problem."

Just like that, my life changes. Within 15 seconds, I go from being sated with the beauty of the autumn day and our perfect little family, to frozen in fear and uncertainty. I try to speak, but the only thing that comes out is a squeak.

"Em, are you there?"

"Um, yeah," I manage. "What kind of problem?"

"Well, what I'd like to do is have you get an amniocentesis in a week or so. That'll tell us whether or not we even have

41

anything to worry about. It's a needle procedure, but don't panic. It's not a walk in the park, but it's not horrible, either. It's pretty quick, and nothing compared to giving birth!"

Her weak attempt at humor in no way diverts the gruesome scenarios my mind has been conjuring up since she uttered the word "problem." She fields the few questions I come up with, which open the door to some pretty frightening possibilities. While trying to wrap my mind around her news, I watch Tom bury the boys in the gigantic leaf mountain they've been constructing. Meanwhile, my world starts to crumble.

I look heavenward, where the earth tones of the mountainside make magical music with the gold and rust-colored leaves of mid-autumn. Our small Pennsylvania town, Rock Face, is a scenic area any time of the year, but especially in the fall. Named for the chiseled auburn crags that grace the east side of Interstate 650, the main highway of our little town tucked away in the southeastern quadrant of the state, Rock Face is home to approximately 10,000 hard-working families who exist in the divide between workaday life and activity driven weekends. We were one of those families five minutes ago. Now we're a family in trouble, and my husband and kids are making fragile leaf piles that look heartier than I feel.

I guess Dr. R. can tell I'm terrified, so she tries to do damage control.

"OK, this sounds scary, I know. But here's the thing. We aren't sure your little one has any problems, but it's best to proceed as if he or she might. That's why I'm ordering the amnio. We'll do an ultrasound at the same time and this will all give us a much more accurate picture of what's going on than we have at this point. If you want, we can wait a couple more weeks and probably be able to tell the baby's sex at the same time. How does that sound?"

I try to respond, then realize she can't hear my head nodding. I mutter that I'll talk to Tom and then call my primary to get the referral for the tests. I pretend to believe her assurances that everything's probably fine and hang up the phone.

I want a new pregnancy!

To my shame, this thought keeps running through my head as I try to think of a way to tell Tom without bursting into tears. I, who bring my kids to pro-life prayer vigils outside of abortion clinics. I, who pray regularly for a baby for my sister and her husband, whose efforts to achieve pregnancy have cost them upwards of $30,000 over the last few years. I, who wasn't thrilled in the first place to learn we were expecting again, but was just getting used to the idea.

I feel smacked down by almighty arms that are, on one hand, forcing me to put my principles to the test, and on the other hand, perhaps punishing me for not appreciating the amazing gift of life I'm carrying.

"Who was that, Em?" Tom calls after dislodging himself from the kids' efforts to obliterate him with leaves.

43

Chapter 10 Tom

"Silence is a true friend who never betrays." – Confucius

My wife, Emma, isn't an emotional person, but I can tell when she gets off the phone that something's up. For one thing, her face is the color of my grandmother's hair after she stopped dying it. For another, she ignores my question about who was on the phone and goes right into the house. After eight years of marriage, I know when to give her space (usually), so I do my best to exhaust the boys, then plop them in front of a video and go into our room to talk to her.

Em is sprawled out on the bed, staring at the ceiling. Her baby bump, as the tabloids love to nickname such things, isn't much bigger than my fist, but the sight of that little knot sends the same bolt of excitement through me that I felt five years ago when the bump that was Kyle first started rearranging Emma's tiny figure.

"OK, Em," I say, "what's wrong?"

Her lips move, but her eyes stay fixed on the dead white paint over our heads. Finally, she blurts out, "That phone call – it was Dr. Rivera. She thinks there's something wrong with the baby!"

I go numb.

In the space of five minutes, Emma pours out the problem, the possibilities, and her panic over what might be.

I like to fix things, like the plate that fell from its place over a bank of windows, leaving a gaping hole in the arrangement Emma carefully created in our dining room. Our older guy, Kyle, freaked out when I shooed him away from the shattered pieces on our hardwood floor. He went on and on about how the four remaining plates would be lonely without it, despite the fact that I told him it was only a dish and Mommy could get another one to replace it. Didn't matter. The kid wouldn't calm down till I got out glue and mended the thing. It looked ridiculous next to the others in all their perfection. There was a big chunk missing in the middle, but Ky-Guy, as I like to call him, let loose with a gap-toothed smile, threw his arms around me, and shouted, "Yay, Daddy!"

I wish stupidly for some sort of glue to repair whatever damage is going on inside of Em's uterus.

I can't think of anything comforting to say, so I just lie down next to her and cradle her the way she likes in the crook of my arm. After a while, I can feel her softly crying. I stroke her cheek.

"Hey, Babe, let's not get ahead of ourselves," I say, hoping that will be enough to calm her. I've been known to say the wrong thing when I try too hard.

"I know, but Tom, what if – what if it's one of those things she said it could be? What if it's the worst-case scenario – one of those awful diseases, er, conditions, that can't ever be fixed? What if he – or she – has a huge hole in his back? What if –"

I'm thinking all those same things, but I have to slow down this train wreck somehow. She's, what, just barely into her second trimester? We can't go on projecting like this through the whole pregnancy, or it'll make us both crazy.

"Whoa there, Babe, let's back the truck up," I say as evenly as I can. "We don't know what, if anything, is messed up. Right?"

45

I look hopefully at her face, searching for something optimistic in her usually serene blue eyes. Today I read nothing but fear.

"Right?" I say again.

"Right," she concedes, but without conviction.

My mouth goes on without my permission, uttering things I want to I believe about the doctor probably being mistaken and everything turning out fine. I finally realize I'm probably making things worse by protesting too much. I force myself to shut up and let the silence soothe her.

We lie that way for 20 minutes or so, till the kids' show ends and they start yelling in the living room.

"Hey, Babe, one of us needs to go in there and settle those savages down. Tell you what. You get some rest, and I'll make dinner and take care of the chuckleheads. Do we have any spaghetti?"

She gives me that winning smile that attracted me to her in the first place, and says she loves me.

Chapter 11 David

"[We receive] no government funds ever. So we can keep sharing the Gospel. Amen." – Karen Hess, Former Executive Director of AlphaCare Pregnancy Center

I can tell this is gonna be a long night.

Jess's impish behavior makes dinner a disaster, and Mary's losing her mind about little things. I make a joke to try to get Jess to drink her milk, but I don't time it right. She decides to comply just when I get to the punchline, which sends her into gales of laughter, spraying homogenized chaos all over the kitchen.

Tanya isn't any help, either. She steadfastly refuses to go to the fundraiser, even though Mary begs her.

"But Honey, you'll enjoy yourself," Mary wheedles while mopping up milk with a dishtowel. "Denny Klein is gonna be there, giving the keynote speech. Did you know he and his wife, before he started playing professionally, they were so broke they considered aborting their second child? We could get a babysitter for Jess –"

"No *baby*sitter, Mommy!" Jess erupts indignantly. "I'm a *big* girl!"

"Alright, Jessica, just a sitter, then. Tanya, how 'bout it?"

Tanya rolls her eyes and gets up from the table. Ironically, the sweatshirt she's wearing has Jacobs's name emblazoned on the back of it, along with the name of the team he pitches for.

It was nice of Jacobs to get them for us. He offered them to all the staff at the pregnancy center and their families. Said it's the least he can do for people who are, as he puts it, on the "front lines" of the battle for life. He even got one in Jess's size – a fleecy thing with a hood – that Mary wanted to put away for Christmas. My wife usually starts shopping for next year the day after Christmas so she can hit all the bargain basement sales, but work's been so busy for her this year, she's running behind. I know she's afraid she won't have enough to put under the tree, and she doesn't want Jess to think Santa shortchanged her. She really is great with money – much better than I am – but in this case, I managed to talk her out of her practicality. I didn't want Jess to see the rest of us bumming around in our hoodies and wonder why she didn't get one.

"Look, Mom, I've told you before, and I guess I'm gonna have to tell you again. I don't have time. Why can't you get that through – I mean, why can't you understand that?"

Tanya's snotty tone isn't lost on Mary, who glares at her with a mixture of anger and disappointment.

I wish she wouldn't be so desperate to drag Tanya to these things. Mary figures anything with a Christian label could be the key that will unlock Tanya's heart and bring her back to church. I favor giving the kid time, letting her grow back into her faith, but when you get right down to it, she's Mary's daughter, and I can only say so much.

"Alright, Tanya, I won't ask again," Mary says in a hurt tone, then turns back to Jess.

"Now, you listen, young lady," she begins, "You finish up your dinner 'cause we've got to get you into the tub. Your father and I have a banquet to go to, so you need to get in and out of that bathtub, lickety split. No silliness tonight. Mommy's been working hard on this banquet, and she can't afford to be late."

I smile to myself, thinking how the benefit for Mary's pregnancy center must mean about as much to Jessica as meeting a baseball player does to Tanya. None of us are sports fans, least of all our teenager.

Tanya starts across the floor, but her sock monkey slipper lands in some milk that escaped Mary's wiping frenzy. Tanya skids, then catches herself on the counter edge, letting loose some choice words in the process.

That does it for Mary.

"Alright, Tanya, that's enough! Take yourself upstairs this instant! Can't you even control your tongue around your baby sister?"

"I'm not a *baby*!" Jess screeches. Her indignation is barely audible over the barrage of fury Tanya's unleashing. Mary begins to cry.

This is my cue and I know it. I put down my coffee mug and pick up Jess.

"OK, little lady, time to head upstairs now. Tanya," I venture, trying to sound authoritative without overdoing it, "let's make this easy on everyone. Let's call it a night, OK? Your mom asked you to go upstairs, so please."

Tanya, looking only slightly less dangerous than Lizzie Borden, mutters "Fine!" and stomps out of the kitchen. Her exit would be more dramatic if her wet monkey slipper weren't making sloshing noises each time it connects with the linoleum.

49

I swing Jess around to my back and head for the stairs, winking at Mary on my way out. She half smiles, then blows her nose on a napkin. As I round the upstairs landing, I hear dishes clanking as Mary hurriedly clears the table and puts away the remains of our meal.

When we reach the bathroom, I say, "OK, Girly, let's get this bath over and done with, so Mom and I can get out the door. Hop to it. First you better sit on the potty while Daddy fills up the tub."

By now Jess is over her tirade about being called a baby and narrates non-stop everything she's doing.

"OK, Daddy, I'm gonna go potty now. Wait, need help with this button."

I give the requested assistance, then turn to test the water from the tap.

"K, Daddy, lifting up the potty lid. Uh oh, there's pee in it. Eeew, it smells bad, Daddy! Daddy, it's stinky! Mommy didn't dump it. No sticker for her! Daddy –"

"Never mind, Hon, I got it!" I chuckle, reaching down and removing the basin. She's right, I note while rinsing the offending article; it does do quite a number on the olfactory senses. I can only imagine how much worse things would be if our daughter were having greater success in the full gamut of potty training.

Mary comes in, rattling off instructions. One thing I love about her – she does let things go pretty quickly.

"Oh, Dave, you'd better get dressed, Honey! We have to be out of here in 20 minutes. Here, I'll finish with you, Miss Jessica."

"OK, but what about you? I mean, don't you have to get ready, too?"

"Don't worry, Dave, I have my whole outfit laid out, and I can do my face while this one's splashing around. Oh, wait, I forgot to get out the pin I always wear to these things. Oh, you know the one I mean, don't you? The one with the baby feet? I don't wanna forget that."

I know the one. A tiny pin with an even tinier stick to fit through her lapel. It has two little gold feet the size of my pinky nail. She wears it to every fundraiser the pregnancy center has. Supposedly, it's the same size and shape of a 10-week-old unborn baby's feet.

"No worries, Hon, I'll get it for you. In your jewelry box, right?"

As I root through necklaces, unattached earring backs, and even a few earrings (it's on Mary's to do list to clean out her jewelry box, but I doubt she'll ever get to it), I wonder about the night ahead. I hope her expectations aren't too high. She's been running this organization on a shoestring budget for years, doing wonders with the pittance she has to work with. She says this annual fundraiser covers about a quarter of their operating expenses, helping to stock their "Baby Boutique" with clothes, baby food, diapers, wipes, toys – you name it. Apparently, the expectant couples take parenting classes (I think they even sneak in some advice from the Bible), and as they finish each course, they earn "Baby Bucks" which they get to "spend" on items in the boutique.

Mary says they hand out stuff like vitamins for the moms to take while they're pregnant or breastfeeding their kids, and don't charge a cent for any of their services, including pregnancy tests and ultrasounds. They offer free counseling for women and couples who didn't plan to get pregnant, and even for people who aborted in the past and regret it. Mary says she's praying they get enough donations this year to start doing STD testing at no cost.

Ah, there's the pin, tucked inside an antique amethyst ring. When I pick it up, for a weird second my mind flashes to Kermit Gosnell, the abortion doctor who got thrown into jail a few years back for keeping his "clinic" about as clean as a barnyard and staffing it with unlicensed personnel and drug addicts. Apparently, his solution to late term babies who were unlucky enough to be born alive during attempted abortions was to jam scissors into their necks and sever their spinal cords to "ensure fetal demise." Somehow the miniature golden feet on Mary's pin conjure up for me the workings of that sadistic monster, who also had a creepy foot fetish, and kept the tiny feet of aborted babies in jars like cocktail sausages.

Mary's voice down the hall sounds harried.

"Jessica Rose, if you step out of that bathtub once more –"

She leaves her sentence dangling ominously. I picture Jess giggling while climbing back into the sudsy water. I need to grab that pin, throw myself together, and get in there to relieve my frazzled wife.

I do a quick clothes change, tie my tie, and snatch up Jess's princess PJ's, which are strewn carelessly over a chair in her room. Marching into the bathroom, I try to sound serious.

"Alright, little lady, you heard your mother. We've got a banquet to go to tonight, so you'd better hop out of that tub right now and into a towel. Hustle your bustle!"

Chapter 12 Tanya

"Every love story has a sad ending." – Barbara Parrish

Well, here goes.

I'm finally about to do it. After 18 months of uninspired dating, I'm ready to break up with Chuck. I know it isn't nice to do it around the holidays, but what am I supposed to do? Keep leading him on? It's not gonna be pretty, but I honestly don't know what else to do, especially after tonight's disastrous evening with Megan and Steve.

I tried to get out of it, but Chuck seemed to have his heart set on hanging out as a foursome, so fine, we went. I knew I'd have a lousy time watching Steve drool all over Megan, and I was right. Poor Chuck. He didn't have a clue.

Afterwards, I just can't pretend anymore. When he drops me off in that vintage eyesore he drives around in, I know it's now or never.

"Hey, Chuck," I begin. My mouth suddenly feels like it's stuffed with cotton. "Can we talk?"

"Sure. What's up? Did you like the movie tonight?"

Can he really be that clueless?

"Yeah, it was fine. I mean, if you like that sort of thing."

What sort of thing? Even I don't know what I'm talking about.

Get on with it! my conscience bellows.

"Well, what I wanted to talk about, uh, it wasn't exactly the movie. I mean, did you notice anything about me tonight?"

54

"Oh, I get it, you're fishing for a compliment –"

"Chuck, I'm not fishing for a compliment! Are you kidding me! Didn't you notice I wasn't having too much fun?"

His face changes. The sly grin he assumed when he thought he knew what I was getting at settles into a sad kind of grimace.

"Look, it wasn't that I didn't like the movie or anything like that. To be honest, I barely watched the movie. I was too busy watching Steve and Megan."

Chuck says nothing. His face seems literally frozen in that sorrowful mask.

"Come on, Chuck, aren't you gonna say something? Don't you wanna know why I was watching them?" I demand.

"Yeah. Sure. Why not?"

Something about his flat tone irritates me.

"Because I'm interested in Steve!" I bark. "That's why I was trying to get out of going out with them! I knew I'd have a rotten time because Steve's all about Megan and *I'm* all about Steve!"

Why did I say that? Was that really necessary?

"I'm sorry, Chuck, I shouldn't have said that," I say, backpedaling as fast as my sense of decency can go. It makes no difference. He just sits there looking sucker punched. He opens his mouth once as if to say something, but nothing comes out. His eyes are two pools of misery.

"I'm sorry, Chuck. Really. I wanted to care about you the way you seem to care about me. I mean, I tried to love you. It's just, I can't force it. I tried. Really. I'm sorry."

Chuck regains his dignity.

55

"I think you better go," he says softly.

"Oh, yeah, I guess you're right," I say, unhooking my seatbelt, and grateful he's not gonna insist on talking it out.

He gives me a parting shot before pulling out of the driveway, which isn't like him.

"I treated you nice!" he declares. Something in the tone of those four words carries an indictment, as if I'm guilty of far more than squashing a case of puppy love.

Mom, of course, wants to play 20 questions when I get in. Why does she expect the blow by blow whenever I come home from a date? David, mercifully, gets her to back off by pretending to want to resume the chick flick they paused when I came in.

My stepfather's really not a bad guy. If his last name weren't such a monstrosity, I might have said yes when he offered to adopt me. But there's no way I can trade in a nice, normal name like Ritter for something that conjures up images of frizzled beards and tusked helmets. I have little enough going for me.

Chuck won't call. He's not the type of guy to come crawling after somebody dumps him, even if that somebody happens to be a girlfriend he seemed crazy about, for reasons which escape me.

I once heard a quote that went something like, "I refuse to join any club that would have me as a member." I think it was Groucho Marx who said it. That's pretty much the way I see this thing with Chuck. I don't even want to be with myself half the time, so I'm not sure what he sees in me. He'll get over it, but now I don't have anyone to go to the prom with. I mean, it's months away, but guys aren't exactly knocking each other down to get to know me.

Maybe I should've thought this through a little more.

Chapter 13 Chuck

"Weakness of attitude becomes weakness of character." – *Albert Einstein*

I enter the house quietly, so I won't get peppered with questions by Mom. I don't feel like giving her the gory details. Doesn't matter. She hears me in the hall.

"Hey, Son, you're home early."

It's an innocent enough comment, and normally I would respond. God knows she deserves all the kindness she can get right now. But I don't have it in me to make small talk.

"Chuck?" she persists. "Honey, is that you?"

OK, I don't want her thinking there's an axe murderer in the house.

"Oh, yeah, it's me, Mom," I manage. "G'night."

"Wait a second, Babe, do you have a minute?"

Just shoot me now goes through my mind.

"Listen, can it wait? I'm pretty tired."

But I hear the floorboards creak and the next thing I know, she's beside me. The coffee stain on her seen-better-days bathrobe goes well with the sick feeling in the pit of my stomach.

"Honey, are you OK? It's only, what, 9:30? I didn't expect you for a couple of hours."

The only way to get her to back off when she's like this is to act tough. I don't wanna hurt her, God knows, but I know from experience this sympathy of hers will turn into pity, and before long, I'll be bawling in her arms. I can't handle that on top of everything else.

Maybe this kind of weakness is what Tanya can't stand about me.

"Look, Mom, if you must know, Tanya and I broke up tonight. That's all. Look, I'm gonna go to bed."

"Oh, I'm so sorry, Sweetheart," she says in that tone I don't want to hear. When I don't respond, she takes the hint. "OK. Goodnight, then. Love you."

She touches my arm, but I brush past her.

I think I'm a pretty rare breed. When I first started dating, my dad took me out for lunch and basically told me to keep my hands to myself. I was a little young for that lecture, as the girl and I were barely in middle school and had to be chauffeured around by our parents to and from the stupid carnival we went to. Still, I took his message to heart because he'd always been a good role model and knew what he was talking about.

Up until the divorce, that is. We used to do stuff as a family, like cutting down our own Christmas trees and having movie and game nights. Both my parents are really hands on, and we had a pretty good upbringing, I guess. They tried to give us morals, too. They put software on our computers so we couldn't look at anything that might give us the wrong ideas. Stuff like that.

Now, though, since Dad hit his mid-life crisis or whatever it is, everything's hit the fan. He lives in a rented room 20 miles away, and Mom's not sure we can keep the house. She's on the internet all the time, trying to find a job. When she's not doing that, she's paying people to help her write a résumé that doesn't look like she spent the last 20 years of her life raising kids. My little brother's started wetting the bed again. The whole thing's a mess.

So, on top of all this drama, Tanya dumps me. And for no good reason that I can see. Like I said, I'm a rare breed. I paid for almost all the stuff we did, for one thing. Show me another guy in this day and age who does that. And I treated her like a lady, a dying art if ever there was one. I never pressured her for a thing.

Well, there was that one time last summer, but that was all her, really. I mean, let's face it, I could've said no, but come on. I'm only human. It was after a movie, a love story she wanted to see. Anyway, Tanya got real "affectionate" and, well, one thing sort of led to another. She joked afterwards that my old Monte Carlo was our cheap motel. I was a little insulted, to tell you the truth. I put a lot of work into that car, and it may not be a bona fide classic, but it is to me. So was the event itself, for that matter. That's not something I do every day, and it was because she was special.

Anyway, we talked about it later, and decided not to go there again. We both have sort of a religious background and kind of regretted it. Doesn't much matter now. She's made it real clear she wants me out of her life.

I wonder if it has anything to do with my name. Hammerschmidt's not exactly a name girls would line up to change theirs to, and it sure doesn't sing with "Tanya." I hear girls try out their first names with guys' last names when they're serious, just to see how it sounds.

But I guess it was only me who was serious.

Chapter 14 Mary

"People shop for a bathing suit with more care than they do a husband or wife. The rules are the same. Look for something you're comfortable wearing. Allow for room to grow." – Erma Bombeck

"Hey, Mar, how's that couple you were telling me about?" Dave asks as we sort through the fridge for tonight's dinner.

"Can you be a little more specific, Sweetie?" I smile. "We do have one or two folks coming through our doors every day."

"Oh, yeah. I mean the ones you mentioned that are pregnant with the disabled kid. The baby who might be disabled. Have they been back?"

Dave's referring to the Coughlins, Emma and Tom. Every once in a while, we have a husband and wife come in together. More often, it's single women who've just found out they're pregnant and are considering abortion. Rarely do they consider adoption and, when they do, most of the time they end up changing their minds. Keeping your baby is the chic thing to do, regardless of whether or not you can provide for the poor thing. Unplanned babies put an even greater strain on relationships that are far from perfect to begin with. Too often, couples whose babies come as a surprise don't know how to parent, and their children pay an awful price for that lack of knowledge. That's why our foster care system is so overcrowded and inefficient. The whole process is heartbreaking for those of us who see it up close and personal. Not least, we feel for would-be adopters who spend thousands of nonrefundable dollars on birth mothers' expenses, too often having their hopes dashed in the end.

But that's not what Dave's asking about. In the Coughlin case, the parents went to their priest for counseling and, thankfully, he referred them to us. Our services are a great option, because this is all we do. We give them facts and alternatives and offer to help them materially and emotionally. Spiritually, too, if they'll let us. When the clergy try to shepherd these kinds of folks all the way through their pregnancies, they sometimes get in over their heads. No minister can be expected to know everything about everything, but the one thing many of them agree on is that abortion is the wrong choice. When they tell people like the Coughlins that, and the parents see no other alternative, they feel judged and sometimes never show up in church again. Then they're worse off than they were before they sought counseling in the first place.

"Yeah, fortunately," I answer Dave's original question about whether the Coughlins ever returned to our center. "Dad seems more committed to staying the course than Mom, though. He seems more optimistic after talking to one of the agencies we referred them to. More hopeful. Mom still looks like she lost her best friend."

Maybe she did, I think after I say that to Dave. There are few things more stressful in a relationship than having a disabled child, and when one parent's on board and the other can't wrap his or her mind around the circumstances – well, things get pretty tense.

"Do they have any other kids?" Dave asks.

I have to be careful how I answer questions like that, because we have a confidential relationship with our clients. If we didn't, they couldn't trust us and that would be the end of that.

"Um, Sweetie, I'm better off just sticking to the general outline of their situation. Y'know what I mean?"

"Oh, sure, Mar, of course. I just wondered because that would affect their decision, too, right?"

"Oh, sure. When there are other kids, the whole family's affected by the child's special needs. Can you hand me the pepper?"

"Here you go," he replies, and I sprinkle some into the meat loaf I'm putting together. He loves the way I make it with seasoned tomato sauce on top. I try to use the leanest cuts of beef whenever they're on sale. I don't want heart disease to claim him at an early age, like it did his dad and two brothers. And he's overweight to begin with, so I try to do what I can to keep him healthy.

"Thanks," I say, then wince when a jolt of pain cramps up the fingers on my right hand. It's the arthritis rearing its ugly, inconvenient head, just when I'm trying to get dinner on the table. Dave notices.

"You OK, Hon?" he asks. "The joints again?"

"Yeah," I answer, annoyed because this condition makes me feel like a grandmother. "It'll pass. Alright, we need to get this into the oven. See if it's preheated, OK?"

Dave's mind won't be diverted. He wants to keep talking about this.

"Hey, Hon, did you ever make an appointment with the doctor about those hands? Why should you have to suffer?"

"I'll get to it, but they're only gonna tell me to take medicine, and you know that's not my favorite thing to do. Hey, how was work for you? We're doing all this talking about my job, and I haven't heard about yours yet."

"OK, change of subject!" he laughs. "It's going fine, I guess. I mean, I survived the last round of layoffs, thank God, but you already knew that. They're putting more on us, though, since they cut the staff. I may have to start picking up Saturdays or staying late some nights. I hate to do it, though. I see little enough of you and Jess as it is. Oh, and Tanya."

I pretend not to notice him adding her as an afterthought. To be honest, she's been so distant lately, it's easy for me to almost forget she lives here, too. She says she's busy with school, but I feel like she's avoiding us.

I don't think she's seeing Chuck anymore, either. She doesn't want to talk about it, so I stay away from the subject. If I'm right, it makes me sad because he seemed like a genuinely nice guy. He even asked me once for my cell number "just in case." I thought that was very foresighted and told him so.

"Wow, Sweetie, I didn't realize things were getting that tough," I respond. I'm about to wipe my hands and put my arms around him when Jessica bounds into the room. She and her little friend have been playing in the living room, but apparently view the kitchen as their new "manifest destiny." This is unfortunate for me, because the other child, also named Jessica, is three years older than our Jess, and sort of acts as a babysitter. She keeps the baby – er, *our* Jess – occupied and helps to tire her out.

"Not happening, ladies," Dave cautions. "The oven's on in here, and we can't have you two getting hurt. Tell you what, though. I'm almost done helping Mom. If you two can stay put in the other room for a few more minutes, I'll take you out on the trampoline when I get finished. How does that sound?"

Both girls squeal with delight at the idea of bouncing around in the great outdoors. It's gotten so cold lately that I can't believe Dave's going to brave the elements with them.

If only Tanya were this easy to amuse.

Chapter 15 Mary

"Then the LORD *said to [Moses], 'Who has made man's mouth? Who makes him mute, or deaf, or seeing, or blind? Is it not I, the* LORD*?'" – Exodus 4:11, the Bible, English Standard Version*

"Hi, Emma, I'm so glad to see you! It's been a while. How are you feeling?" I ask when Emma Coughlin shows up at my office. In truth, I hadn't expected to see her again. I've been doing this work long enough to know when a woman wants out, and this one definitely wants out. She doesn't have to say the words to me. I can read it in her face, hear it in what she's not saying. My only hope is the fact that her husband, Tom, seems committed to raising this child, come what may.

"Oh, OK, I guess," she answers flatly. She looks down at her hands, fumbling with her wedding ring.

Actually, I rarely counsel expectant moms anymore. My job involves a lot of fundraising and paperwork. I do a lot of behind-the-scenes stuff because we are, in fact, a business, and we do have a bottom line. I also spend a fair amount of time commuting to my job, which is in the city. Most of our clients eke by under the poverty line and have little education to better their circumstances. That's one of the reasons they consider abortion. They see no future for themselves, let alone their children.

It astonished me to learn that quite a few churches in our vicinity actually support these moms aborting rather than choosing adoption for babies they feel they can't raise. Apparently, there's less of a stigma associated with taking a child's life than giving it a chance to live in someone else's home. Good thing no one ever told Moses's mother that, or she might have opted to hold on to her son even though that would've meant being slaughtered by Pharaoh's henchmen. Then who would have led the Jews out of Egypt?

Tanya's right; I do preach too much.

In any event, sheer luck brought the Coughlins into my path for counseling. No, that's not accurate. I don't believe in luck any more than I believe in the tooth fairy (although if Jessica asks, I do believe in that gossamer-winged sprite). I think it was a divine appointment. They came in the day before Thanksgiving. Emma said she passes our building on the way to her office, and thought since she had a short day at work because of the holiday, she'd drop in. I later learned her priest put in a good word for us, too. Since she and Tom had met for lunch that day, they came in together.

I was hoping for a short day myself, as I had stuffing to make, a table to set, side dishes to start, and a three-year-old who wasn't going to make any of that easy. I had sent most of my small staff home early to get a jump on their holiday preparations, so it fell either to me or the peeling wallpaper to welcome these folks. I said a quick prayer asking the Lord to put more time in my day (I swear he's done just that on some crazy mornings when I couldn't get out the door) and dove into the trenches with Emma and Tom.

They returned once after that, and I haven't seen them since. Frankly, I feared the worst, but seeing Emma today gives me hope. Her belly looks fuller, but her face, sadder.

Like I said, I'm really not a counselor. But I'm a veteran of unplanned pregnancy, and well acquainted with fear.

I wait patiently for Emma to speak. This is the first time she's come in without Tom, and I'm thinking she might feel freer to say what's on her heart if I don't press her. I've learned there can be great value in silence.

After a few minutes, tears start to fall. She angrily brushes them away and apologizes.

"Emma, would it be alright if I give you a hug?" I ask gingerly.

She hesitates, then nods. I hold her for what feels like a long time, then sit back down in my chair.

I decide to risk it.

"Wanna tell me what's happening?" I venture.

More tears.

"The baby has spina bifida. Well, you knew that, right? Well, we were hoping they'd be able to do surgery in utero, but that's not gonna be an option. Certain things have to be – oh, it doesn't matter, you don't need the details, just take my word for it, they can't do it. They *won't* do it. So that means he's gonna have hydrocephalus, too – do you know what that is? In the old days, they called it 'water on the brain.' So, they're gonna have to put a shunt in his brain. That's a tube that drains off the extra fluid. Oh, and the shunts don't last forever, so he gets to have *more* surgeries when that happens."

Her brow furrows as she lets her sarcasm sink in.

"Bottom line, we're gonna be stuck with, I mean, we're gonna have a kid that'll walk temporarily if at all, need tons of surgeries, have to have catheters and enemas all the time 'cause his plumbing won't work –"

"His? You mean you've found out your baby is a boy? Oh, sorry, I didn't mean to interrupt."

"No, that's OK. Yeah. Yeah, it's a boy. My little guy, Kyle – he's been calling him Matthew, so I guess that's his name. Do you have any more tissues?"

"Here," I say, handing her the box. "You can hold on to it. There's plenty more where that came from! Please, go on."

"Thanks," she sniffs. "Well, my husband, Tom – you met him – he's being the Rock of Gibraltar. Says everything's gonna work out. He has it in his head that we're gonna train our two older boys to come alongside us and help with their brother, that we'll all be this big, happy family of overcomers, and then when we're too old to take care of this kid, our older boys are just gonna swoop in and take our place. Can you believe that?"

"Hmmm," I begin. Emma jumps in while I'm pondering my response.

"Tell me, Mary, do you think that's fair? Or even realistic? Seriously?"

I pray, *Lord, give me wisdom.* I have no idea what this mother wants to hear, and even less what God wants me to say.

"I don't know," I say finally. "I don't know your boys – they're very young, aren't they?"

She nods.

"Yeah. Four and two. Well, the older one's almost five. But I don't know how they'll turn out, whether they'll want to care for a disabled brother or not. The other thing is –" Emma breaks off momentarily, then continues, "the other thing is, *I* don't want to care for a disabled baby! I don't want my whole life turned upside down by a child I never asked for in the first place! When I did accept that I was pregnant again, I wanted a girl! Doesn't anybody care what *I* want!"

Her outburst startles me, but I know it's important to remain calm. I study my aching fingers and wait for her to continue. She looks at me expectantly.

Tag. I guess I'm "It."

"Emma, you came here for a reason. Why, do you think?"

She blows her nose and swears.

"I have no idea, Mary! I had nothing else to do on my lunch break – God knows, I can barely eat these days – so I figured I'd stop in, I guess. Oh, sorry, I didn't mean to be rude."

"No offense taken, Em. Go on."

She blows her nose and continues.

"Well, we've been doing our homework, you know, we got in touch with some of the agencies you sent us to last time. Remember you gave us that list?"

I nod.

"Well, I found this other group online. Prenatal Partners, they're called. Oh, and then I contacted the Spina Bifida Association, too. They have a Facebook page for parents of spina bifida kids, and one thing led to another, and we got to talk to this woman who was born with it, and that was really helpful. The woman's name is Lisa Jane – she told us to call her L.J. – and when

I talked to her I felt sort of, I dunno, stronger somehow. Like, because she's been living with it all these years, and she's really amazing, maybe our baby would grow up to be amazing, too. Y'know?"

I nod.

"She didn't pull any punches, either. Told us she had tons of surgeries like our guy will have to have. Even told us she maxxed out her insurance a couple of times! Said her parents had to get a lawyer to make her school district get on board with helping her. Like, the school didn't wanna put in a railing outside so she wouldn't fall going down the steps on her crutches! Stupid stuff like that. Oh, yeah, and she said she gets extra hot because her body's thermostat doesn't work right, and the school would complain 'cause she had to wear tank tops, like as if that's the worst thing a girl can wear these days, and –"

Emma's voice trails off. I wait.

"Here's the thing. This woman, she has the best outlook. And she's so smart. Got through college – well, it took her a long time, but still – she just never gave up on herself and never quit. I'm trying to remember how she put it. It was something like, 'Some people think my life is all misery and woe, like a melodramatic horror story.' But she said she doesn't see it that way. She figures everybody has bad moments, not just disabled people."

Another pause. I leave the lull alone.

"She did admit she's having trouble finding a job. Like I said, she graduated college, but y'know, it's hard for most people to get jobs these days, let alone someone with a disability. She's pretty

71

tough, though, said she's not giving up. She said something really inspiring, too. I'm trying to remember how she put it. Something like, 'God didn't bring me through all my surgeries and help me get through college so I could sit around and complain about how tough the job market is!'"

I nod and smile.

"She gives a lot of credit to her parents. Apparently, she has this really awesome family where everybody helps out, not just her mom and dad. She has, I don't know, two or three brothers and I think a sister. They know someday she may need to live with them – the parents are pretty open with the rest of the kids – and they're working on a plan where they'll help her in shifts, sort of. The parents built an addition onto the house where everything's handicapped accessible, so she can do a lot more for herself. She'll still have to get aides from the outside and all, but she's just OK about the whole thing. Doesn't feel sorry for herself at all. Very practical, really."

I nod. Seems my best sentences in this conversation are unspoken.

"The best thing, though, and I think this is what really got Tom – the best thing she said was along the lines of, why rule out a person's potential based on a possible prognosis? I mean, her parents knew before she was born that she was gonna have problems. Just like us with Matt. But they just figured, what with the way technology's always changing and all, I guess they figured, why not give her a shot?"

At this point, Emma looks at me as if she expects a response. Again, I pray. Then, right in the middle of this intense conversation, the Lord zaps me with a revelation.

Maybe if I pray before talking to Tanya, things will go better.

I compartmentalize that information into the maternal section of my brain and mentally shift back to professional mode.

"So, all this sounds very encouraging, Em. That's wonderful! I'm proud of you for doing all that research."

Ouch! Why did I say that? This is a grown woman I'm talking to, not one of my daughters. Guess I didn't completely shift gears after all. Fearing I'm coming off condescending, I try another approach.

"So, it seems like you're pretty upset today, though. You were very honest a little while ago about not wanting to raise Matthew. Do you wanna talk about that?"

Her eyes fill up again.

"Well, just because L.J.'s family has all the money in the world to remodel their house and all, Tom and I don't have that kind of money! We don't have thousands of dollars to be putting in wheelchair ramps and buying special vans and taking time off from work to run this kid to doctor appointments all the time! I have a full-time job and so does Tom! Our kids are in day care as it is! What day care is gonna jump at the chance to take on Matthew? This whole thing is just impossible! I don't know how to *do* spina bifida, and I'm pretty sure I don't wanna learn! Oh, Lord, why can't I do this! Some great mother, not wanting to raise her own child!"

She breaks into heaving sobs. Her already running mascara slides down her cheeks in an ashen trickle. She wipes her eyes with an overused tissue and takes a deep breath.

Lord, what do I say now?

If she's expecting me to join her in beating herself up, she'll have a long wait. I know firsthand the kind of doubts mothers feel when confronted with an unplanned pregnancy. I can't begin to imagine what it's like when you find out, on top of that, your child will never do all that typically abled kids do, and may not even live very long.

I take a gentle tone and wade in.

"Emma, you are where you are. No amount of self-flagellation is gonna change where you are. The important thing is you're researching and moving forward. What's the next step, do you think?"

She smiles weakly.

"I don't know, Mary. I mean, they have more tests lined up. I swear, if they ultrasound me one more time, my bladder's gonna release Lake George all over that office! And those MRI's, I feel like I'm in a coffin. Can't stand 'em. I've used up all my personal time from work, don't know if they'll let me use sick time for all these visits. Guess I could ask HR. Thing is, it's pretty hard to stay on top of things at work with all this going on. And the boys, Kyle and Kevin, my guys, they're great, but I'm so wrapped up in my, I don't know, pain, I guess, that I feel like I'm not there for them. Tom's being an absolute saint and I almost want to kill him for that. How can he accept this so easily? Why isn't he furious with me!"

More crying. I get up and put my arms around her. Professionalism be hanged, this girl needs a mother's touch.

"Oh, Honey, how could he be furious at you? You're –"

"No, you don't understand, I want him to be furious *with me*, not *at me*! We should team up in our fury! We have every right to be furious! Why can't he see that?!"

Suddenly, she laughs at herself, and I take a chance that it's OK for me to laugh with her. Before I know it, we're hugging and I'm telling her I don't have all the answers, but I'll be there for her.

She smiles and says she'd better clean her face and go back to work. I walk her to the door and ask if it would be OK for me to call her to see how she's doing. She says she'd appreciate that and gives me her cell number. We hug once more and say goodbye.

I think about my own two girls with their working limbs and unshunted heads, and breathe a prayer of thanks.

Chapter 16 Tanya

"If I had conceived these twins naturally, I wouldn't have reduced this pregnancy, because you feel like if there's a natural order, then you don't want to disturb it. But we created this child in such an artificial manner — in a test tube, choosing an egg donor, having the embryo placed in me — and somehow, making a decision about how many to carry seemed to be just another choice. The pregnancy was all so consumerish to begin with, and this became yet another thing we could control." – Expectant mother "Jenny," quoted in "The Two-Minus-One Pregnancy" published in The New York Times, August 10, 2011.

I sit down at the keyboard and type the header for my report at the upper left-hand corner:

Tanya Ritter

Senior Project

Abstract and Works Consulted

Dr. Chase - Block 2

December 2, 2017

I really hate getting started. Mom says I'm a good writer, but that's only after I get rolling. At least this only has to be one page.

I take a break to pick at some loose skin on my left forefinger. My hands always get really chapped in the winter, no matter how much hand cream I slap on them. The dangling piece of flesh comes off, and the finger starts to bleed.

Great, Tanya. This is what always happens. Satisfied?

I wrap a tissue around it and go back to work, typing the title:

Selective Reduction: Pro Side

I consult my notes, which are not organized as well as they should be. I can't help it. It drives me crazy trying to sort facts into categories. I just write stuff down and let it sort itself out later. But Dr. Chase says we'll lose credit if we don't arrange the notes *just so*. He likes to brag that he went to Princeton, so I guess he knows what he's talking about. Personally, I'd rather have a needle jabbed into *my* heart than to have to follow such ridiculous rules.

I check my finger before diving in. The tissue has done its job; I toss it onto the desk next to the computer and adjust my position in the chair.

OK, I need an intro, but it's hard to argue the case for selective reduction. Anyone who's ever read anything it about can see it's cold at best and creepy at worst. Doctors start recommending the procedure when a woman ends up with what they call a "high- or higher-order pregnancy," which are fancy terms for when she's carrying three or more children. Most often this is caused by fertility treatments that result in broods like the Gosselins. When doctors realize they've created such a huge pregnancy (at a cost of thousands of dollars not covered by insurance), they start talking about "reducing" it, which means stabbing the hearts of one or more of the babies with a lethal injection!

But wait, it gets better. They leave the remains of the "reduced" babies in the uterus, so the living ones develop next to

77

the decaying corpses of their brothers and sisters, which supposedly get absorbed by the womb. They rationalize all this by the argument that the health of the mother and babies is at greater risk than in "singleton" pregnancies (only one child).

I force myself to write the opening paragraph:

Selective reduction is the process of eliminating fetuses in a higher order pregnancy, which means 3 or more fetuses are being carried. This is done to protect the life of the mother and lives of the babies that will be carried to term. Often the babies have been conceived through fertility treatments, but there are too many to be carried safely.

I backspace and change "babies" to "fetuses," which is how all the articles refer to them. I continue the paragraph:

Doctors inject the hearts of fetuses to be killed with a needle containing potassium chloride, which gives them cardiac arrest.

I replace the word "killed" with "reduced," like it says in the articles. For the life of me, I can't see how it's anything but killing, but Dr. Chase is very big on accuracy. I continue:

That means the heart stops beating. The fetuses that are most easily reached or seem to have abnormalities are injected first. In some cases, parents can choose which ones are injected based on sex preference.

I thumb through more notes. This would probably be a lot easier if I had used the notes function in the works cited program our school librarian taught us to use. Instead, I have to wade through my own handwriting, which is like trying to decipher the Rosetta Stone.

Stop griping, Tanya. You have to get this done.

More keystrokes to explain the background of the procedure:

Dr. Mark Evans was the first to perform selective reductions in the 1980's. He is quoted as saying, "The finished product has a much better chance of surviving... Look, you never want to dehumanize it, because then you get cavalier. You have to keep the big picture in mind. We're not losing one. We're saving some." (Mundy).

The hard part of this project for me is arguing the pro side of this horror show. I didn't want this topic to begin with, but there were a limited number of choices, and by luck of the draw, we were one of the last pairs to pick. My debate partner, Sophia, said there was no way she could argue the pro side, so I got stuck with it.

Tanya, just DO it!

I force myself to think like Dr. Evans, and resume typing:

Reasons to support reduction are: a) higher order pregnancies have more of a risk of premature birth and birth defects than singleton (1 fetus only) or twin pregnancies; b) some parents, such as blended families, already have several children and don't want so many; c) the parents have usually paid 1,000's of dollars to get pregnant by fertility treatments, so they should have the choice of how many they want to keep; d) it's the parents' responsibility to pay for reduction, so they should be allowed to spend their money the way they want to; e) the more fetuses there are, the more chance of birth defects, which may result in non-productive citizens.

I reread that paragraph to see if it sounds convincing. I guess it's as scientific sounding as I can make it.

Finally, I type the wrap up:

In conclusion, selective reduction is a safe, reasonable alternative when higher order pregnancies occur. Since abortion has been legal in the U.S. since the Roe v. Wade court ruling in 1973, selective reduction is a logical extension of that court case.

I retrieve the list of citations that the works cited program produced for me as I went along (our librarian really is a genius), cut and paste it into the end of the paper, and I'm mercifully done.

Works Consulted

Affordable Fertility Treatments. *Center for Human Reproduction*. Center for Human
    Reproduction, 1 Jan. 2014. Web. 28 Oct. 2014.
    <https://www.centerforhumanreprod.com/pdf/chr_ivf_uninsured_to_50k_us_2014.
    pdf>. Procedures and costs of fertility treatments, such as in vitro.
Blackwell, Tom. "When is Twins Too Many?" *National Post*. National Post, 11 Jan. 2011.
    Web. 11 June 2014.
    <http://www.nationalpost.com/news/When+twins+many/3960709/story.html>. Use
    of fetal reduction in twin pregnancies.
"Fact Sheet: Induced Abortion in the United States." *Guttmacher Institute*. Guttmacher
    Institute, July 2014. Web. 6 June 2015.
    <http://www.guttmacher.org/pubs/fb_induced_abortion.html#1>. Abortion stats: "In
    2011, 1.06 million abortions were performed, down 13% from 1.21 million in 2008.
    From 1973 through 2011, nearly 53 million legal abortions occurred."
    Source: Jones RK and Jerman J, Abortion incidence and service availability in the
    United States, 2011, Perspectives on Sexual and Reproductive Health, 2014,
    46(1):3-14
"Fetal Development: Stages of Growth." *Cleveland Clinic*. Cleveland Clinic, 30 July 2010.
    Web. 11 June 2014. <http://my.clevelandclinic.org/healthy_living/pregnancy/hic-

fetal-development-stages-of-growth.aspx>. Fetal development from conception through ninth month.

Gleicher, Norbert, MD, et al. "Fertility Treatments and Multiple Births in the United States." *New England Journal of Medicine* 370 (2014): 1069-71. Web. 11 June 2014. <http://www.nejm.org/doi/full/10.1056/NEJMc1400242>. Rates of multiple pregnancy occurrence after in vitro and other fertility treatments. Complications in multiple births.

Mayo Clinic Staff. "Diseases and Conditions: Premature Birth Complications." *Mayo Clinic*. Mayo Clinic, 27 Nov. 2014. Web. 9 Feb. 2015. <http://www.mayoclinic.org/>. Results of premature birth, including cerebral palsy.

Mundy, Liza. "Too Much to Carry?" *Washington Post* [Washington] 20 May 2007: n. pag. Print. Excerpted from Mundy's book, *Everything Conceivable: How Assisted Reproduction Is Changing Men, Women, and the World,* published by Alfred A. Knopf. Fetal reduction in higher order pregnancies.

Padawer, Ruth. "The Two-Minus-One Pregnancy." *New York Times* [New York] 10 Aug. 2011, Magazine: 1-7. *The New York Times*. Web. 11 June 2014. <http://www.nytimes.com/2011/08/14/magazine/the-two-minus-one-pregnancy.html>. Reduction of twin pregnancies.

"Pregnancy Ultrasound." *Medline Plus*. Bethesda: U.S. National Library of Medicine National Institutes of Health, 2014. *Medline Plus*. Web. 11 June 2014. <http://www.nlm.nih.gov/medlineplus/ency/article/003778.htm>. Prep, risks and results of ultrasound.

Saletan, William. "After-Birth Abortion: The Pro-choice Case for Infanticide." *Slate* 12 Mar. 2012: n. pag. *Slate*. Web. 28 Mar. 2015. <http://www.slate.com/articles/health_and_science/human_nature/2012/03/after_birth_abortion_the_pro_choice_case_for_infanticide_.html>. Analysis of Journal of Medical Ethics article by Alberto Giubilini and Francesca Minerva, where they propose the idea of post-birth abortion.

Seligson, Hannah. "Data Murky on Fertility Rates." *New York Times* [New York] 28 Apr. 2014: n. pag. *NYTimes.com*. Web. 11 June 2014. <http://well.blogs.nytimes.com/2014/04/28/data-murky-on-fertility-rates/>. CDC and Society for Assisted Reproductive Technologies's live birth records. Compares in vitro cycles to actual births.

Transvaginal Fetal Reduction in a Quadruplet Pregnancy with 1 Sac Containing a Monochorionic Diamniotic Twin. By Sevellaraja Supermaniam. *YouTube*. N.p., 13 June 2010. Web. 11 June 2014. Ultrasound with narration and music of a fetal reduction.

"Your Growing Belly and Baby: A Timeline Through Pregnancy." *WebMD*. Ed. Nivin Todd, MD, FACOG. N.p.: n.p., 2012. N. pag. *WebMD*. Web. 11 June 2014. <http://www.webmd.com/baby/interactive-pregnancy-tool-fetal-development>. Timeline and photographs of fetal development.

Chapter 17 Tanya

"If you tell a big enough lie and keep repeating it, people will eventually come to believe it." — *Joseph Goebbels*

I heave a sigh of relief after Sophia and I wrap up our debate for senior project. All I can say is, thank God I only have to do this once!

Now I just have to survive the Q&A session where Dr. Chase and the class get to grill us. All the students have to log a certain amount of questions after peer presentations to prove they were paying attention. If they don't document that they asked at least five questions over the course of debate week, their own grade suffers. The debaters have to hold their own against the class's challenges with halfway intelligent answers – Dr. Chase calls this "defense of position," and says we'll thank him when we get to grad school. Right now, I could care less about grad school or even my bachelor's degree. I just want to get out from behind this podium!

Easy does it, Tanya. The worst is over.

To be honest, I'm less worried about the follow-up than I was about presenting. Some of the kids this week have been pretty unprepared for Q&A, but Dr. Chase hasn't been too hard on them. I guess he knows we're all just trying to pass this class so we can graduate.

"That was very well done, Ms. Ritter and Ms. Antonini," our teacher begins in that scholarly voice of his. "Your positions were well researched, and your arguments made sense. I think I speak for the whole class when I say you both convinced us that you held the positions you advocated. I'm curious, though. Would either of you be comfortable revealing your actual views on the issue?"

Sophia and I look at each other. Where's he going with this?

I wish for the hundredth time that I'd been able to squeeze into my dress pants. I hate to admit it, but Mom was right; I shouldn't have waited till the night before to plan my outfit. I look like a tormented fish in these loose pants that flare at the bottom, while petite Sophia in her pencil skirt shows off her perfect legs.

My partner finds her voice first.

"Well, um, I'm pro-life, so it was relatively easy for me to argue my side. I can't speak for Tanya, though."

I could kill Sophia at this moment. I know she's not trying to throw me under the bus – she's too sweet for that – but how am I supposed to respond to that?

I know what Mom would want me to say. Her whole existence seems to scream "pro-life." It's her life's work, and Dolly and I are living proof that she's willing to put her money where her mouth is.

But my research has given me a lot to think about. Abortion's been legal since 1973. If it's so terrible, how could our whole country let it go on and on for generations? Selective reduction just seems like the logical next step after abortion.

Besides, we have all the technology to help women get pregnant, and doctors can't help it if too many embryos implant. I mean, the couples are the ones taking all the chances, when you get right down to it. I read in a major newspaper that it costs around 12 grand for just one round of fertility treatments.[1] Then the patient has

83

to turn around and spend another 10 grand or so to reduce if they get more than they bargained for.[2] To me, the whole thing seems wasteful. But, hey, it's their money.

Plus, it makes sense for couples who already have children from earlier relationships and only want one together; why should they be saddled with more than they can handle, even twins? And in large pregnancies, one or more of the babies is bound to have birth defects, which doctors screen for before doing the reduction. They aim their lethal needles at the hearts of those babies first, so the parents don't have to deal with disabled kids. If all the kids seem OK, they just see which ones they can reach most easily with the syringe, or even which sex the parents prefer to keep.

But if I admit reduction might not be a bad thing, am I being disloyal to Mom?

Dr. Chase is sitting there, waiting for me to comment. I look down at my hands, and notice my thumb is bleeding. I guess I've picked it into oblivion while I've been up here, waffling over how to respond. I shove my hand into my pocket, hoping no one has noticed the blood on it.

Dr. Chase breaks into my thoughts.

"Ms. Ritter, what about you? Would you care to share your actual views on the procedure you just argued so convincingly for?"

My tongue sticks to the roof of my mouth. I don't mind giving him an answer; I just don't want to sound like an idiot while I'm doing it.

My mind flashes to a quote from a fertility expert, who uses the words "take home baby rate," as though he's equating reproduction with grabbing KFC for dinner. Dr. Evans, the guy who thought up the whole reduction procedure, calls the babies that make the cut – the ones who don't get needles jabbed into their hearts – "the finished product," as if he's describing a jar of pickles or something. In the next breath, he says he doesn't want to "dehumanize" the "finished product," because he doesn't want to get "cavalier."[3] I'm no rocket scientist, but his whole attitude sounds pretty dehumanizing and cavalier to me!

To get through the project, I had to decide there was no point in my getting worked up over it, since it has nothing to do with me. I sort of put aside Mom's views – the ones she wants me to have, too – and tried to think like all the medical people who believe this is a good idea. But here I am being asked by my Princeton educated teacher to *really* pick a side. Truthfully, the whole thing boggles my mind, since there seem to be good reasons for and against.

I have to say something. I open my mouth and pray something half sensible comes out.

"Well, um, it's a pretty tough call, actually. There's a lot of good reasons *to* do it, but there's also many, I mean, lots of reasons *not* to."

Please let that satisfy him! Please let him just turn the class over to the next set of debaters!

It doesn't, and he doesn't. His mouth twitches, and he comes back with, "But Ms. Ritter, you just argued extensively for the pro-reduction side. Your analysis in your research paper was spot on. You really sounded convinced. Was that all just for show?"

My underwear is beginning to slip uncomfortably down below my belly fat. So much for the "muffin top destroyer" claims that came on the packaging. My muffin top seems to be overrunning the undies, so thanks for nothing. Not only that, but I'm starting to sweat, and I worry the foundation I'm not used to wearing will start dripping down my face in little beige raindrops.

I have to think fast and find some way to get off the hot seat. For some stupid reason, the advice they always give us when we take multiple choice tests leaps to mind. They say the first answer you think of is probably the right one.

If that's the case, I guess I'm with Mom, because what's going through my head is a sickening quote from Dr. Evans's ultrasound technician – herself a breastfeeding mother. She said, "I don't particularly like doing the reductions. I find it very stressful. With every patient, I think, *If it was me, what would I do?* Some of these people tried to get pregnant for the past five years and prayed to God. And now that they are pregnant, they are telling God: You gave me too many. I sometimes feel like we are playing God, and that is very emotionally stressful. It's a very hard procedure, because the baby is moving, and you are chasing it. That is what is very emotional -- when the baby is moving and you are chasing it."[4]

I take the leap.

"Well, I guess what bothers me about reduction is it sounds a lot like the slave traders," I begin, mentally praising myself for hearkening back to Dr. Chase's area of expertise, history. "It sort of reminds me of the way they loaded as many slaves onto the ship as they could carry, even though they knew a lot of 'em wouldn't survive the journey."

"Go on. How is that like reduction?" he persists.

I'm feeling more and more flustered, and without the carefully scripted arguments Sophia and I had worked out, my answers are becoming less coherent.

"Well, I guess, um, because the embryos get implanted, I mean, transferred, um, into the, y'know, the uterus, and there are too many of 'em to, um, manage, I mean, so they just get rid of some of 'em. Well, it's not exactly like the slave ships, but you know what I mean, right?"

"We're listening. Finish making your point," Dr. Chase demands.

"Well, um, in the case of the slave traders, they just let 'em die – the slaves that were piled on top of each other on the ships. In the case of the embryos, they just implant, er, transfer too many and kill off the excess. To me, it seems kind of heartless."

Dr. Chase draws himself up in his chair and stares at me. With his white hair and Coke bottle glasses, he sort of reminds me of an angry owl.

"But Ms. Ritter," he says, "how are the two analogous? In the one case, you're talking about something which took place centuries ago, which all educated people now agree was a national disgrace. You're comparing that to a modern medical procedure which, if not done, could jeopardize the lives of innocent mothers and children. I'm having a hard time seeing any similarities."

87

Because you don't want to, you old goat, I want to scream. Instead, I stand there looking foolish with my underpants riding down and my makeup running like a faucet. Later, I know, at home in front of the mirror, all kinds of clever answers will come to me; now, I can think of nothing except what my classmates must be thinking of me.

Sophia, bless her heart, tries to come to my rescue.

"Dr. Chase, I think what Tanya means is –" she begins, but he cuts her off.

"The question was directed at your *opponent*," our teacher states emphatically. "One does not argue the opposing side in a debate."

"But, Dr. Chase," Sophia persists, with more gumption than I would've given her credit for, "she *is* arguing my side. I had the pro-life, er, *con* side, remember?"

"You'll have a chance to reply later," he responds, then stares back at me.

I know what I want to say. It goes something like this: *Look, Dude, neither one of us wanted to defend this barbaric procedure, but one of us had to! You asked me for my honest opinion, so I'm giving it to you. If you don't like it, go back to the Arctic with the other snowy owls and leave me alone!*

But that bit of honesty, though it would be immensely satisfying to deliver, would also be the death of my GPA. Q and A time is a hefty portion of the grade, and I have to pass this class. I have no choice but to suck it up and do damage control.

I can feel tears beginning to blur my vision. I feel sick. Maybe the best thing would be to concede the point and let him move onto his next victim.

"Well, uh, I guess you're right. I guess maybe it is for a good reason – the procedure. I guess my reasoning was, uh, wrong."

Now can I sit down? I pray.

But Dr. Chase refuses to relinquish the power he holds over me.

"Does the audience have any questions or comments?"

John Sickles raises his hand. Now, here's a pit bull I don't want to go up against. I've seen him pulverize previous debaters and even a teacher on one occasion.

This kid really oughtta consider a career in law, I remember thinking after watching him destroy the unfortunate debater who had argued that climate change was a myth. John had hacked away at the kid's logic until the poor guy looked like he'd dropped a load in his pants. I know Dr. Chase believes he's preparing us for the rigors of college life, but that's no excuse for the way he looked on passively that day like a spectator at a gladiator fight. The difference, of course, was that in those ancient contests, both participants usually had weapons; here in the school arena, Sickles showed up well armed, while the other poor idiot might as well have been defending himself with a balloon sculpture.

"I'd like to know how Tanya – er, Ms. Ritter –" Sickles corrects himself, remembering they're supposed to address the debaters with formality, "can compare a mass of chromosomes that hasn't yet developed into a person to an African American human being on a slave ship."

I wince. I remember coming across information which could shut this guy up. Facts like when the fetal heartbeat can first be detected. When is it? Six weeks? And that doesn't take into account that the heart actually starts beating somewhere around the third week, doesn't it? That ought to prove the thing is more than a "mass of chromosomes." And how do we define a baby in the first place? I can't help but wonder why the pro-choice crowd calls it a "glob of tissue" when it comes at an inconvenient time, but it's "a bundle of joy" when people beg God to let them get pregnant. When people announce they're expecting, no one ever congratulates them on their "product of conception," but on having a baby! How quickly the terminology changes, though, when the kid messes up its parents' plans. And if a baby is only a baby when its parents want it, how come pregnant women are considered mothers-to-be, even if they opt for abortion?

All these thoughts ramble through my mind but won't form a rational sentence in this forum where so many unfeeling eyes are on me, waiting, it seems, for their gladiatorial catharsis. My only defender has been silenced by the man in charge.

I plead with my brain to come up with something intelligent, but instead hear myself blurt out, "Remember that book we read in middle school – *The Giver*?[5] Remember what that society did to inconvenient babies? They 'released' them! Release meant killing them! Doesn't 'release' sound an awful lot like 'reduce?'"

Silence. Sickles just glares at me with a scornful expression. His quietness seems to convey that my emotional response doesn't even deserve an answer. He's "resting his case," I guess.

Hoping the ordeal is over, I dare to rest my mind for a few seconds. But John must sense I've let down my guard. He opens with round two.

"Ms. Ritter, what does a fiction book about a dystopian society have to do with fetal reduction? You're making irrelevant statements."

Now I'm getting mad. Just because this joker's gearing up to be editor of a law journal is no reason for him to be taking shots at me.

"John, I mean, Mr. Sickles, I'm just making a comparison. The society in *The Giver*, they, I mean, the leaders, didn't value life, so they picked and choosed, er, *chose*, who got to live and who got to die. I'm just saying that's not all that different from reduction."

"Fine, but how about giving us some *facts* instead of your *interpretation*," he sneers that last word, "of a middle school novel."

Mercifully, the bell rings. With this tangible reminder of where we actually are (a high school classroom as opposed to a courtroom), Dr. Chase drops his formality and dismisses the class.

"Good stuff today, gang. Mr. Zeppo and Ms. Klinger, you're up Monday with physician assisted suicide. Lookin' forward to it. See ya!"

I run into the bathroom and throw up.

⚔⚔⚔⚔⚔⚔⚔⚔

Author's note: The sources Tanya refers to in this chapter are cited below:

[1]http://well.blogs.nytimes.com/2014/04/28/data-murky-on-fertility-rates

[2]http://www.nationalpost.com/news/When+twins+many/3960709/story.html

[3]http://www.washingtonpost.com/wp-dyn/content/article/2007/05/15/AR2007051501730_5.html

[4]ibid.

[5]Lois Lowry, *The Giver* (Boston: Houghton Mifflin, 1993).

Chapter 18 Tanya

"Blessed is the servant who loves his brother as much when he is sick and useless as when he is well and can be of service to him." – Francis of Assisi

As if I'm not upset enough after my own debate debacle, I have a feeling this next one's gonna give me nightmares. Carl Zeppo and Zara Klinger are presenting on physician assisted suicide, and oh man, is it bringing stuff up for me. Literally.

As Zara speaks, I find myself back with my grandparents in their room – the one at the top of the stairs that's been mine ever since they died. When they were alive, I used to squeeze into their double bed between them, and Granddad would tell me bedtime stories. When I got too big for that, they invited me to set up my sleeping bag and camp out on their rug whenever I wanted. Mom was fine with it as long as I got to sleep on time, and Grandma and Granddad always turned off the TV the minute I crept into their room. I remember thinking that I wouldn't want to turn off a show in the middle, but if it bothered them, they never showed it.

While Zara's making the case for physician assisted suicide, my mind switches gears and I can smell the disinfectant that permeated Grandma and Granddad's room in their final years. I can hear the tiny "pppft" sounds coming from the oxygen machine and see the long cord snaking across the bedroom floor, tethering their elderly, ailing bodies to what was left of their lives.

They both got pretty sick, ending up on hospice with visiting nurses, that kind of thing. Both were unconscious at the end, which was really sad, except Mom said they could probably still hear us, so we whispered in their ears about seeing them in heaven, and prayed they had accepted Jesus into their hearts so that would actually be the case. At the time, I bought everything Mom said about such things, but now I'm not so sure.

I guess Zara's argument reminds me of all this because her main selling point hinges on physician assisted suicide being a "humane" alternative for the sick and elderly. "Death with dignity," they call it, as opposed to the messiness and inconvenience (not to mention expense) of having to be taken care of. According to Zara, quite a few states have legalized patients' rights to choose the time of their own deaths, and doctors are supposed to help by supplying some sort of lethal injection. So much for the Hippocratic Oath.

The way Carl tells it, though, from the con side, sometimes there's a big push from family members and society in general for such people to hurry up and die so everybody else can get on with their lives.

When he says that, I feel the breakfast burrito I consumed two hours ago rise up in my throat. I will myself to keep it down by recalling the last time I saw Grandma alive.

"Read to me, Tiny Tanya," she urged. That was her affectionate name for me as long as I could remember, and she'd no doubt disregard my protruding gut and still call me that today. Her cancer-ridden body had made it impossible for her to get out of bed. Macular degeneration and cataracts had done their worst, and she could barely see.

"OK, Grandma," my younger self replied while settling into the chair by her bed. I opened my backpack and pulled out the novel my fourth-grade class was reading. "This is great! I can get my homework done and still hang out with you!"

Looking back, I remember the plot bored even me and probably sent Grandma more quickly into her pre-death coma. But if the book made her yawn, she never let on.

"Oh, Sweetheart, you are just what the doctor ordered!" she beamed, squeezing my hand. "How did you get to be such a good reader?"

Evidently, she hadn't picked up on the mispronunciations and skipped sentences my teacher was always calling me on. To her biased ears, I was reading Elizabethan English flawlessly.

I shift in my seat, trying to focus on the here and now. Zara and Carl have caught a break. Sickles the Interrogator is absent today. With any luck, he's caught something non-contagious but terminal. I'll be the first to send flowers to his funeral.

Despite my best efforts, my mind wanders again. This time it's two years after Grandma left us, and pretty much a bad rerun: Granddad in his final days, and Mom again muddling through with the help of hospice nurses and home health aides. But everyone on the medical team was home sleeping when Mom could've used help that November night at 2 AM.

I woke to hear Granddad sounding agitated, insisting on going to the bathroom by himself. He wasn't strong enough to get out of bed on his own, but what he lacked in physical strength he made up for in sheer will.

95

"Shhh, Dad, you'll wake Tanya," I heard Mom saying as I made my way to the doorway of his room. By that point, she was fumbling to get his 200-pound frame onto the bedside commode. Even at age 12, I realized this wouldn't end well. I instinctively stepped in to take some of the load. Mom flashed me a smile that warmed the dark room like sunshine, and said she'd never been prouder of me.

After that, I kind of became her right arm. I mean, I still went to school and everything, but when I came home, I would ask Mom what I could do to help. She showed me how to change his adult diapers when he got too weak for the commode, and together we would roll him back and forth so we could fasten the strips of tape on the sides. I won't say it was pleasant, and I know it made Granddad feel weird, but in a strange way, I think he felt good that we cared enough to do something like that for him.

One day when I got home, Mom was in a state trying to get somebody to hang out with Granddad so she could do some errands. She looked older that day than I had ever seen her, and I could tell she'd been crying.

"Don't worry, Mom," I reassured her. "I'll stay with Granddad. Everything'll be fine."

Two lines formed between her eyebrows while she considered this.

"I don't know, Tanya. It's a huge responsibility."

I kind of pushed the issue, reminding her how much I had already done for Granddad, and that I'd been staying alone for short periods for quite a while. I could tell she was still undecided, so I rested my case with, "Besides, Granddad's not going anywhere, is he?"

That did it. She smiled indulgently, grabbed her purse, barked a few orders, and flew out the door.

Granddad was still pretty alert at this point, unlike how he was at the end when the drugs controlled both his pain and his mind.

"Hey, TT Pot," he began, using his pet name for me. I didn't like it, but never had the heart to tell him.

"How'd you like to hear a story? Just like when you were a little girl. It's been too long, don't you think?"

"Sure, why not?" I answered, not knowing that would be the last time he'd ever tell me one. I knew I couldn't relax like I used to as a kid, when his bedtime stories would put both him and me to sleep. Still, I lowered the sidebar of his hospital bed and cozied up to him as best I could without disturbing the cord from the oxygen tank, which wound its way across the floor and ended in two prongs that had an annoying habit of slipping out of his nose.

"Oh, Tanya, don't ever make the mistake Channing did!" he cautioned me, referring to the title character in the story, an overly curious young chimp who wandered away from his family and got lost in the forest.

"Well, you know what happened next. Channing had a close call with a huge leopard! Poor thing had to run for his life and scurry up the tallest tree he could find! Things were looking pretty bleak for poor Channing until –"

A coughing spell interrupted him. I gave him a few sips of water and waited for him to continue.

"Lucky for Channing, along came his rescuer, and you know what his name was!" Granddad laughed and waited for me to answer, as I had done every one of the thousand times he'd told me this story.

"His name was Stanley the Silverback!" I cried with the gusto Granddad expected.

"That's right, TT. Stanley chased off that old leopard just as the big cat was about to climb up the tree after Channing!"

Here, Granddad clapped his hands in triumph and heaved a sigh of relief, just like he always did at this point in the story. I've never been quite sure who was most terrified by Channing's close call – the chimp or my grandfather.

Granddad continued on for a few minutes, describing the reluctant friendship that developed between the two. Stanley had his hands very full leading his own group of apes, which, of all things, is called a "shrewdness". Granddad always cracked up when he referred to Stanley's family as his "shrewdness" – he never got over the silliness of that name!

Anyway, Stanley wasn't really looking for a new best friend, but Channing attached himself to his new hero and held on for dear life. Granddad told me about some of their adventures until he started to sound hoarse, so I gave him more water.

"Thanks, T," he said gratefully. "Now, where was I? Oh, yeah, we were talking about, um, lemme see –"

"It's OK, Granddad, you need to rest," I said, seeing he was fading.

"No, no, it's OK, T," he protested. The spirit was willing, but the flesh was weak, and he started rambling like he used to when he got too tired. I guess the dark room and warmth of the covers made him sleepy, and he always ended up nodding off and mixing bits of his dreams into the story.

"Well, you see, Channing went to the coronation, and the royal family were all there, too, of course –"

I couldn't help it, I started to laugh. It was just like old times, but with painkillers added in.

I let him drift off, silently filling in the details he had left out. For some reason, I wanted to finish the story in my head. I'm not sure why. Maybe it was my mind's way of putting some finality to the last story my grandfather and I would ever share.

Granddad slept for about half an hour, but then I began to detect an odor I knew only too well. I considered my options. There was a good chance Mom would get home soon, so maybe it could wait. But then Granddad started squirming, trying to get comfortable, and I knew only one thing would accomplish that. I wrestled an adult diaper out of the full package and went to work. At first, he resisted, saying he could wait till Mom got home, but from the smell of things, I knew sooner would be better than later.

I patted his arm and tried to sound confident.

"It's OK, Granddad. We'll get this on in no time."

With a weak smile, he relented, and 20 messy minutes later, the deed was done. It wasn't on straight, and shortly after I finished, a yellow trickle made its way down his left leg via the gap where his hip met his thigh. But my pride was unconquerable. When Mom walked in the door, she burst into tears, saying I was the best daughter anyone could ever have, and she wished she could do something to reward me.

She didn't realize she just had.

So, listening to Zara's case for assisted suicide, all I can think of is those are the moments I'd have missed out on if that option had been available when my grandparents were dying. Sure, my life might've been easier if I hadn't gone through all that stuff, but no one can tell me those two old people didn't have something rich to contribute even from their death beds. I count those last days with them among the sweetest in my life, and if I could have them back, I'd gladly tuck in next to them in those God-awful hospital beds and be just as content as I was camping out on their rug when I was a kid.

Suddenly, my throat feels like it's got a huge glob of peanut butter stuck in it, and I catch a tear escaping from my eye. I wipe the back of my hand across my cheek, and swallow hard. It's no use. The lump is there to stay.

I force myself to listen to the Q and A. Let me tell you, Dr. Chase doesn't grill Carl and Zara the way he did Sophia and me. He just makes them clarify a couple of points, then everybody asks their stupid questions, and we move on to the next pair of debaters.

I slam the door on other memories that threaten to unleash themselves at this inopportune time. There's one thought I can't chase away, though – I wish Dolly could've gotten to meet those two wonderful people before they died.

Chapter 19 Mary

"The needs and heartaches of women, men, and whole families surprised by an unplanned pregnancy are as many and varied as they are. The staff and volunteers of pregnancy resources centers, also known as crisis pregnancy centers, offer a wide and equally varied menu of services and resources – many of them free. Besides pregnancy tests and counseling with a peer counselor... many pregnancy centers are now staffed by medical professionals and offer services such as testing for sexually transmitted diseases right in their facilities. Other pregnancy centers reach out into their communities with presentations and classes aimed as much at prevention of unplanned pregnancy as helping women and men in them."—Dianne E. Butts, <u>Deliver Me: Hope, Help, and Healing through True Stories of Unplanned Pregnancy (p. 193)</u>

Tanya's not been herself lately. That is, she's been less like her new self lately.

My daughter hasn't been her old self for some time – the Tanya that used to sing with me when we walked down a dark street so we wouldn't think about what might be lurking in the shadows; the girl who helped me nurse my parents gently into their graves with nary a complaint or even a hint that she was in over her head; even the big sister who was so excited when Jessica was born that she made a "Welcome Home, Mom and Dolly!" sign. That girl seems to be lost to us, at least for the foreseeable future. But just when I thought I knew what to expect – a sullen, often snarly young woman who, nevertheless, carried traces of the loving Tanya who

102

apologized when wrong and forgave when right – somehow, that new Tanya has been replaced with a stranger who says little and is almost a ghost in our house. When she comes in from school or work, she immediately goes up to her room without so much as a hello, unless Dave or I initiate it.

Something's bothering her for sure. She doesn't seem to be seeing Chuck, anymore, and isn't going out with friends, either. She hasn't gone to church since the day Seth and Vicki took her out, and unfortunately, I don't think they've followed up with her. So much for pastoral concern. On top of everything else, she looks terrible. She drags herself around in baggy sweats, and her hair needs shaping, but I don't dare mention either one of those things. And her face, her beautiful face, is all broken out most of the time.

I'm so worried about her.

I also can't stop thinking about Emma and Tom Coughlin, that couple we're working with at the pregnancy center. They're heartbroken since finding out their baby will be born with spina bifida. That means he'll be born with a hole in his back and another condition, hydrocephalus, where the baby's head swells and has to be shunted because the spinal fluid isn't circulating properly. They got a lot of information from their doctor and tried to explain the possibilities to me, but I can't take everything in. What I am grasping is, they're terrified and looking to us for support.

One thing I did manage to digest is that their little boy will likely have issues with incontinence and ability to handle schoolwork – part and parcel, I suppose, of doctors probing around in his central nervous system to try to correct what they can after he's born. Emma's husband puts up a brave front and tries to reassure his wife that all will be well if they work as a team, but Emma continues to look shell-shocked.

More tests await the frightened couple as their growing team of doctors – living near Philadelphia means access to all kinds of specialists and teaching hospitals – strives to determine the best way to proceed with Emma's high-risk pregnancy.

If she'll let me, I can continue to be a sounding board and offer support to Emma. I just wish I could do the same for my own daughter.

Chapter 20 David

"A family is a place where principles are hammered and honed on the anvil of everyday living."– Charles R. Swindoll

"Daddy, you're funner than Mommy!" Jess announces after we leave the grocery store.

"Oh, now, don't say that, little lady," I scold, trying not to show my pleasure at being the "most favored parent" of the day. "You have the world's greatest mom, and don't you forget it!"

"But Daddy, Mommy won't buy me things in the store. And her don't always buy me a horsey ride," she whines.

She has a point there. Mary's a lot more frugal than I am and doesn't seem to realize the cost-benefit ratio of a 99-cent candy bar when it comes to keeping a kid happy in the aisles.

My other secret weapon is the mechanical horse in the front lobby. Jess knows if she behaves, she gets a ride at the end of the trip. So, of course, she begs for something in every aisle, but I keep reminding her of the gold at the end of the rainbow, and she settles down. She keeps chattering like a cricket, but at least she knocks off the hounding.

I can't help feeling like the good guy, even though I know Mary's better at handling money than I am.

I wish she would take it easy about finances. We're not rolling in dough but we're doing OK. I know she worries I'll be laid off, but I would think she'd have a little more faith about the whole thing. She's much more tuned in to church and the Bible than I am, although I do agree on the basics. It just surprises me that she sweats small stuff like a candy bar for Jess in the grocery store. It's such a small investment, and makes things so much easier.

So Jess gets her "horsey ride" and everything's right with the world as far as she's concerned. I shoot some video of her loving life on the back of a plastic stallion who gallops about as fast as the Galápagos Tortoise we saw at the zoo.

When we get home, I give her a couple of light things to carry inside, which thrills her beyond words. You should see her traipsing through the door with her hands full of toilet paper.

After we get the groceries put away, I say, "OK, Jessica, it's time for your nap."

She isn't fooled by my attempt to sound authoritative by using her full name. Instead, she gripes, "But Daddy, I'm not tired! I wanna build a fort with you!"

"No way, José. You have a date with the Sandman, and that date is now!"

But she knows I'm a pushover about things like that, and sure enough, she gets away without taking one. Not that she naps much anyway. The babysitter says she's lucky if she can get the kid down for 20 minutes. Still, I know Mary wants to keep it going as long as possible, but since she isn't home, I make the executive decision that a possible 20-minute nap isn't worth the inevitable 30-minute battle.

So we build a fort in the dining room instead. She grabs some sheets off her bed and drags a bunch of her stuffed animals in, and we have quite a time of it. Then she insists on putting on her princess dress. Mary found the pink and white getup at a yard sale, and Jess would live in it if we let her. After a while, she says, "Daddy, gimme an upside-down horsey ride!"

Remembering what a stickler Mary is about manners, I say, "Excuse me, little lady, what was that again?"

"Horsey ride, Daddy!" she demands.

"Sorry, I can't seem to hear you. What was that again?"

She wrinkles up her brow, then shouts, "Horsey, Dad, *Horsey!*"

OK, she's not getting it the subtle way.

"Jess, what's the magic word? I'm pretty sure my hearing will clear up as soon as you say it."

"Oh!" she says knowingly. "Puh-*leez!*"

"Well, isn't that amazing, now I can hear you loud and clear!" I laugh, assuming the position. I lie on my back, motioning her to come balance her belly on my feet. I suspect from a distance we look like a set of scales that can't decide which side is gonna topple first. It's such a hoot to see her flailing around, pretending she's scared, when we both know she's loving every minute of it. She gets a real kick (OK – pun intended) out of it when I bend my knees and threaten to send her rocketing towards the ceiling.

That's about as close to being a soccer star as I'll ever come. Even if I lose the 30 pounds the doctor's always on my case about, my coordination has always lacked – well, *coordination*. The great thing about Jess, though, is she couldn't care less. She doesn't want a sports star or an athlete or even someone who can walk a straight line. She just wants her daddy, and, for some unfathomable reason, she seems to be glad I got the job!

I have to admit, she came much earlier in our relationship than Mary and I had expected, and what a shock that was. Really threw me till I was able to wrap my mind around it.

Best surprise I ever got.

What a contrast between Jess and Tanya. If Jess is Beauty, her sister's getting more like the Beast every day. Tanya's surly and Mary can't stand it. I can't, either, to be honest, but I try to play it off like it doesn't matter. Mary doesn't know how to do that. When Tanya gives me one word answers and hoofs it up to her room, I let her be. Mary can't do that. She's gotta keep asking the kid if everything's alright and how can she help.

If Tanya wanted help, she'd ask for it. What she wants is to be left alone. She didn't even want a fuss made over her birthday last week. It was all Mary could do to get her to say yes to a cake. Poor kid must really be miserable.

I love my wife and I love my daughter – no, *daughters* – but why didn't anybody ever tell me how complicated it would be living in a house full of women?

Chapter 21 Tanya

"I think togetherness is a very important ingredient to family life."
– Barbara Bush

"C'mon, Tanya, why don't you join us?" Mom begs as she zips Dolly into her jacket. It's the fleece one with the Teddy bear hood that Dolly would wear year-round if Mom let her. Mom tries to hide it, but I see her wince when she's struggling with the zipper. She takes both hands away from Dolly's coat for a minute and cups her left fingers over the right knuckles. I consider asking if she needs help, but then she goes back to what she was doing, so I guess whatever it was must have passed.

"No, I have homework to do," I answer, heading for the stairs.

"But Sweetheart, you're missing all the lights this year. You used to love that."

She frowns when she says that, and for some reason that makes me boil over. I don't even know why.

"Look, *Mother*," I say, with emphasis on that last word, "I have a ton of homework, for one thing. Don't you remember how teachers try to cram all the tests and projects in right before Christmas break? And for another thing, I feel lousy. I'd appreciate it if you'd get off my back!"

I expect her to start issuing a lecture, but she just takes on a hurt look and turns her attention back to my sister.

"Now, you listen, Jessica Rose. When we get to the Christmas house, you must hold Mommy or Daddy's hand at all times. There are a lot of people there, and we don't want you to get lost. If you won't hold a hand, we'll get right back in the car and come home. Understand?"

Jess nods mischievously. I figure they'll be back soon.

It's almost Christmas, and I'm so not in the spirit. Mom's reference to what locals call "the Christmas house" doesn't help any. It's in Marley Bank, one of the fancier neighborhoods near Rock Face, the not-so-fancy area where we live. The owners of this house must have more money than brains because they attach lights to every last inch of their house, garage, windows, you name it. Oh, and they have all these blow ups – snowmen, the Grinch, and of course the big guy in red. David hates blow ups. He's always threatening to pop them with a BB gun after dark. I think he'd better get over it, though, because Mom's talking about grabbing some on clearance after New Year's.

Last Christmas, Chuck took me to the Christmas house. They had this giant snow globe with penguins inside, and a shed-sized Santa's workshop, and free-standing glass cases with mechanical elves painting toys and stupid stuff like that. For some reason, I was a lot more into that sort of thing last year. Chuck thought it was very romantic to sort of get lost in the crowd – there's always a crowd around the place – and just chill with his arm around me, watching all the characters do their thing. I kind of got into it and felt that starry-eyed sort of wonder and wanted to be close to him, too. Well, not really him, because I just never felt that way about him – not once during the whole year and a half we dated. But *someone*. And since he was the only one asking, I went

110

with it. It actually was pretty romantic, now that I look back, and when we went back to his house later, his mom had done some baking, and the whole house smelled like chocolate and peppermint and holiday magic.

I wish everyone would stop being so happy. They all want me to get in on the traditions they're trying to start with Dolly. All of a sudden, Mom can't get enough of baking cookies. You'd think she's trying to put Mrs. Claus out of business. When I was a kid, she did slice and bake or break and bake. Now that's not good enough. She learned how to wield a rolling pin and now she's not happy unless she, Jess and the kitchen are covered in flour and fighting over who gets to lick the beaters.

I consider apologizing to Mom for the snotty comment I made, but for some reason, I don't want to. I start to go upstairs, but she calls after me, "Tanya Elizabeth, could I have a word with you?"

I hate when she uses that formal tone of voice, like she's talking from the heights, so I snarl back, "Yes, *Mary Ann*, I'm right here."

"Dave, will you take the baby – I mean, Jessica – out to the car? I'll be right there," Mom says in a frighteningly controlled tone.

David shoots me a nasty glance but does what Mom asked. When he and Jess are gone, she turns to me. Her eyes are slits of fury.

"Tanya Eliz –" she begins, then backtracks. "Tanya, why are you trying to ruin the holiday for everyone?"

"Oh, Mom, get over yourself!" I bark. "This family can have a perfectly fine Christmas without me participating in every stupid tradition you dream up!"

When I was younger, she would've let me have it if I'd have said something like that. But she hasn't spanked me since fifth grade, when I caught up to her in height and strength. The last time she tried it, I held her off with one hand while suppressing a giggle.

"Tanya," she says in a quivering voice, "that remark really hurt me. In fact, your whole attitude lately hurts me. Deeply. At one time, that would have mattered to you. I wonder if it does now, or ever will again."

With that, she takes herself out the door and into the holiday nonsense.

I feel bad that I'm making her miserable, but I can't seem to help it. It sort of takes some of the sting out of the way I've been feeling since I broke up with Chuck. I don't miss *him*, exactly, but it stinks not having anyone.

I better shake off some of this gloom and start doing something about my appearance if I ever want romance in my life again. I've gained weight, and none of my clothes fit right. I refuse to buy new ones until I shed some pounds. Ironically, my stomach's not as jiggly as it usually is. I have gym every day this quarter, and I guess the stretches they make us do are firming me up, despite the weight gain. Even though I'm not eating much junk food, my face is a mess. Maybe I should stop fighting Mom when she suggests going to a dermatologist. It's just such a pain, though, and makes me feel like a little kid when I have to go with my mommy to the doctor.

Wait a minute. Now that I'm 18, maybe I can go alone. If she'll let me have the car, why not? That would make the whole thing a lot more bearable if she wasn't tagging along into the exam room, basically holding my hand.

When she calms down, I'll ask her.

Chapter 22 Mary

"Parenting is an impossible job at any age." – Harrison Ford

"OK, Tanya, here are the insurance cards. This one's mine, and here's Dad's, er, David's. Now, listen, there's something called the birthday rule, which means they bill the one whose birthday comes first in the calendar year first. Mine comes first, so they have to bill my coverage first. Tanya, are you listening?"

The impatient look on her face tells me the question was unnecessary.

"Yes, Mom, now just give 'em to me so I can get going, or I'll be late. I'll figure it out!"

You'll figure it out, eh? I want to say. *Wait till you see all the forms they have patients fill out. Then you'll want my help, and maybe – just maybe – I won't be available.*

Instead, I toss them onto the table by the door and walk out of the room.

Tanya's appointment with the primary doctor is this afternoon. He won't send her to a dermatologist until he sees her first. I really hate bureaucracy! I'm glad she's doing something about her skin because it's worse than it's ever been, poor child. I want to help her so badly, but she doesn't want anything to do with me. She won't even let me take her to the doctor. Miss Independence.

I need to relax and take David's advice. He's always telling me to give her space, let her grow. When I protest that she'll grow away from me, he goes into that cliché about if you love something you have to let it go. I know he doesn't mean permanently, but just to loosen my grip. But it's so hard.

I thought it would be so easy to change my focus to Jessica, and in some ways it is. Watching her change from a toddler into a little girl is refreshing, even though she's exhausting. That probably seems like an oxymoron, but it really isn't. Any parent knows that joy and fatigue go hand in hand when you're raising a child. She's sweet, innocent, interested in everything I do, and dying for me to join in with everything she does. Those first two aspects of her personality touch my heart and make me want to pour everything I've learned into her little mind, perhaps doing a better job than I did with my older daughter. The constant togetherness, though, which I should cherish because my job keeps me away from her so much, leaves me little time to myself and to keep up with the day-to-day details of life. Too often, I find myself sticking her in front of a screen to keep her occupied.

Tanya, in contrast to her sister, is difficult, world weary, couldn't care less what I'm doing, and definitely doesn't want me sticking my nose into what she's doing. Interestingly, though, in some ways it was easier raising Tanya, probably because she was all I had to focus on. I had no husband or other children to think about. I sometimes feel like I'm shortchanging Jessica, what with my career, marriage, and Tanya's problems. I'm so glad Jess has David, who really delights in her. After he got over the initial shock of becoming a father, he jumped in with both feet and he's been aiming for Father of the Year ever since.

"Oh, Tanya, wait a minute!" I call, realizing I haven't given her money for the copay.

"What!" she groans. Something in that one word infuriates me, so I answer, "Oh, nothing. Be careful driving."

Let her pay her own copay if she's going to be such a brat.

Lord, may my better instincts prevail!

Chapter 23 Tanya

"Cure sometimes, treat often, comfort always." – Hippocrates

I follow the nurse into a sterile-looking room with a digital scale and a fax machine.

"Up on the scale," she commands, yanking the back of her cranberry-colored scrub shirt down over an enormous behind.

Holding my breath, I watch the numbers jumble around before settling at 171. Great! Nine pounds higher than last summer. At this rate, I should try out to be a blimp in the next Thanksgiving Parade.

Seeing the look of shame on my face, the nurse responds, "Could be worse," in what I take to be a weak attempt at comfort. For the first time, I realize she's a human being too, despite her business-like manner. It dawns on me that I probably look scrawny to this rotund woman, whose massive breasts droop almost to her naval, while her lower half could
pass for a corseted army tank.

"Thanks. I guess you're right," I mutter, following her into the examining room.

I sit down on an examination table in obedience to her hand gesture, and immediately make a hole in the wrapping paper stuff that's supposed to shield me from any germs left behind by the last patient. She motions that I should extend my arm for the blood pressure cuff. Her conversation skills could definitely use a refresher course from communications 101.

When she sits down to type my numbers into a computer, the pant legs of her too-tight scrubs ride up, revealing a jaw-dropping sight. Spider veins crisscross her bare ankles and buckle-topped foot, reminding me of the purple-lined roadmaps on my GPS. She catches me staring, and any sympathy she may have felt for me seems to evaporate into embarrassment.

"Doctor will be right in," she calls over her shoulder while high tailing it out of the room.

I'm irritated to be here. I don't know why my primary doctor can't just write me a referral to the dermatologist. No, he has to play Super Doc and insist on seeing me first. For crying out loud, he just saw me last summer for a physical. Everything was fine then. Why shouldn't things be fine now? I bet he just wants another chance to bill the insurance company. What a racket.

"Well, hello, Tanya, long time no see!" Dr. Edelstein jokes when he pops into the room 20 minutes later. That's another thing I love about going to doctors. They make you wait twice – first in the waiting room, then again when you're half undressed and feeling the North Wind wafting through your backless gown. At least this visit I've been spared the humiliation of disrobing.

"Doc, I was just here in August!" I respond, having a hard time keeping the annoyance out of my voice.

"So you were. Well, what brings you here today?" he continues in a less jovial tone.

"My mom wants me to see a dermatologist. I've got zits all over my back as well as my face. We've tried all the standard stuff, and nothing seems to work. She thinks I need the big guns."

"I see. Well, let's find out what kind of shape you're in, shall we?"

He takes out his stethoscope and places it on my back.

"Breathe in. Good. Now hold that breath. Nice. OK, let it out nice and easy. Good, the lungs sound fine. Your vitals are all normal."

He turns to my chart on the computer screen. When he looks up, an awkward expression crosses his face.

"OK, Tanya, I do have to caution you about your weight. I think we talked about this last time you were in, too. A lot of people your age are developing conditions when they're overweight that used to be reserved for old guys like me! I wouldn't want to see that happen to you. Have you tried –"

He stops in mid-sentence because I burst into tears. I don't know why, except I guess I figured he was gonna ask if I'd seen a nutritionist or tried this diet or that food plan, and I'm just sick and tired of trying to lose weight. Mom's always all over my case about it, half the girls at school look like super models, and I'm just sick to death of the whole subject of thinness. I don't think I'll ever be thin. At least not thin enough.

I get control of myself, apologize for being emotional, and tell him I'm working on it. He seems relieved not to have to comfort me and moves on to another subject before I can have a relapse.

"OK, how's your cycle?" he sputters. It takes me a minute to realize what he's talking about, but then the light dawns.

Duh, Tanya, you think you're so smart, but you can't even figure out when a health professional is asking you about your monthly nightmare.

"Oh, uh, it's, um, a bit screwed up, actually. I haven't had it for a while. Probably 'cause I've been dieting. This happened once before when I wasn't eating very much. It came back eventually."

"Hmmm," he responds, then strokes his chin. He hesitates, then says, "OK, Tanya, I've been seeing you for years, and this is the first time your mother hasn't come in with you. Are you sure there isn't some other reason you're here today?"

His voice is a mixture of fatherly concern and something like accusation. I stare at him dumbly. Then it comes to me.

"Doc, you must be kidding! No way! You can't seriously think –"

My voice trails off, as does any sense of what to say next.

"OK, Tanya, let's connect the dots. You've gained almost 10 pounds since August, yet you say you're dieting. You're not menstruating. You wouldn't be the first girl this ever happened to. I have to ask, could you be, uh, are you –"

"No!" I snap indignantly. "No! I most certainly am not!"

A little voice is whispering in my head that that isn't completely honest. There was that one time with Chuck. But nobody gets pregnant the first time, right?

"OK, take it easy. Well, look, it won't hurt to order blood work to make sure your lipids and sugars are where we want them, that kind of thing. I could order a pregnancy test, too, if you want. Dermatologists have to rule out pregnancy to put you on certain

120

acne drugs anyway. They have to, by law. We'd just be getting it out of the way. It's entirely up to you."

I know he's pretending to believe me, trying to let me save my pride, and I'm grateful for that. I try to sound casual as I answer, "Sure, why not? Might as well get it over with."

I leave the office in a daze. My head is throbbing, my palms are sweaty, and I feel sick. I want to go home and sleep through the rest of the winter. Hibernation is sounding better and better. I also want to hug my mom and have her stroke my hair the way she used to when I was little and afraid. Instead, I grunt "fine" when she asks how the visit went and flee to my room.

I'm getting pretty good at this lying thing.

Chapter 24 Chuck and Tanya

"The absence of an eternal perspective makes you vulnerable to losing heart." – C. J. Mahaney

I do a double take when I look down at the phone and see Tanya's text. It's weird timing because not long ago I dreamed about her.

Her mom must still be refusing to buy her a smart phone because she's still texting in that abbreviated, punctuation-less prose I used to jokingly call "Tanya-ese." I recall with no small degree of satisfaction how ticked off it used to make her when I would talk text a perfect message while she painstakingly typed a choppy one on her prehistoric slide phone.

Her message says, *Can u call asap its impt*

Hearing from her after all these months makes me angry. Foggy fragments of my dream find their way into my head. I shudder.

I keep her waiting.

After an hour, she texts me again: *I really need to talk to you*

Forty-five minutes later, I reply, *What's up?*

I imagine the sound of her phone's spoon-on-crystal chime that signals she has a text. Almost instantly, my phone sends out three rapid-fire taps, meaning she's responded.

Can u meet me somewhere we hv to talk

I let 10 minutes go by, then answer, *What's this about?*

I gotta talk to u in person cn u call or meet me

Five minutes later I text, *Fine. I can be at Starbucks in half an hour.*

I envision her fingers zigzagging furiously over the keypad.

Ok ill b there she types, then adds *thx*

Traffic is light, and I get there first. I'm sitting in their dining room, twiddling my thumbs, and my mind is going in freaky directions. It's the first time I've ever wished for something stronger than coffee in this place.

Remnants of my dream resurface, in which a frightened Tanya is pleading with me to help her haul something away. The item is in a big, red trash bag like the kind they put hazardous waste in. Tanya has mascara running down her face, which is odd because she rarely wears makeup.

Whatever's in the bag must be heavy because it's too much for her to handle alone. She needs my help and is begging me to drag it away.

Now there's a change of pace, I say to myself. *I never begged her for anything, but in a way, I was always begging her. She never had to beg me to do anything. I was always ready to drop everything to give her a driving lesson or take her to the mall or even take her annoying sister to the park.*

In my fading dream, the girl I used to love is making promises we both know she won't keep. If only I'll help her, things will be good, and we can live happily ever after.

Yeah, right. But like a fool, I believe her and help her.

Believing promises, I'm starting to realize, is like accepting a check drawn on an empty bank account. Fat lot of good it did my mom to believe Dad's promises all those years.

****

"You grew a goatee!" I exclaim when I catch sight of Chuck. Well, a partial goatee, at least. He bypassed the mustache but has a beard of sorts sprouting under his mouth. Chuck trying to look more mature isn't working for him; his whiskers have shaped themselves into a pitchfork-type deal, and they're reddish, contrasting oddly with his yellow hair.

"So, what's so important?" he begins, ignoring my outburst.

"I'm fine, thanks, how're you?" comes out of my mouth before I can stop it. I counseled myself beforehand to be calm and controlled. His reluctance to answer my texts made his position clear. Still, I do need his help.

"Look, you text me after all these months and expect me to come running. I don't know what you want from me."

He's guarding himself, I realize. Or maybe he's moved on, even seeing someone else. It doesn't matter. This conversation has to happen.

Suddenly, though, I feel awkward, not knowing how to introduce what has to be discussed.

"Do you want some coffee or something? On me."

"No, Tanya, I wanna know what you need from me. I really don't feel like sitting here drinking coffee with you after two months. I've got work to do."

Breathe, Tanya, I coach myself. *He's obviously not over this. Just get it over with.*

"I may be pregnant," I blurt out.

He stares at me, the tight expression he's been wearing replaced with shock and disbelief. Then his eyes shoot down to my gut. I don't look pregnant, just fatter than usual. He won't get any confirmation there.

"No way," he says finally. "How can that be? It was only the one time."

"I'm not a hundred per cent sure," I backpedal, trying to ease the tension my statement and this whole meeting have created.

"Whaddaya mean you're not sure!" Chuck barks. His voice is a biting whisper.

Now I'm getting flustered. He's right. I should've gotten the blood work done before dragging him into this. But I need someone to help me think through what to do, and Chuck's good at that. He's always been levelheaded, even when he was helping me learn to drive stick shift in his beloved Monte Carlo. When I made beginners' mistakes, stalling out the manual transmission, he kept his cool. Boy, the tables sure have turned. I used to be the controlling force in the relationship, but he's showing a lot of backbone now.

"Look, I'm sorry," I whisper back. "I'm not sure what to do. That's why I called. Whaddaya think we should do?"

He puts a hand to his brow, covering those uninviting brown eyes.

"Chuck?" I venture.

125

"I'm thinking. No, I'm praying, if you wanna know the truth. What are we gonna do?"

Something in me rallies. Bringing him into the secret is somehow making me feel less terrified. For the first time since my visit with Dr. Edelstein, I feel like I can breathe.

"The doctor wants me to get a blood test."

He explodes in another acid-y whisper.

"You mean you could've had blood work and didn't even bother?! Why are you texting me, scaring the crap out of me, if you haven't even bothered to find out for sure?! What are you, just tryin' to play games with me?!"

That's when I understand why he's being so nasty. Just when the wound was starting to heal, here I am opening it back up again, a hundred times bigger and with a brand, new twist. I feel like Jack the Ripper.

"No, I was too scared. Or in denial. Something."

He pulls out his phone and his fingers start zigzagging over the screen. I'm about to ask him what he's doing when he starts firing questions at me.

"OK, are you tired all the time?"

"Yeah, I guess so. I mean, it's been a horrible winter. I thought I was just beat from all the shoveling."

"How 'bout irritable?"

"I dunno. No more than usual, I guess. You know how it is living with Jess."

For the first time, he smiles and half laughs.

"Yeah, I guess that's a no brainer!"

I relax a little.

"Cramps?"

"I dunno. No, I guess."

"Heartburn?"

"No, unless I eat Italian or spicy. But that's the same as always."

"It says 'frequent heartburn.' Should I put no?"

"Then yeah. I mean, put no."

"Sore legs?"

"No."

"Stomach big after eating?"

"What? That's a weird question. I mean, I feel full, yeah, but I don't know if my stomach's any bigger."

Chuck snaps at me.

"Look, I didn't write this stupid test, and I'm not the one who thinks they're pregnant! Just answer the questions!"

The calmness I've been allowing myself to feel for the last couple minutes evaporates. He isn't happy about this, I realize, and doesn't want to be part of it. He's just trying to be noble.

"Increased body temp?"

"I have no idea. I never take my temperature unless I think I'm sick."

"That's another one. Feeling sick in the mornings?"

"Not especially."

"Frequent urination?"

I feel myself turning red.

"What? Lemme see that!"

"That's exactly what it says!" he barks and begins quoting. "'Are you experiencing frequency of urination?'"

"I don't know. Maybe. A little more than usual, maybe."

Chuck looks up briefly.

He seems embarrassed to ask the next question, as if he already knows the answer.

"Have you lost weight?"

I fold my arms across my bulging belly and shoot him a disgusted look.

"What do *you* think?"

He clicks a response, then looks stricken.

"It says you're pregnant," he says slowly.

Chapter 25 David

"Where grief is fresh, any attempt to divert it only irritates." –
Samuel Johnson

Tanya's on the war path. She's raging because Mary and I
just broke the news about having to put down our beagle, Ralph.

He's the moochiest dog I've ever met, and unashamedly so.
He'll jump up on your chair if you leave it for an instant, scarf down
your whole plate of food, and beg for seconds while you're yelling
at him.

We got him from a rescue place right after we got married.
Sort of a consolation prize for Tanya, I guess. Right from the
beginning, they've been an item. He sleeps with her every night and
whimpers when she goes out.

Mary and I feel awful, but we really don't have much
choice. The vet costs are skyrocketing, and we're still afraid I might
not make the cut in the next round of layoffs. But trying to explain
that to Tanya is like suggesting to the Hatfields that they oughtta go
have a beer with the McCoys.

When Tanya takes a breath from her fury, Mary grabs the
chance to try to reason with her. I gotta hand it to my wife.
Normally, if Tanya were letting loose with those kinds of words,
Mary would be all over her. I guess she realizes that underneath
Tanya's conniption is a breaking heart.

"Sweetheart, you know how sick he's been," Mary says
soothingly. "The vet says he probably has cancer. Those awful
seizures and nosebleeds could be just the tip of the iceberg. I know

this isn't what you want to hear, and God knows none of us wants to go this route. But the poor animal is suffering, and we just don't have the money to make him better. If that's even possible, I mean."

Instead of Mary's words calming Tanya down, she goes into overdrive.

"Yeah, well, if you wanna murder my dog, you can count me out!" she shrieks. "You'd find the money to treat Jessica if *she* was having seizures, don't tell me you wouldn't!"

Mary opens her mouth to let her have it but stops when she notices the weird look that crosses Tanya's face. It's as if she shocked even herself with that last comment.

"Never mind, I didn't mean that. You know I love Dolly," she back-pedals. "But how can you do this to Ralph?!"

Her face twists into a mask of wretchedness. Mary reaches out to hug her, but she lashes out again.

"How much money have you raised over the years to save drug-addicted babies? You were so burned up when I lost that bottle full of money for your beloved pregnancy center! You'd move heaven and earth to save every deformed, unwanted baby that comes across your doorstep, but you can't come up with a few lousy dollars to save my best friend!"

She pauses, then spits out five more words: "You are such a hypocrite!"

That's when I put my foot down.

"Listen, Tanya," I say in a voice I usually reserve for Jess's insubordination, "it's not OK for you to talk to your mother like that. Your mom loves Ralph as much as the rest of us. She's just as brokenhearted as you are."

It's rare when I confront Tanya, and I don't think she was expecting it. The "if looks could kill" analogy crosses my mind when she turns to me, her face a mixture of hatred and pain. Mary looks as if she wants to intercede for Tanya but holds off when I put up my hand. I have a long fuse, and I try to stay out of their mother-daughter stuff, but I won't have her trash talking my wife, especially when it comes to Mary's commitment to life. There's no way she would agree to put Ralph down if she didn't think it was the only way.

Tanya swears and stomps out of the room. Mary collapses in tears. I offer comforting words which she brushes aside, saying I should have left Tanya alone to express her grief in whatever way she needed to. I tell her that would have been tantamount to agreeing with Tanya's slurs, and ask how she would have liked it if I had stood by silently while her daughter attacked her. We argue in circles, always coming back to the fact that I don't understand Tanya.

I give up and leave to go get Jess from the sitter. I want to be with someone who wants to be with me.

Chapter 26 Tanya

"No one ever told me that grief felt so like fear." – *C.S. Lewis*

Life stinks.

That's my considered opinion, after 18 years on this dreary, nonsensical, unfair planet.

Mom and David are gonna put Ralph to sleep. He's *my* dog. I love the way he curls up with me in bed. He even lets me cradle him like a baby, which is no small undertaking – he's a big, awkward amalgamation of fat and fur. I don't even mind when he grabs my spot when I get up for a drink or to pee. He looks at me with those devilish brown eyes and moves over when I tell him to. He understands everything I say to him. More to the point, he understands me.

He loves to wait for me at the front door. We have a glass paneled storm door that Ralph loves to look out of, like a sentinel or something. One time we forgot to lock it and Jess ran out when no one was looking. Ralph somehow knew she wasn't safe and howled his head off to warn us. I can always hear him barking in that low, moan-y voice of his when I pull up in the driveway. Then he gets all excited and wags his tail when he sees me coming up the walk.

Ralph's pretty much my best friend. The thing I love most about him is when he's lying down on the rug and I'll say to him, "You OK, Buddy? Are you good, Ralphie?" and then he'll wag his tail at high velocity like a windshield wiper. Doesn't matter how many times I ask him; he never gets tired of playing the game.

And, oh, how that dog can eat! Doesn't matter what or when. We actually have to keep the kitchen trash can off limits in the cellar way so he can't get into it. Once Mom got an emergency phone call and had to leave in a hurry. She had the trash can out in the open because she was tossing scraps into it as she was cooking. When she came home, he had knocked over the whole thing and strewn chicken bones, potato skins, and other disgusting debris all over the downstairs. We had to call the emergency vet because we were afraid he might have eaten some of the bones. Let me tell you, it wasn't a pretty sight solving that problem. Let's just say the backyard got well fertilized after that disaster, and guess who got elected to clean up the mess. I complained a lot, but to tell you the truth, I love him so much, I would do that and a lot more for him if I had to.

To top everything off, I found out a Christian singer I used to be really into is going through all kinds of divorce drama. His wife's claiming he has a porn addiction and cheated on her. He doesn't seem to want to walk away quietly, and is firing back with all kinds of allegations of his own.

Somehow, with everything that's going on with Ralph and my body, I decide to take it out on Mom about the singer, whose stage name is X Granger. I know it's crazy. I should be trying to find out for sure whether or not I'm pregnant, but I keep thinking it can't be possible. If I go get it confirmed, I'll have to figure out what to do, and I can barely hold it together as it is.

When I tell Mom about Granger's messy, so-called Christian life, she looks positively stricken. I know it's mean, but I can't help snarking at her, "So, what do you think of your God now? His followers sure do a great job of following him, huh? Oh, and by the way, I haven't heard from Pastor Kaplan – or anyone else at that church, either, for that matter – since that 'intervention' you staged, so please don't do that again."

When I turn to walk away, she stops me in my tracks.

"Tanya Elizabeth!" she calls after me. When she starts out that way, I know I've crossed the line.

"What?" I growl. I know I'm being really snotty with her lately, but somehow it makes me feel less horrible about Ralph when *I* bark at someone.

Her tone changes. Instead of laying into me, which I deserve, she sort of appeals to me.

"Tanya, Honey, I know you're hurting about Ralphie. We all are. Believe me, it's the last thing your fa – I mean, Dave and I want to do. I can see you're miserable.

"Honey, I've been where you are. But, Sweetie, God is only a whisper away. And yes, Christians do disappoint us. Regularly. I'd say, over the course of my lifetime, I've been more disappointed than not in the church and the people in it. But I learned a long time ago, I'm not following flesh and blood. I'm following the opposite of those things. If I put my faith in Granger or (here she inserts the names of other well-known church people), I'd have quit the church a long time ago.

"David coined a phrase which I'll never forget when we were car shopping," she continues over the objections I'm starting to raise. "Please, Sweetheart, let me finish. Then I promise to listen to you. Deal?"

"Fine," I mutter, assuming the most exasperated expression I can manage, and wondering why she called me "Sweetheart" when I'm being so rough on her and her God.

"Thanks, Honey. Anyway, you remember recently when we were trying to find a minivan? Well, I guess Dave's a better judge of character than I am, or maybe he's just bought more used cars than I have. Anyway, I was really liking the salesman, and he was giving us a really smooth sales pitch. When he left us alone for a few minutes, I was sort of singing his praises to David. You know what he said to me? 'Mary, I can't afford to fall in love with the salesman.'

"And guess what? He was spot on. We looked it up, and it turned out we'd have been the third owner, the report was full of alerts – the car was a lemon!

"Dave was right. Just because you like someone's message, or the way he's delivering it, that doesn't get you off the hook from doing your homework. You've gotta look at the facts, and check out the product itself, not the guy who's pitching it.

"The thing is, Christians are people, and people are made of dirt – you remember God created the first people from the dust of the earth, right? – come to think of it, maybe that's why our actions are often so dirty. Well, that's not really accurate, because everything God made was good, so I guess that would include even the dirt we were made of."

I hate when she does this. She always gets caught up in every little detail and takes forever to get to her main point. My face must show irritation because she jumps back on track.

"Well, never mind that. We've all said and done things that were wrong. You of all people know about some of the mistakes I've made. But those same mistakes have turned out –" her voice catches in her throat, "well, they've turned out to also become my greatest gifts. They humbled me, and somehow God turned around what could have been an awful mess and made it into a glorious girl named Tanya Elizabeth Ritter."

I grab the opening she's just given me.

"Oh, so I'm a mess? Thanks a lot! I suppose –"

She surprises me by coming right back at me, but not in a mom-ish way, just firm and commanding.

"No, Tanya, that's not what I meant, and you know it. You're the furthest thing from a mess. You have a lot of growing still to do – we all do – but there's no doubt in my mind that God has great things in store for you. David and I both believe that. Can't you see how much we love you? You've always made us so proud. And you always will."

Something in me breaks. I start to bawl like a baby. I don't know why. I let her put her arms around me, and even put mine around her.

I wish I could tell her I might be pregnant. But how can I disappoint her when she just said I'm the greatest thing since the microwave? To be treating her so rotten, then have her tell me how special I am, then spring this news on her?

I can't bring myself to do it.

Chapter 27 Mary

"True prayer is not a mere mental exercise, nor a vocal performance, but it is far deeper than that — it is spiritual commerce with the Creator of heaven and earth." – Charles Spurgeon

I catch Dave just as he's about to take Jessica to visit his aunt in the nursing home. Bless his heart, he always makes time for what's important. Me, I'm always so busy trying to fit everything in after I get home from work – laundry, meals, errands, *life*. Dave helps with all those things, too, but somehow God seems to stretch his hours so that he squeezes in stuff no one else gets around to.

"Dave, Honey, can we talk for a minute?"

"Sure, Mar. Aunt Carol's not going anywhere," he chuckles. "What's up?"

This isn't something I do well, but it needs to be done.

"Well, um, I wanna say I'm sorry for the other night. The thing with Tanya."

He wrinkles his brow.

"What are you sorry for? You weren't the one dropping four-letter words!" he jests.

That's one of the things I love about Dave. He makes it so easy to be human. He never holds my failings against me.

"I know," I smile, "but I gave you grief about trying to back me up with Tanya. I shouldn't have argued with you about that. You were only trying to help."

Dave puts his arms around me and kisses the top of my head.

"Listen, Hon, she's upset about her dog. I get that. We all are. It's just, I try not to get into your stuff with her, but when she starts attacking you like that –"

"You're right, Sweetheart. And you do a masterful job of being Switzerland!" I joke. "You must have teeth marks all over your tongue most of the time!"

"Well, maybe a few bicuspid bites anyway!" he retorts. "But listen, I know you're walking a tightrope with her. How can I help?"

I pause. How *can* he help? How can *anybody* help?

"I don't know, Honey. I really –"

I start to laugh.

"Well, by golly, there *is* something you can do to help! I'm starting to do it myself, as a matter of fact, and it's only taken me 18 years to figure it out! I got this wonderful inspiration recently when I was talking to one of my clients – the one I told you about, the lady whose poor baby has so many problems. I didn't know what to say at one point, so I just kind of prayed my way through the conversation. I really felt God's guidance as to what to say and how to say it. And when. Y'know what I mean?"

"Yeah, I guess," he answers. "You're better at that sort of thing than I am, though."

"Well, maybe we could both practice. If Tanya has another meltdown – no, *when* she has another meltdown, 'cause we both know she's gonna have one – how 'bout we both try to remember to

139

pray as it's happening? Pray for each other, pray for her, pray for wisdom?

"Ooh, I forgot to tell you! We had a conversation yesterday about poor Ralph again, and I actually remembered to do that when she was getting hysterical, and it worked wonders! She actually sort of poured her heart out to me about some other stuff, instead of just screaming at me! Somehow, I was able to remain fairly calm and say what needed to be said, and not just react. If only I could do that every time!"

"Mar, that's terrific. Way to go!"

"Yeah, well, like I said, it's only taken me 18 years!"

"Well, listen, who knows, by the time Jess starts acting up, maybe we could write a book or something! We could call it, I dunno, 'Reflections of a Driven Insane Parent on How *Not* to Raise Children!' Got a nice ring to it, don't you think?"

I pull his face down to mine and plant a kiss on his five o'clock shadow.

"Hey, is that the best you can do?" he whines.

I grab him and show him just how much better I can do.

Chapter 28 David

"When grace is joined with wrinkles, it is adorable. There is an unspeakable dawn in happy old age." – Victor Hugo

"Don't worry, Hon, I'll give her a healthy lunch!" I call to Mary. Jess and I wave goodbye while pulling out of the driveway.

"See that you do!" she retorts with a smile. We both know it's a promise I won't keep, but we also know she'll come home with a full belly and a full heart.

"OK, little lady, no unstrapping yourself today," I warn Jess while settling her into her car seat. I toss her "big girl bag" – which, unbeknownst to Jess, contains an extra pair of undies and even a few pairs of throwaway underwear, just in case – onto the seat next to her. "We need to keep you all buckled in, safe and sound, so we can get to see Aunt Carol real fast."

As soon as the words are out, I know I've blown it. Jess figured out how to unbuckle her car seat awhile back, and I'm much better off if I pretend it never happened. Sure enough, I hear the telltale sound, followed by a mischievous giggle, seconds after the words leave my lips.

Pulling over, I practice my serious face. Part of the problem, as Mary frequently reminds me, is that the kid knows I think her hijinks are hilarious. Oh, I always win in the end, but I can't help laughing when she gives me those dimples and tries to look innocent. Mary says I'm "reinforcing unacceptable behavior," but I'm only human. What guy could resist that angel face?

"Alright, Jessica Rose," I begin, using her full name as Mary does when she means business, "we are going to turn right around and go home if you're gonna pull this stuff. Do you understand me?"

"OK, Daddy!" she giggles, then attempts to refasten herself. Funny thing: she's got the unbuckling down pat, but don't ask her to redo the thing. Then she's all thumbs.

"Never mind, Baby. Daddy'll get it. Your job is to leave it alone. Got it?"

"Got it!" she squeals, then proceeds to undo it several more times before we take off. Each time, I try to assume the look Mary gives her that always stops her dead in her tracks, but whatever it is, I clearly don't have it. I finally have to do a 180 with the car and pretend we're going back home.

"No, Daddy, please, I'll stop!" she begs.

"No, it's too late," I tease, trying to maintain my poker face. "Guess Aunt Carol and Molly will just have to miss out this week. That piano will just have to stay silent and miss your little fingers playing 'Twinkle, Twinkle, Little Star.' It's so sad, but –"

Her screams of heartbreak prove I have her where I need her. Not that I like to play that card, but I have to get this to go my way somehow. God knows, I can't have the cops pull me over and find out I have an unstrapped toddler in the backseat. I could have her watching an X-rated movie on her little tablet, no problem, but heaven forbid I bend a safety rule that the government in all its wisdom imposed on parents. What's the law now, kids have to be in booster seats till they go to the prom, something like that?

"Alright then. No more unbuckling, or home we go. Got it?"

"Got it, Dad!" she chirps in that way she has.

When we push open the glass door, the stench bowls us over as it always does. Jess asks her usual question.

"Daddy, how come Aunt Carol's house smells like diapers?"

"I know, Jess, it's kinda stinky. That's because she lives in a nursing home, remember? Sometimes old people have to wear diapers, too."

"But why, Dad? Aren't they potty trained? Maybe I could teach 'em."

I will myself not to laugh. Looking down at her questioning eyes and the solemn look on her face, I know that even cracking a smile would deflate her. As I gaze at her creamy, perfect skin, the contrasting image of Tanya's acne-ridden face involuntarily enters my mind. Before I can catch myself, I grimace.

"It's not that, Sweetie. They do use the potty if they can. But some of them can't always make it in time, and they have accidents like you did that time, remember? So, it helps if they have a grownup diaper on."

I should've known that wouldn't be the end of it. Lately, Jess has been taking more in, remembering conversations we had previously. It blows me away how her mind is expanding. The first thing she says when she hops onto my aunt's lap is, "Aunt Carol, do you wear diapers?"

I try to do damage control.

143

"Jess, that's not polite! We don't ask Aunt Carol questions like that!"

My aunt grew up during the Depression, so I guess she knows a thing or two about not taking life too seriously. A boisterous bellow escapes her lips, causing the crepe-y folds of her neck to jiggle like an accordion. That gives Jess permission to laugh, too, and the two of them sit there howling like idiots for a good 30 seconds.

"Well, I'll tell you a little secret, Honey Bunch," my 80-something aunt begins, "I have been known to wear an adult diapie when I go on a trip!"

"Daddy, Aunt Carol wears an adult diapie on trips!" Jess blurts out. I make a mental note, once I stop cackling, to tell Mary when we get home. She'll be relieved to know the rule we taught Jess about not keeping secrets from Mom and Dad has sunk in.

"Aunt Mary, what's an adult diapie?"

This produces more snorts and snickers from the wheelchair, and I give up hope then and there of having any sort of adult conversation.

The thing I love best about Aunt Carol is her outlook on life. She doesn't waste time wondering why senseless things happen; she just absorbs them, comes to a place of acceptance, and shares whatever perspective she's gained with those who are still struggling. For instance, when my brother, Lenny, died way too young, she called to console me. By that time, Al was gone too, as well as my mother. That left only my brother, Jack, and me to represent our family. Aunt Carol must've known how unfair it all

144

felt to me. She didn't say much except she was sorry, and she loved me, but at the end of the call, she made herself available in no uncertain terms.

"Davey," she said, "you have my phone number. Use it. I'm always here for you. Sometimes you just need to talk to somebody with white hair."

I've never forgotten those four sentences. I guess that's why, when she broke a hip and had to move to this God-forsaken place, I made it a point to come visit her regularly. It's good for Jess and for me. Somehow, I feel closer to my parents when I look into that beautiful, wrinkled face.

"Aunt Carol," Jess says with excitement, "wanna see what's in my big girl bag?"

"I sure do, Honey Bunch. You got any secrets in there?"

"No, no secrets," Jess replies solemnly. "We don't keep secrets, right, Daddy?"

"That's right, little lady!" I affirm, then remember the aforementioned emergency items Mary snuck into the bag right before we left. They'll do more than give lie to what I just said; they'll hurt Jess's "big girl" pride.

"Hey, Jess, can I see what's in your bag first?" I say, knowing it's a dumb ruse and probably won't work anyway. But it's all I can think of on the fly.

To my surprise, she agrees and hands it over. When I peer inside, I see the soft toy that's lived on Tanya's bed ever since I moved in. It's a floppy yellow thing that seems to mean almost as much to her as Ralph did. I think Mary said she's had it since she was a little kid.

"Hey, Jess," I begin, "what are you doing with Fluffy? Does Tanya know you have this?"

"No, Daddy, it's *Puffy*!" Jess counters.

"Oh, OK, I stand corrected. Does she know you have Puffy? Your sister will be pretty upset when she sees it's missing."

"No, Daddy, Tonna gived it to me."

"Now, Jess, what did Mommy and I tell you about making up stories? That's called 'lying,' and Jesus doesn't want you to do that."

"No, Daddy, Tonna did give it to me. 'Member when I cutted my finger? Tonna gived it to me to make me stop crying. Puffy's mine!"

With that, she snatches up the item in question and proceeds to brag on all its wonderful features to my long-suffering aunt.

At this point, Aunt Carol's friend, Molly (they refer to themselves as fellow inmates), pulls her wheelchair (they call them their chariots) alongside Aunt Carol's in the solarium. I decide to table the Puffy discussion, making a mental note to discuss it with Tanya when we get home.

"Well, how's my little punkin' today?" Molly asks my daughter.

Jess isn't crazy about Molly, she tells me, because the 300-pound woman has long, wiry whiskers poking out from her double

146

chin. Still, I've taught her to be polite, so she answers earnestly, "I'm fine, Molly, and so is Daddy."

"Well, I'm glad to hear that, Punkin', and would you like to play a song today? Would you like to learn a song about a star?"

That's the one thing Molly has going for her in Jess's eyes: she taught piano for years, and she gives my daughter an addled coaching session every week. I'm not sure who's more to blame for the ramshackle-ness of the lesson – Jess with her wiggles and giggles, or Molly repeating the same thing 400 times. Each week she re-teaches her "Twinkle, Twinkle, Little Star," and each week Jess reminds her that she's already learned it. Molly apologizes, then starts all over again with the same song. The memory section of Molly's brain is caught in a spin cycle that the neurons simply can't overcome.

Jess has a kiddie keyboard at home, and she dutifully fools around on it after the lesson. I'm no help, having the musical aptitude of a turnip, but I always tell her she's wonderful and that Molly will be proud next time we see her.

As usual, Aunt Carol smiles and squeezes my hand as we watch Jess pound the ivories. That old upright has definitely seen better days, but it serves the purpose for the hymn sings St. Philomena's sponsors at the home every third Sunday. The way Jess talks about it, you'd think it was a baby grand; I guess, compared to her mini keyboard, it is.

When Aunt Carol starts to nod off, I know it's time to go. I scoop up Jess, cue her to say goodbye, and cart her off towards the exit with my usual promise of chicken nuggets and fries. In minutes, we find ourselves out in the sunshine, away from repetitive piano lessons and the pungent but well-earned smells of humanity.

Chapter 29 Tanya

"Our greatest joy… is her greatest pain." – Adoptive parents Paul and Cheryl Wilkinson, regarding a birth mother's sacrifice

I overhear Mom and David talking when I'm coming through the living room. They're in the kitchen, as usual. Normally I don't bother to eavesdrop – their conversations just aren't that interesting – but lately I've been catching some juicy tidbits that pertain to me, so I guess it's worth it.

Oddly enough, they're talking about Puffy.

"Mar, the funniest thing happened when we were visiting Aunt Carol," David begins. "Jess had that special toy of Tanya's in her bag. Y'know, the yellow one? She said Tanya gave it to her. Do you know anything about that?"

"Oh, darn!" Mom exclaims.

"What's the matter, Hon?"

"Oh, it's nothing. Just this stupid arthritis. Gets me when I least expect it. Let me put this knife down for a few minutes and –"

"Well, here, let me take over," David offers. He's such a Sir Galahad.

"Oh, you're sweet," Mom replies. "Here, let me show you. You have to cut against the grain, like this. It's easier. See what I mean?"

"OK, Hon, I get it. Now let me do it, or your hands are gonna keep bothering you. Why don't you just get the rest of the stuff out of the fridge or something?"

I hear David's distinctive chuckle.

149

"What's so funny?" Mom asks. I can tell she's smiling with him. I, on the other hand, am not smiling. Are they or are they not gonna get around to talking about me?

"Oh, nothing, really," David replies in such a way that it's obvious what he's writing off as *nothing* is very much *something*. "I was just remembering the first time you invited me over for dinner. We were having beef stew then, too. Do *you* remember that, by any chance?" he asks mischievously.

"Well, of course! You don't think I'd forget the first meal I ever cooked for you, do you?"

"Hmmm," he muses. "'Cooked' is a relative term! I wonder if Tanya remembers it. Did I ever tell you what happened when I got there? I must've been a few minutes early, and she opened the door. Well, 'opened the door's' a relative term, too, now that I think about it!"

"It was pretty funny, come to think of it," Mom chimes in. "As I recall, I got to the apartment a bit after you did, and Tanya had you out in the hall!"

"Yes, she did!" my stepfather laughs. "Said you wouldn't let her open the door for 'strangers.' I didn't see much point in reminding her that by then she'd been on at least three or four dates with us – remember how you used to love bringing her along?"

"Well, yes," Mom confesses. "It was kind of a protective thing, I suppose. Made it hard for a man to try anything when my daughter was right there in the rear-view mirror! Maybe not so smart, in retrospect, because what if Tanya had liked you but I

150

couldn't stand you! Then, if I had broken up with you, and she was all attached to –"

"Or if *I* had dumped *you!*" he jokes.

"Oh, that, too!" Mom admits, laughing. "In any case, it gave me the opportunity to see how you were with her, and how the two of you got along."

"Well, anyway, so Tanya has me out in the hall, and she's talking to me through this two-inch opening created by the chain lock! By the way, did you ever stop to think that that wouldn't be much of a deterrent if somebody really wanted to get in? I mean, how hard would it be to bust through a chain lock?"

"Well, of course, Sweetheart. She wasn't supposed to even open the door! Believe me, we had quite a discussion after you left."

"Ah, the truth comes out!" he chuckles. "Well, anyway, the bottom line is, she gleefully reports to me that you ran out to the store to pick up canned beef stew that you planned to pass off as your own! Now it all makes sense, because I'm getting a distinct smell of burnt *some*thing wafting through the crack in the door! Well, little does our mischievous, little Tanya realize that burnt food equals love to me. I told you my mom used to let pots boil over on a regular basis, didn't I?"

"On many occasions, and I love her for it!" Mom laughs. "Every time I ruin dinner, I thank the Lord for that darling woman and all her burned meals! That poor woman, it's a wonder she got anything done at all, trying to raise four boys all by herself."

"Hey, we weren't that bad! My brothers did a pretty amazing job of –"

"I know, I know," Mom pacifies him. "Your brothers did a great job after your dad died. No question about it. You turned out to be Mr. Wonderful, and it's all thanks to them and your wonderful, food-burning mother! Now, let's hear the rest of the story about Tanya and the beef stew!"

"OK, smart aleck, here's the punchline. She's trying her best to discredit you, and I come back with, 'That's OK. I'd rather eat canned food with you and your mom any day than have a gourmet meal with, I don't know, Princess Kate!'"

"Oh, Dave, you're my hero!" Mom gushes.

If this lovefest gets any sweeter, I may throw up.

"Well, your daughter didn't think too much of it. Remember how she sulked through that first dinner? Made me feel about as welcome as the measles!"

"Well, never mind that. We got together in the end, and that's all that matters."

Just then, my little sister gallops upstairs from her playroom in the basement and, of all things, she's dragging Puffy with her. She trots past me, says, "Hi, Tonna," and waltzes into the kitchen. That jogs Mom and David's memory about their original topic of conversation.

"Hey, little lady, we were just talking about you!" David says in his usual merry way. Doesn't he ever get tired of being the Good Humor Man?

"Yes, Jessica, we were," Mom adds. "Your father and I were just wondering what you're doing with Tanya's Puffy. You know that's her favorite toy. Did she give you permission to take it off her bed?"

I'm annoyed that Mom's referring to Puffy as "it" instead of "him" – I know it's stupid, but he and I have been together since I was a baby, and it doesn't seem right to de-personalize him like that. On the other hand, it isn't fair for them to blame Jess. She's telling the truth. I did give him to her.

As Dolly begins to state her case, I emerge from the dining room, hoping they won't notice the fact that I've been listening the whole time.

"Leave her alone, you guys. She's telling the truth."

Mom gets a look on her face like I just told her a flock of geese is moving into the house next door. I don't know why, but I start babbling.

"Listen, it's no big deal. I mean, I'm way too old for stuff like that anyway. She was crying that one day when she got hurt, so I let her hold him. Seemed to make her feel a lot better. So, I just told her she could keep him. I mean, it's not like I can't visit him anytime I want to, y'know? Not that I would want to. I mean, let's face it, I'm 18, for cryin' out loud. How long can a person sleep with a –"

For some reason, Mom starts crying. Not bawling, but just little tears swimming around inside her eyes. She's gonna get carried away, I just know it. She always does.

"Tanya, you angel!" she sort of blubbers. "I know how much that toy meant to you! And for you to give it to your sister! Oh, Child, you are just too precious!"

David's cutting up meat, trying to look invisible. I guess he doesn't know what to do when Mom gets all emotional, either.

"Thanks, I guess, but it's really not that big of a deal. I mean, it's not like I'm getting rid of him. I mean, Puffy lives with Jess, and Jess lives with us, so it's kind of like I still have him anyway. He's just sort of, I dunno, in her custody. Like she, I dunno, adopted him or something. I mean, as long I have Dolly around, I'll always have Puffy around, in a way. Y'know?"

Now Mom totally gives in to the waterworks. She throws her arms around me and hugs me tight, saying all kinds of things about how amazing I am. Finally, Jess gets jealous and grumps, "Hey, what about me, Mom?"

Mom laughs and turns her attention to Dolly.

"Oh, you're very special too, sweet girl," she coos. "You are the best younger sister anyone ever had! I'm just so proud of both my girls!"

That does it. If only she knew what I was keeping from her. I start to cry right along with her.

"Oh, it's OK, Tanya, Sweetheart. You don't have to be embarrassed. Your fa – I mean, David and I, we're both really proud of you, aren't we, Dave?"

He looks up from the meat, which he's been cutting into smaller and smaller pieces to avoid getting involved in all this sentiment. He looks at me awkwardly, then rallies.

"Yeah, Tanya, your mom's right. That was a really nice thing you did."

He goes back to fumbling with the meat. If he makes the chunks any smaller, we're gonna have beef paste for dinner. I decide to help him out.

"Listen," I say through tears, "I'm not all that perfect. I mean, thanks and all, but I'm still the pain in the a – I mean, *butt*, Tanya that I've always been. I mean, yeah, Puffy means a lot to me, but I guess Jess just means more."

Dolly saves the day.

"Yeah!" she cries. "Jess means *more!*"

David scoops her up, and Mom and I fall into a bear hug with the two of them.

How can I ever tell them?

Chapter 30 Tom and Emma

"You cannot contract to sell a baby. If they legalize this contract they may soon start bringing poor women in from other countries just to be breeders... Nature's laws have to supersede man's law." – *Mary Beth Whitehead on her groundbreaking surrogate mothering court case*

"So, how's work been going, Ted?" I ask my brother-in-law after filling my plate with a variety of unhealthy holiday goodies. We're having a post-New Year's celebration with Emma's sister, Linda, and her husband, Ted. Em hasn't been herself since we got the diagnosis about Matthew, and I thought being with her sister would cheer her up. She and Linda have been close since they were kids, and Ted's not a bad guy, either.

We have to celebrate a week late because both of our kids took it into their heads to contract the flu on the 31st. So, instead of watching the ball drop on New Year's Eve, we watched our younger guy, Kevin, spill his guts – literally – all over the living room rug. I told Em I would clean it up, but she likes to do everything a certain way. So instead, I "de-grossed" Kev in the tub while Em scrubbed the mess, her swollen belly sagging over the foul-smelling carpet. Tears stood in her eyes. She wouldn't admit she was upset, but I know my wife.

Ted, who works for a graphic design firm in the city, responds to my question about work.

"The job's OK, I guess. Everything's hectic, what with the downsizing and restructuring, but I'm just glad I didn't lose my job with the layoffs last summer. It's just a pain to have to put in ten to twelve-hour days because they let so many people go and won't fill any positions."

I'm not one to complain, but I feel an odd responsibility to chime in with some negativity of my own. Misery loves company.

"I hear you, man. School's the same way. They're not laying people off *yet*, but they're sure taking their pound of flesh with all this state testing and the department of education breathing down our necks about every little thing. We're working day and night to prove the district's making 'adequate yearly progress.' Meantime, the burden's all on the teachers. The parents say, 'Jump!' and we have to say, 'How high?' You wouldn't believe what we go through to keep everyone happy."

Lull. Once we hit our stride, Ted and I can converse for hours, but it always takes a bit of doing to find a topic of mutual interest.

"How's Emma feeling?" he asks, then realizes we're there to have fun and not discuss weighty subjects like bad prenatal diagnoses. "Oh, sorry, man, you probably don't feel like talking about that tonight."

"Nah, it's fine," I answer. "She's doing OK. We're both getting used to the whole thing. Gonna take some time. What about you guys? What's the latest?"

He laughs in a humorless way.

"Ha! Now there's a subject that should be off limits! I thought the adoption system was screwed up, but it's running like clockwork compared to the foster care system. We had yet another glorious visit with Danny's birth father, where he showed up half an hour late and threw a huge fit when the social worker told him he couldn't see the baby. He knows the rules, but I guess they don't apply to him."

Ted's referring to the 18-month-old they've been fostering for the past six months. Danny is Ted's sister's son, and he's had a rough start in life. His mom's on drugs and the dad has been arrested I don't know how many times for dealing. The guy's clever, though, and the cops can never seem to make the charges stick.

The sad part is Ted and Linda want to adopt the little guy, even though he's a real handful. The poor kid clings to Linda like glue, doesn't want to let her out of his sight. Screams bloody murder if she even leaves to go to the bathroom.

They've spent gobs of money over the past four or five years trying to adopt, and it always blows up in their faces. Twice they got real close, only to have the door slammed shut in the end. That's bad enough, but to add insult to injury, all the money they shelled out for fees and the birth mothers' expenses goes up in smoke. It's the only business I can think of where you know up front the whole thing's a long shot. No refunds, no guarantees.

Ted seems to be waiting for a comment, but I'm not sure what to say. I just shake my head and roll my eyes in sympathy.

"But wait. It gets better. After he huffs and puffs and the social worker has to pretty much throw him out of the office, she turns to us and says, 'Mr. and Mrs. Genovese, I don't want you to get your hopes up. In spite of Mr. Sanders' behavior, in all likelihood, he'll be granted custody in the long run. I'm sorry to have to tell you this, after all you're doing for little Danny, but I've been doing this job for a long time. That's usually the way it works, unless he ends up in prison. The system really does try to reunite children with their biological families.' Can you believe that?"

"That is really criminal," I say with disgust.

****

From across the room, my sister, Linda, hears Tom use the word "criminal," and picks up on it.

"Emma, speaking of criminal, you mind if I run something past you?" she asks me.

"Go for it, Lin."

"OK. Well, you know Ted and I have really been robbed with this adoption business a couple of times now, right? Well, we've actually been considering going in another direction."

This piques my interest. It might be nice to think about someone else's parenting problems for a change. I go over and over the situation with our unborn Matthew constantly in my mind. Sometimes I can handle it, and I feel like it's actually doable. Other times, I turn into a gelatinous mess of tears and terror. Let me focus on poor Linda's issues tonight.

"Yeah, I can't disagree with you there. You guys have really been through the wringer with the traditional route. I can't blame you for looking for other options. By the way, Danny seemed to go down easier tonight than last time we were here. Is he coming along?"

"I hope so. Yeah, I think he is getting better in that area. He's such a cuddle bug at times, but other times, he throws these wild tantrums and we don't know how to calm him. It's like he has two different personalities. Do your kids do that?"

I have to think about how to answer that. My boys are no different than most children; when they don't get their way, they scream and fuss. What I've noticed about Danny, though, is he becomes almost hysterical and is pretty much inconsolable until he exhausts himself and falls asleep. In my heart of hearts, I think Linda may be in for much more than she bargained for if she adopts this child.

Fortunately, Linda continues before I have to think of a diplomatic reply to her question.

"Well, anyway, I was starting to tell you about our plans." She hesitates, as if weighing whether or not I can handle the subject she's about to introduce.

"The thing is, I don't want to be insensitive. With all you're going through, maybe this isn't the time to –"

"No, of course it is, Lin. I want to hear it. Definitely."

"Well, alright, if you're sure. We're prepared for the fact that we may not get Danny. Ted's sister doesn't want to be bothered with him, and she's not clean anyway, so she's not gonna put up a fight. But Danny's father really wants custody of him, and he'll probably win even though he's a really bad apple. It's a disgrace. But we've been through so much, it would be criminal to quit now. So… you've heard of artificial insemination, right? Actually, the term they use is 'intrauterine insemination.' Well, the doctor we've been talking to thinks that might be a good idea for us. He says it's pretty affordable, and if that doesn't work we can try in vitro – but that costs a boat load."

This catches me off guard. The little I know about reproductive alternatives makes the whole business seem like an engineering project. *"Concocting a pregnancy"* is the phrase that springs to mind. Fortunately, it stays in my brain rather than exiting my mouth. How dare I, for whom pregnancy happens almost as often as sock changing, make that kind of judgment on my poor sister, who's desperate to raise a child – anyone's child.

She's waiting for a response. I think fast and decide the safest place to go would be finances.

"So … how much are we talking? If you don't mind my asking, I mean."

"No, not at all, you're fine. In the neighborhood of 10 to 15 thousand. The place has a sliding scale. Our paper work's not all in yet, but they'll give us all the numbers when it is."

I groan.

"Wow, that *is* a bundle. Do you guys have it?"

"We're working on getting a loan. Those two failed adoptions set us back a lot. They don't give refunds, you know," she adds with disgust.

"So, it sounds like you guys are pretty set on this."

"Well, like I said, it's our contingency plan if things don't work out with Danny."

I'm afraid to ask too many questions, so I just emit a non-committal "Hmmm."

161

Linda pauses for a minute, then seems to make up her mind to tell me everything.

"Worst case, we hire a surrogate."

After picking my jaw up from where it landed somewhere under my rib cage, I say, "You mean somebody else to carry your baby?"

"Yeah, basically. I mean, it would be ours, really. I mean, my egg and his, y'know. Just somebody else to sort of, incubate, in a way."

A siren goes off in my head.

"Wait, what about that case 20 or 30 years ago? What was it called? Baby X? Something like that. Where the birth mother sued to keep the baby 'cause she changed her mind. Remember that? Honey, you don't need that kind of trouble."

"Yeah, Em, I know what you're talking about. 'Baby M' was the case. Trust me, we're not going there. We read up on this stuff and talked to a lawyer. That happened 'cause it was actually her egg and she didn't wanna give up her own baby, so the courts felt she had a case. What we're considering is the surrogate would just be a carrier for Ted and me. The entire whole, um, embryo would be from us. See the difference? I don't think we'd have a problem."

Another news story is gnawing at me, but I'm having trouble bringing the details to mind. I remember reading about a couple who provided a frozen embryo for a surrogate to carry, but then wanted to back out when they learned the baby would have birth defects.* I start to look it up on my phone, but then I realize Linda

162

wants a sounding board, not an opinion. Besides, this is getting into the realm of too much information, more than I feel I can handle. When she brought up the subject, I wanted to be a good sister and support her, but now her infertility issues are getting all mixed up with my concerns over my situation. I don't feel strong enough to weigh all the ethical implications of what she's proposing while struggling so much with my own moral dilemma.

I do what women do best. I change the subject.

"Hey, I could really go for a chick flick. What are you in the mood for?"

I pretend not to notice the hurt expression on her face, and snatch up the remote the way Kevin grabs for his pacifier. Tom calls it his personality. We really have to wean him off of that thing.

****

Author's note: The case Emma can't recall involved a Connecticut couple who insisted their surrogate have an abortion when ultrasound revealed severe birth defects. The surrogate mother moved to Michigan, where her rights as a surrogate trumped those of the biological parents. The child was subsequently adopted by an outside couple (http://www.cnn.com/2013/03/04/health/surrogacy-kelley-legal)

Chapter 31 Mary and Tanya

"I find it impossible to subscribe to a philosophy that believes that the destruction of human life is a legitimate solution to a problem that is mostly social, economic and psychological. In reality, most women 'choose' abortion because they believe they have no other choice. Women who experience unplanned pregnancy also deserve unplanned joy." – Patricia Heaton

"Hey, Tanya, Sweetie, could you help me unload the groceries?" I ask tentatively. We're both just coming in the door, and I'm never sure which Tanya I'm going to get: the one who gave Jessica her favorite stuffed toy to comfort her, or the one who jumps down my throat at the slightest provocation.

"I guess," she grouses, but without much conviction. So far, so good. I'll take it.

"Thanks, Hon. David asked me to pick up a few things for the New Year's party they're having at his work – who ever heard of an employer throwing their big party after the holiday? I guess they figure everyone's too busy before Christmas. Anyway, I bought more than I planned to. No surprise there. You know how I am – go in for bread and milk, leave with ten bags. Aren't you glad you don't have to tag along when I shop anymore?"

Mary, you're talking too much. Relax.

"Um hmm," she agrees without further comment. I thought she'd at least make a quip about how ungodly long I take with all the coupons I use. She used to call me "the coupon queen of Rock Face." Instead, we stroll out to the car in silence.

Count your blessings, Mary. At least it's not an angry silence.

I've been wanting to talk to her. Could this be the right time?

Lord, things have been so much better since I started asking You to steer our conversations. Please, show me whether to proceed.

As if by grand design, she comes out with, "By the way, I got an 'A' on my senior project paper."

Hallelujah! As usual, Lord, You're right on time.

"Tanya," I crow, "that's fabulous! I'm so proud of you!"

I consider asking how she did on the debate portion of the project, but decide I'm better off letting her volunteer that information if she wants to. Instead, I say, "I'd love to read it if that's OK. You know I love reading your papers – especially the 'A' papers!"

"Yeah, sure, if you want. It's kinda long, though – almost 13 pages. Maybe you should just read the abstract. That's only one page."

"Nonsense!" my lips reply, but my mind is thinking, *When do I have time to sit down and absorb 13 pages?* I've been known to binge-read Tanya's schoolwork when I take the rarer than rare sick day or vacation, but neither of those things is forthcoming at the moment. I couldn't call out now even if I had three hernias and a brain tumor. We lost our receptionist, and our counselor just had a baby three weeks early. If only that child could've stayed put till he was due, his mommy's replacement would've been on board.

165

Funny how tending to our own families gets in the way of our helping other people's.

Note to self: get to Tanya's paper asap. Maybe the next time Dave and Jess go to visit Aunt Carol.

"I know. How 'bout I start with the abstract, and work my way up to the whole paper? Sound good?"

"Sure, whatever. I'll grab it for you after we unload."

Here's my moment, a perfect segue.

"Hey, Sweetie, speaking of unloading, can I get something off my chest?"

She looks at me suspiciously.

"No, no, it's nothing you did!" I reassure her. "This one's all on me. No, I just wanted to apologize for dragging you into so many things you didn't want to do. For instance, I really had no business trying to force that meeting with you and Pastor Kaplan. I see now it was a mistake. The only reason I can give is I care so much about your well-being, spiritually and otherwise. It means so much to me that at times I forget you're a young woman, and that I've given you the tools to decide this important matter for yourself. I screwed up. Plain and simple. I tried to force a solution to something that was much better left in God's hands."

I pause, fumbling to make room for the gallon of milk in our over-crowded refrigerator. Dave's right. I could feed the whole population of a third world country on what I refuse to throw away.

I'm a bit uncomfortable that Tanya's not responding, so I continue babbling away like a rushing spring on a hot summer day.

166

"Don't get me wrong: you know I believe a person's relationship with God is the most important thing to cultivate. It's the difference between life and death, when it comes to eternity. You know what I believe and what I live by: that we have to accept in our hearts – I mean, deep down in the gut, not just between the ears and the intellect – but to know in our core that we're doomed without Jesus. That He's our, I dunno, life preserver. That Jesus, or as Pastor Kaplan says, Yeshua, is the Son of God and the only one who ever lived a perfect, sinless life. That He took our punishment in our place on that cross, and the only thing we can add to that perfect sacrifice is gratefulness and a 'pay it forward' attitude to the rest of the world. That it doesn't matter how our good deeds stack up against our bad ones, but the fact that Christ's one ultimate good deed settled the score with God once and for all. You know I believe all those things, and I believe they're just as true for you as they are for me. But…"

I look at my daughter. Her shoulders are arched. I'd better back off.

"OK, as Dave would say, let's back the truck up. I'm up on my soapbox again. You know how I get. Anyway, Honey, bottom line is I love you, whether you believe these things or not. I believe them, with all my heart, and I pray for you daily and hope you'll find these truths to be just that – truths you can live by and shape your life around, as Dave and I try to do."

She winces at Dave's name. I'd better quit while I'm ahead.

OK, I need to say one more thing to hopefully drive my point home.

"Anyway, Honey, thanks for letting me apologize – sort of!"

I laugh, hoping to reduce the wall I just started to rebuild with my overzealous comments. "Most of all, I want you to know I love you – and Jessica, for that matter – I love *both* my kids for *who* they are, *how* they are, *as* they are. End of story.

"And thanks, Hon. For giving me a break and just for – oh, I don't know, for forgiving your trying-too-hard mama."

She continues removing groceries from a reusable tote bag that it's a miracle I remembered to use. Taco chips, potato chips, a tub of dip. Fat and cholesterol, let me introduce you to Dave Gullickson's arteries.

"Tanya?" I probe.

"Yeah, no, you're fine," she answers with something unspoken in her voice. Is that a tear forming in her eye?

"But?" I fish.

****

When Mom comes out with the apology and all that sermon stuff, I'm shocked. Not that she doesn't apologize. She's pretty good about that, for a parent. It's just, I've been so off the rails lately, I'm amazed she would take any responsibility for the tension between us.

"No, you're fine," I repeat, trying to think whether to tell her she's gonna be a grandma a lot sooner than she thinks. The test at the clinic confirmed it. She's being so sweet, maybe she'd even understand.

But how can I tell her that, not only did I allow this to happen – OK, I *invited* it to happen – but I also went to one of those places to get it confirmed. I know how Mom and I guess every crisis pregnancy center worker feels about clinics that help people with a lot more than family planning. I've heard her gripe about them lots of times, claiming they're more interested in doing abortions than any kind of family planning. That may be true, but they've been around an awfully long time, and if they're so terrible, why would the government be helping to fund them every year?

When I searched around on the web and, after a few quick clicks, found out I could get a test done there for free without having to go through Mom and David's insurance, I went for it! Who wouldn't? All I had to do was bring in a few documents and they helped me fill out this application for some kind of state insurance that covered everything. I didn't have to pay a cent, and most importantly, Mom and David will never find out.

I go for light over heavy conversation. I'm not ready to tell her, not when she's just starting to like me again.

"It's no big deal," I say. The finger I've been picking at starts to ooze. I reflexively pop it into my mouth, momentarily forgetting how much I detest the nasty taste of blood.

"It's not just that, Tanya," she adds. "I know I've been in your business too much. Putting pressure on you to do things that matter to me when I know you're trying to grow up. I mean, not *trying*, you *are* grown up. You're 18, for heaven's sake! I'm sorry about twisting your arm to go to the Christmas house and the pregnancy center banquet…"

She keeps talking, but I lose track of what she's saying. I'm thinking about the stuff on the clinic's website about pregnancy

169

centers like Mom's. It says they tell lies and use tricky tactics to force people to keep babies they're not ready to raise. If that's the case, Mom's sure been playing on the wrong team my whole life.

"Tanya? Earth to Tanya!" she jokes. How long have I been out of it?

"Oh, sorry. I guess my mind wandered. What were you saying?"

"Maybe that's for the best!" she laughs. "I was giving a speech, sort of, so maybe it's best your mind drifted. No, I was just saying that I tried too hard to make a perfect family memory with the Christmas house, but I forget that nothing's ever perfect. No family will ever be perfect, especially ours! Oh, sorry, I didn't mean anything by that! I mean, we all try our best, but –"

It's painful to see her floundering like that, so I bail her out.

"It's OK, Mom. I know what you mean."

"Thanks, Sweetie. I guess what I'm trying to say is, we may never be perfect, but nevertheless, we can be good at being a family. And Tanya, *you* are good. You are *enough*. Just as you are. You will always be enough. For me, for David, for Jessica. For God! You were fearfully and wonderfully made, as the good book says, and you not only please me, you *delight* me. You were and always will be my firstborn, and I will always love you just the way you are. Can you forgive your overbearing mother for trying too hard?"

She reaches out to hug me. I fold myself into her arms.

I'm more confused than ever. If the staff at the clinic are right, then people like Mom are just trying to con people like me into making the biggest mistake of our lives by keeping a baby that maybe isn't even a person to begin with. I give Mom credit for living out her ideals, keeping Jess and me, but her life probably would've been a whole lot better if she had planned us.

Isn't that why places like that exist in the first place – to help people choose when and if they want to become parents? And didn't the Supreme Court recognize that when they legalized abortion in the 70's?

Well, one thing's for sure. This isn't the time to tell her.

Chapter 32 Chuck

"You cannot escape the responsibility of tomorrow by evading it today." – Abraham Lincoln

The other shoe has dropped.

Tanya got her pregnancy confirmed, and we're sitting in my Monte Carlo with the windows up and the heat on full blast (which in this car means a couple degrees higher than freezing), trying to plan our baby's future.

"Chuck," Tanya says, then clears her throat, "Chuck, what are we gonna do?"

That better be a rhetorical question, because I don't even have a lousy answer. Fortunately for me, she follows it up with a long diatribe.

"I don't have the heart to tell my mom and David. I mean, they're going through so much with my little sister. You think she *used* to bounce off the walls? You should see her now! Even David, with all the stuff he does with her, even he can't tire her out. I honestly think Mom should break down and take her to see someone to find out if she has ADHD or something.

"Plus, our house is just so small. I don't even know where we'd put a baby, even if I could tell them. My mom's using the basement for an office, and you have to step over things to get to the washing machine, there's cords all over the place from her computer and fax machine and –"

She continues rambling, but I stop listening. I'm thinking of all the reasons my house isn't an option, either. I cut her off.

"I'd love to say my folks would help us, but I can't. They're in the middle of a pretty wicked divorce. You knew about that, right? They can't even agree on custody of my little brothers, let alone adding a baby to the mix."

"Oh, man, that's rough," she says without much sincerity. I guess she's too wrapped up in her own problems to have much left over for anybody else. Besides which, she's busily picking at her right thumb, which already looks like it went through a meat grinder.

I'm this kid's father – it sounds so weird to say that – and I feel like I need to do something. Take responsibility somehow. But how?

I trip over a few words, then start over after mustering what little courage I have.

"Listen, you know how I always felt about you. I know I was pretty rude when you first called me outta the blue to tell me all this, but, you know, I was still pretty mad about the way you dumped me and all. I mean, do you think we oughtta consider … I mean, maybe if we tried to do this together …"

Tanya's eyes soften. Those and her smile were the first things I ever noticed about her. When she uses them the right way, you sort of forget she hasn't got the greatest body. She reaches for my hand. I reach back, cautiously.

"Chuck, you really are great, you know that? I know school and work are kickin' your butt, how hard you're workin' to get through school. But if you're saying what I think you're saying, getting married would only make it harder. I can't do that to you. I mean, I *won't* do that to you."

At least she doesn't think I'm talking about just living together. She ought to know me better than that, but I can't assume anything about Tanya anymore. I feel an odd mixture of disappointment and relief, then wonder if I should try to pursue it. What's she expecting? Does she want me to try to convince her?

Thank God, my subconscious kicks in.

This is no time to play games, Hammerschmidt. Neither one of you is in a position to get married. Leave it alone.

"Yeah, I guess you're right," I respond, "but where does that leave us?"

"Well, what about adoption? Whaddaya think about that?"

The idea stuns me, like the ice bucket challenge everyone was doing a few years ago. A buddy of mine challenged me to do it on social media, and I've gotta say, those polar bears must be certifiably nuts. When I felt that freezing water and those cubes cascade over my head and slosh down my back, it was like a million tiny, *painful* needles boring into every inch of my shivering flesh. When I watch the video of me pathetically jerking and twisting when the water hit, I don't know whether to laugh at my idiocy or pummel my sorry self into a coma.

I hope the mess I'm currently in finds me better able to handle myself than I did that day.

I look at Tanya. She's wrapping a tissue around her thumb.

"Hey, Chuck, you don't have a Band Aid, do you?" she asks sheepishly. It's then that I notice traces of blood soaking through the tissue.

"Oh, man, that's gross! You made it bleed!" I blurt out. She starts to cry.

I feel bad. I've never made her cry before. I've never made anyone cry before.

"Look, I'm sorry. I didn't mean anything. It's just, I wasn't expecting... I mean, I forgot you like to do that. I mean..."

I can either keep on fumbling for the right words, or I can reach over and hug her. I go for the hug.

Her body feels limp in my arms.

After a minute or two, she settles down. I say, "OK, are you good now?"

She nods her head.

This weird little exchange has given me the few seconds I needed to rally from her suggestion that we consider adoption.

"OK, getting back to your question, adoption never occurred to me," I begin. "I mean, I never had to give anything like this any thought, but if I did, I guess I'd have to say a parent should raise his own kid. I mean, you're not serious, right? I mean, give our baby away? To strangers?"

The thought of handing our child over to some unknown family frightens me, especially with all the creeps in the world these days. With our luck, our baby would end up living with some unhinged school shooter.

175

"They wouldn't have to be strangers, Chuck. I heard there's a way, I mean, this guy my stepdad works with, his name's Ted, he and his wife, I think her name's Lisa –"

"Tanya, what're you talkin' about?!"

"I'm saying people get to choose who's gonna adopt their kids these days! My stepdad was talking about it at dinner one night. And if you change your mind, you don't have to go through with it. That's what I was trying to tell you. My stepdad's friend and his wife – no, her name wasn't Lisa, it was Lydia or something like that –"

"Tanya, who cares what her name is! What's this got to do with us?"

"Linda! That was it – Linda! Anyway, this guy, Ted, and his wife, Linda, they got picked a few times to adopt people's babies, but at the last minute everything fell through."

She laughs in a nasty way.

"Guess you have to have tons of money and a famous last name to adopt these days."

I feel myself getting irritated. We don't have time to play games.

"So what? What's that got to do with us?"

"What it's got to do with us is, we could sign up for adoption, but we could still change our minds in the end if it doesn't feel right. And I think David said the people have to pay for everything for you, too, so it's a good deal. And even if you change your mind, they can't get a refund of what they put out. Even maternity clothes, stuff like that. It's really a great deal –"

176

"Yeah," I say contemptuously, "for everyone but the kid. He gets shoved off to live with strangers 'cause his own parents don't want him. And the poor people who have to pay all that money – it costs a lot, doesn't it? – they end up getting cheated. We're not talking about opening a bank account and then closing it after you get the freebies. We're talking about people putting out major bucks to raise somebody else's kid, then they lose out. What a horrible thing to do."

I don't think she's really for or against adoption. All she wants is some kind of plan.

I glance down at her ragged nails and her face sprinkled with zits. I probably don't look like any prize either, after not sleeping the better part of a week.

Tanya takes a deep breath, then switches gears.

"Um, Chuck?"

"Yeah?"

"Um, what about, um, I mean…"

Me, still patient: "Yeah?"

Tanya, hesitant: "I'm not sure how to put it. Gimme a minute."

Me, less patient, and getting nervous: "*What*, Tanya?"

"Alright, I'll say it. Abortion!"

Now I know what being hit by a train must feel like.

Dumbstruck, I stare stupidly at the girl I used to love. When I finally get my bearings, the only words that come out are, "You're kidding, right? I mean, you can't be serious, right?"

Tanya, defensively: "Don't look at me like that! I'm not some kind of a monster, but we've got a real problem here! I'm looking for ways to solve it!"

I can't speak. I literally can't believe what I'm hearing. All kinds of things are hitting me at once. The woman I once thought I loved is turning out to be nothing more than a selfish, spoiled child. And a murderer, at that. In one sentence she's shown me a side of herself I never knew existed.

I was brought up to believe all life was sacred, that God and God alone could take a life. I don't necessarily accept all the church's teachings, but I do know right from wrong. At least I thought I did. Anymore, who knows? Still, this might be right for someone else, but I don't see how it ever could be for me.

I try to calm myself down enough to respond rationally.

Think, Chuck. She's the mother. She can probably do this without your permission, so you'd better get a grip, man.

"Tanya, let's think about this. You're talking about getting rid of a baby. *Our* baby."

I look at her face. I might as well be looking at a stone. I search my brain frantically for something that might convince her.

"Tanya, that's not who you are."

Her eyes flash.

"Wait a minute, Chuck. Let's think about this another way. I did a big research paper – you know, that class I have to pass to graduate – on this medical procedure called 'fetal reduction.' What it is, sometimes when women have trouble getting pregnant – don't we wish *we* had that problem – they get all these fertility treatments and then they end up with too many babies and they have to kill, er, *reduce*, some of 'em so the mother and other babies can –"

"Tanya, what does that have to do with this?! With us?!"

She starts to cry again. Only this time it feels like she's pulling out the oldest trick in the book, to use on the dumbest guy in the world. Even so, I put my arms around her and pull her to me. The way I used to when things were right.

"I'm sorry, Hon, er, Tanya," I say. "I just don't understand what you're saying. How could you even think of killing our baby?"

She collects herself.

"That's another thing," she responds. "Lots of people – reasonable people – don't believe they're babies until they're born. There's even some who believe they're not really even *people* till they're old enough to reason. That's why it's OK to reduce 'em. If there are too many fetuses – actually, they're called 'products of conception' until they're born – if there are too many to survive, they just stick a needle in 'em, and some of 'em die, I mean, *get reduced*, so the rest can survive. It's pretty humane, when you think about it. Like the way they take out criminals by lethal injection."

I pull away. I feel my face twisting into a mask of revulsion. She keeps rambling on about how she used to believe her mom was right about a fetus being a baby, not just a bunch of cells, but she's thought it all over since doing that research project and hearing all those other opinions. I wonder if she really changed her mind, or if she's just scared to death because we're in this huge mess. It doesn't matter. I have to try to make her see reason.

"What? No! Tanya, that's just *wrong*! Can't you see that?! Criminals get lethal injections because they've done something wrong! Innocent babies shouldn't be executed like that! Man, how can that be legal!"

"Of course, it's legal!" Tanya screams, sounding hysterical. "Abortion's been legal for, what, 40 years? What's the difference, Chuck? I'm just making the point that, even if you don't believe in abortion, if you look at it from the reduction standpoint, it's really to save the others. And the mother, too. It's risky to carry all those babies around. So that's not all that different from what we'd be doing 'cause we both have to go to school and get our lives started, right, and y'know…"

I have to shut off my mind from the rest of what she's saying. Any feeling I ever had for her has been blown to smithereens in these few short minutes. I no longer care whether I ever see her again, but the fact remains. She's the mother of my child.

Idiot! I whip myself. *No one forced you to go to bed with her. You did that all by yourself. You could've said no.*

Maybe it's the stress of the situation, but I start to laugh. The irony is ludicrous. I'm the guy, I didn't want to get involved that way in the first place, (well, I wanted to, who doesn't want to, but I wouldn't have if she hadn't started things). Now, here *I* am having the regrets. Isn't that supposed to be the girl's role?

You're even more of a moron than I thought you were. How could you be so stupid? Not only doesn't she love you, she doesn't

even love the baby she's having. Nice going, Buddy. You picked a
real winner for the mother of your kid.

We argue a while longer, but in the end, we just table the discussion. Neither of us can think of a way to tell our folks what's going on. I can't bring myself to add more stress to my mom's plate, and Dad's the last guy on earth I would trust with this – or anything, for that matter.

So we do nothing.

Chapter 33 Emma and Tom

"It seems to me clear as daylight that abortion would be a crime."
— *Mahatma Gandhi*

I call Lacey, the counselor at an online group I found that supports parents who've gotten bad news about their pregnancies. At least this time I get through the conversation without blubbering like a fool.

"Hello, Emma, it's nice to hear from you!" she chirps when I identify myself. I think I can hear her beaming on the other end of the phone. "What can I help you with?"

"Uh, well, I guess I should just get right to the point. My baby's been diagnosed with spina bifida, I think I told you that last time –"

"Yes, I remember," she responds sympathetically. "I'm so sorry. Can the doctors do anything to improve your baby's health before he or she is born?"

"He. I mean, it's a boy. His name is Matthew."

"Matthew. I love that name. I have a son named Matthew also. Did you choose that name because it means 'gift of God?'"

Startled, I reply, "No. No, we didn't. In fact, I didn't even realize that's what it meant till just now when you said it. My son started calling him that out of the blue one day, and it just stuck. How 'bout that?"

More beaming on the other end of the line as she repeats her question.

"Emma, can the doctors do anything to help Matthew while he's in the womb?"

"No. No, they can't. That's why I'm calling, actually. This woman I work with, when she heard about my situation, she whipped out her phone and started looking up the diagnosis. She's one of those annoying people who can't mind her own business, and when she found out all the problems he'll have, she started talking about 'saying goodbye early.' Can you imagine? I'm sitting at my desk trying to get work done when she just invites herself into my life. I was, like, 'What are you talking about, Ruth?' and she kept yammering on about wouldn't it be kinder to the rest of the family and even the baby himself if we all just 'said goodbye early' instead of letting him be born with all those problems.

"I finally said, 'Ruth, what are you talking about, saying goodbye early? I haven't even said hello to my baby yet and you're telling me to say goodbye. What gives?' Then she said something about couldn't they 'interrupt the pregnancy' and wouldn't that make things easier for all of us. I said, 'Ruth, I don't have the faintest idea what you're talking about. Can you please speak English!'

"That's when she looked down at my stomach with sort of a scowl and all of a sudden it dawned on me. I said, 'Ruth, are you suggesting I abort my child?' She said, 'Oh, Emma, of course not! It's not an abortion. I know someone who had it done. It's actually called a medical termination because the fetus will have such poor quality of life and won't be able to contribute much to society. It's really in the best interest of everyone.'"

"Oh, Emma, I'm so sorry that happened to you!" Lacey exclaims. "What did you say to her?"

"Well, after I talked myself out of stabbing her with a letter opener, I calmly said, 'Ruth, it's a little late in the pregnancy to be considering an abortion, because that *is* what you're talking about, even if I believed in them, which I don't. In fact, my husband and I are going to a prayer vigil outside of an abortion clinic this weekend with our two sons. Would you care to join us?'"

Lacey returns to beaming. I can feel the rays emanating through the phone line.

"Oh, Emma, that's priceless! People can be so insensitive, can't they? What did she say then?"

"Oh, she started going on about how those places do a lot of good for women and family planning – you know the arguments. As if they don't perform – what is it? – something like 350,000 abortions every year with the help of taxpayer money.

"Anyway, I decided not to stand there and argue with her. I simply said, 'Ruth, I have a great deal of work to do, so please excuse me.' And she stomped off."

"You, Emma, are a force to be reckoned with!" Lacey hoots with more merriment than the situation warrants.

I should be proud because this woman is saying all the right things, but instead I feel horrible. Reliving the conversation with Ruth underscores a lot of the "suggestions" my rapidly growing team of specialists keep urging. Maybe that's why I blurt out, "Well, if I'm so right, how come this feels so awful? I mean, maybe they're all right and Tom and I are wrong. Maybe this is a horrible mistake, and we should just do the compassionate thing, like the doctors keep saying, and –"

"Emma, you and Tom *are* doing the compassionate thing," Lacey says emphatically. "You're doing the *right* thing. Anyone who tells you it's compassionate to end the life of your child is dead wrong. Parents don't get to choose the health of their children any more than they get to choose their hair color or foot size. Those things are determined by God, and only he gets to decide when it's time to say goodbye."

She lets her words sink in.

"I wanna believe that," I choke, "I really do. I wanna believe that woman the spina bifida organization put me in touch with, the one who says her life's worth living even though it's not what her parents expected. But she's got so much help and her family's so supportive and they built this accessible wing on their house just for her and –"

I must sound desperate because Lacey breaks in.

"Emma, I'm sorry, could I interrupt just for a minute?"

I take a breath.

"Sure."

"Sorry. Thanks, Emma. I just want to tell you a little story, if I may. I know what you're going through. I brought a child into the world who only lived for a few years. She had a chromosome abnormality that kept her from walking and talking, but it didn't keep her from loving and being loved. In fact, we called her the 'teacher of our souls' because we grew so much just from being around her and caring for her.

"Like you, I had older children, and I wondered how caring for Kelly would impact our family. But guess what I found out? Our family grew stronger and closer because of Kelly! My older kids helped out when they weren't in school, and the little ones treated her like she was their own personal doll. They called her 'Jelly Belly Kelly' because she had this round little tummy like Winnie the Pooh! I know it was because my husband and I set the example of loving Kelly, not *because* of what she *could* do, but *in spite of* what she *couldn't* do."

"Wow. I mean, that's really great, but see, I don't think I have the strength you and your husband seem to have. My husband, Tom, he's a tower of strength, but I feel so beside myself. I mean, sometimes I feel on top of it, like 'Bring it on! I can do this.' But the rest of the time – most of the time, if I'm gonna be honest – I feel completely out of control, like there's a train heading straight for me and I've gotta dodge it quick or it's gonna crush me. Y'know?"

"Yes, Emma, I do know. I questioned myself, too. Can I tell you what helped?"

"Please do!"

"Do you know who Corrie ten Boom was?"

"Corrie ten Boom? The name's familiar, but you'd better refresh my memory."

"Sure. She grew up in Holland before World War Two. She was a deep-thinking little girl, raised in a very religious family. At a young age, she was worrying about some things that frightened her little heart. Her wise father gave her a wonderful way to look at them.

"Corrie used to go with him on business trips into Amsterdam. They would take the train to get there. So, to comfort his little girl, Corrie's father said, 'Corrie, when do I give you your ticket for the train into Amsterdam?' That was easy. Corrie replied, 'Just before I get on the train.' Her daddy replied, 'And that's when God gives us the strength we need, Corrie. Just when we need it.'

"Guess what, Emma? Corrie's faith was tested when she grew up, and she laid her life on the line to protect Jewish people who were being hunted by the Nazis during World War Two. She found she had the strength just when she needed it – not a minute before. She went on to survive a concentration camp and become a world-famous author and speaker.

"See what I'm saying, Emma? Does the story make sense to you?"

I can't answer because of the tears filling my eyes.

****

"Mommy, can I hold the sign today?" Kyle asks, wide-eyed and earnest.

Emma and I teach our kids they have an important role to play in the prayer vigil. We bring both kids most of the time to this weekly gathering outside a branch office of one of the nation's largest abortion providers.

When Em was expecting Kevin, she and our older guy would hold the sign together, with little Kyle as often as not perched right on top of her baby bump. Sometimes passers-by make negative comments to the pro-lifers; interestingly, though, no one seemed to want to take on a woman with one baby in arms and another on the way. Em seemed proud in those early days to be such a visible symbol of the value of life. Lately, though, I think her growing belly brings her only grief and powerlessness.

The only reason we're here today is because Kyle's been asking why we haven't been going to the "prayer fingie." That's Kyle-ese for "prayer thingie," which is his name for the vigil.

When our son asks for the sign, Emma absent-mindedly hands it to him. It's a nondescript white placard on which she and the kids stenciled red, glittery lettering that says simply, "Life Matters." It's about as big as Kyle and pretty much blocks him from view.

Little Kevin sleeps next to us in his stroller.

"Mommy, where's the music lady?" Kyle wonders aloud.

"I don't know, Honey," she answers from wherever she's zoned out to. He's referring to Sarah, the pro-choice woman who invariably shows up to protest the praying crowd. She carries a sign that reads, "Keep your rosaries off my ovaries" on one side, and "My body, my choice" on the other. She's gone from dancing to tunes only she could hear through ear buds to regularly blasting loud music of a pretty rebellious nature, while we pray-ers clasp our prayer beads. More than a few pro-lifers have taken exception to her music and her presence, even calling the cops when the volume threatens to drown out our appeals to the Almighty. Still, she shows up religiously, and holds her own in any debate that comes her way.

"Oh, here she comes!" Kyle remarks with what sounds like relief. I guess for kids, routine is all that matters. He has no clue she's on the opposing team, and he's sure not ready for us to tell him that.

Before long, one of the regulars is doing verbal battle with Sarah. The argument today centers on why Scott Peterson was found guilty of murdering both his wife, Laci, and unborn child in 2002. Since partial birth abortion (birthing a second or third trimester baby, feet first, then piercing the skull and sucking their brains out with a catheter so the head deflates like a balloon and slides easily through the birth canal) was legal when the crime took place, little Conner Peterson could've been legally aborted any time prior to delivery. How, then, could the father be held liable for killing that which had no legal right to live until it exited its mother's womb?

Sarah responds that the baby had technically been "delivered" when its body was found along with Laci's, thereby affording it the rights of a person.

See what I mean when I say she can handle herself?

"But don't partial birth laws let Scott Peterson off the hook?" the pro-lifer retorts. "If the mother had the right to abort right up until the point of delivery at the time of this case, why shouldn't the father have that same right? I mean, if it isn't a baby until it's out of the womb, how can we send this guy to jail for destroying a 'blob of tissue?'"

"When he killed the mother, the baby hadn't been delivered. Therefore, he should've had the same right to kill his child as its mother had. And how could he murder something that wasn't alive to begin with? If we're gonna say it's a human being in the womb, then fine, the mother dies and with her, the baby, and he's responsible for both. But how can we say he killed a non-living clump of cells, if that's what we're calling it?"

I understand where the pro-lifer's going. He's trying to get Sarah to admit that, on some level, reasonable minds realize it's ridiculous to label the "clump of cells" living or non-living based solely on whether or not it's left the birth canal. A beating heart is a beating heart, regardless of whether it's inside or outside the uterus. To my mind, partial birth abortion – any form of abortion, really – turns what should be the safest, most comforting place in the world into a torture chamber. Once you accept the whole brutal process as murder, you find that sadistic Peterson guilty regardless of what the law said at the time.

I'm tempted to jump into the debate, but I don't want my preschoolers to hear their daddy discussing such brutal facts of life so early. Little Kyle's so tightly clutching the sign he and Emma made. For now, it's enough that he knows life matters. He doesn't need to know how cheaply it's defined in some circles.

The next round is about blood types.

"How could a mother and unborn child have two different blood types unless they were two separate, viable entities?" the pro-lifer contends. Sarah retorts that blood types are no different than hair or eye color, for example. Since fetuses inherit characteristics from both parents' genetic codes, of course the fetal blood type may vary from its mother's.

Around and around they go.

Without warning, Kevin jolts awake in his stroller and begins to wail. Emma reaches for the baby, while I swoop down and gather up Kyle and the sign he so proudly brandishes.

"Seems like somebody's hungry," Em says, fishing around in her baby bag for a sippy cup and the snacks she brought.

"Me, too!" yells Kyle. Em's hand emerges with a goldfish-shaped tub of something or other. She starts doling out goodies into their chubby hands. Both kids fall silent.

My problem-solving skills have been working overtime for the last month. I know Em wasn't thrilled to learn we were having a third kid in the first place, let alone another boy. The news of Matt's condition along with everything else really blew her away. God knows how long it's gonna take her to adjust to this new normal.

That's really the point, though, in my mind: God *does* know. I don't consider myself as much of a holy roller as the crowd around me, but I do believe in the inherent value of life. I have a gut-level faith in God, and the minimal religious instruction I got growing up all comes down to one thing: God makes life and only he can take it away.

So, I've been thinking. Before becoming a teacher, I ran a construction business. All my experience on job sites with mess-ups and unforeseen complications that were sure to cost frugally minded homeowners more money taught me to look for workarounds. There's more than one way to skin a cat, and I can usually find most of them. When I worked in the business world, if I hadn't been able to stretch a buck till the first president screamed for mercy, I'd have had to shut my doors at the first sign of trouble.

Is there any way she could stay home and take care of the kid? I keep asking myself. Maybe, if we got rid of cable and our landline – and only ate on weekends. We could pull the kids out of day care, that would sure cut expenses, but who knows how many new medical bills are coming our way for Matt? Plus, her insurance is better than mine. Not to mention the fact that Emma likes her job for the most part, even though she gripes there are never enough hours in the day.

What if I stayed home? I ask myself. *John Lennon did it with his kid. Why not me?*

Because you don't have John Lennon's money to pay for whatever help this poor kid's gonna need, that's why, the sensible side of my brain replies. *You're only a so-so history teacher who lots of times can't handle other people's kids, who don't have life-threatening health conditions, let alone two toddlers and a newborn with a hole in his back.*

Whoa, there, dude, you're jumping the gun, I remind myself. *There's no guarantee the baby's spinal cord will be hanging out like spaghetti. There's more than one type of spina bifida, and we could get lucky. Doesn't seem like it from the ultrasounds, though. No way around it, Poor Matt's gonna need serious help. And even if we could afford live-in help, we couldn't expect an outsider to go to constant doctor appointments and fight with the school when the time comes for that. That's a parent's job.*

There's got to be a way! I keep coming back to that after going around in circles like this ad nauseam. It would be easier if I could talk to Emma about it, but I don't think she's ready to go there.

Strange, I conclude. *Guys always get a bum rap for being non-communicative. Here I want to sit down and try to figure out a way to handle this, and she's a basket case any time I even broach the subject.*

Kyle's frightened voice interrupts my silent conversation.

"Daddy, what's happening?"

"Whaddaya mean, Ky-Guy?"

"Tom, aren't you hearing this?" cries Emma. "We've got to get the kids out of here so they don't pick up those words," she gasps, trying frantically to tie all her loose ends together.

Turns out a couple have taken on the priest leading the pro-life camp. They're spouting virulence, their dialogue littered with four letter words and crude suggestions of bodily contortions that would be physiologically impossible to perform. A crowd's starting to form on the main square where the vigil is held, and bystanders are chiming in. Some agree with the epithets being hurled at the pro-lifers, adding in a few of their own; several pro-lifers shoot back less graphic but equally obnoxious insults. A precious few condemn the nasty speech and plead for cooler heads to prevail.

I briefly consider my options. I could try to make an appeal for reason. I'm pretty good at that, can usually calm and de-escalate troubled situations in the classroom. My little guy, though, seeing the distress in his mom's face, is now tugging on my sleeve and urging, "C'mon, Daddy. We gotta go!" Our younger guy, his hunger temporarily abated by the crackers Emma fed him, must need a diaper change. He's throwing a fit.

I look back at my wife and read fear in her blue eyes. I suspect she's less concerned about the language being spewed than the possibility of violence breaking out. Rage often seems to be companion to conviction.

Once, when I was on the football team in high school, a fight broke out when a jock took to towel-whipping a smaller teammate in the locker room after practice. At the time, my impression was that it was all in good fun, but the victim didn't take it that way. The little guy's reflexes were fast, that's why he had made the team, and the jock found his mouth bloodied by a quick clip to the lower jaw. One thing led to another, and punches flew. The big dude was pummeling his irate teammate, whose face was red with fury now that he no longer had the advantage of the surprise element. I saw an opening when the original assailant got caught off guard by an even bigger player, who valiantly launched himself into the middle of the heat.

Instinctively, I yelled, "Man, what're you guys doin'! You're supposed to be on the same team! Save it for the field! The coach is gonna bench all of you if you don't knock this off! We can't afford to lose any of you, or we're gonna lose the game tomorrow night!"

Somehow the combination of being body blocked on the one hand and reasoned with on the other subdued the combatants. Their arms stopped flailing, and they grudgingly slinked away from each other.

At that moment, I realized the power of the spoken word. For sure it hadn't hurt that the third guy had jumped into the altercation, but the fighters were still clawing at each other till I threw in my two cents.

The same instinct that drove me in that locker room 20 years ago is telling me to intervene now. My family, though, clearly needs to be removed from this tense situation.

I look at Emma and say one word: "Wait."

Chapter 34 Mary

"The best-laid plans of mice and men often go awry." – Robert Burns

"Dave, would you have time to read something?" I ask as he chops onions for tonight's dinner.

"Sure, Hon. What are we talkin'? A newspaper article or an epic novel?"

"Very funny!" I reply. "Somewhere in between. It's the paper Tanya wrote for her senior project. It's over ten pages. I've been trying to get to it for a week now, but I'm swamped with the latest fundraising letters. And Jessica's been –"

As if on cue, my younger daughter yells from the living room. She's been playing happily for all of ten minutes in the nook Dave fixed up for her. If only we had a playroom! I can't let her use the basement because that's where I have my "office," if you can call it that. There's too much down there that she can get into.

Dave did the best he could with his limited handyman capabilities, but it still looks pretty ramshackle. He hooked several baby gates together, then used them to portion off a section of our living room. He taught Jessica how to latch and unlatch the gate mechanism – boy, did she feel like hot stuff when she mastered that! Dave then secured some shelving with cubbies for her toys to the wall opposite the gate. I'm praying they don't fall down! The one time he tried to anchor bookshelves to our bedroom wall – well, let's just say it wasn't pretty when I went to dust.

"Hey, little lady, what's up?" Dave calls in response to Jessica's summons.

"Daddy, come see what I did!"

Dave wipes an onion tear from his eye with a dishtowel – I wish he wouldn't do that – then we trot out to see what our little girl is up to.

What *isn't* she up to? We only left her to her own devices for ten minutes – *ten minutes!* – and she's got the couch cushions on the floor of her nook, Puffy under an afghan on said cushions, every toy from the shelves in a circle around Puffy, and an open container of kids' paint on the coffee table.

Where do I begin?

OK, Mary, remember she's only a toddler. You can't expect her not to test limits. Pray before you launch into a lecture. Maybe it'll go better.

"Jessica, remember Daddy and I told you that *this* is *your* play area," I begin, pointing to the gated section, "and the rest of the room is for us grownups?"

"I 'member, Mommy," Jess says solemnly, "but Puffy was tired. He gots a tummy ache. He needed a bed. And covers. And toys."

I suppress a smile and look at Dave, who isn't even trying to hide his amusement.

"We understand, Honey, but next time ask us before you start taking things from the living room into your play area. We'll tell you if it's alright or not. Got it?"

"Got it!" she says merrily.

197

"Now, what's this paint doing here? That's supposed to be used only with Mommy or Daddy. And it definitely doesn't belong on my coffee table," I chide, striding over to retrieve it.

Alas, the best laid plans... I slip on a mini ambulance that must have gone rogue – the one toy that escaped Puffy's circle of friends. I go careening into the coffee table, splashing avocado colored paint all over the couch, carpet and my shoes for good measure.

Dave leaps in to do damage control.

"OK, little lady, we have a big mess to clean up now because you disobeyed Mommy's – I mean, *our* – rules! Mommy and I are very upset! What do you have to say for yourself, and how are you gonna help fix this?!"

Jess bursts into tears, which really isn't fair, because I'm the one with green paint all over my new white slippers, and I'm the one whose living room looks like the Incredible Hulk just exploded in it.

For once, Dave holds firm. I've got to give him credit. He doesn't let her manipulate him the way he usually does.

"That's enough of that, young lady," he lectures her. "Tears aren't gonna work this time. Now, you need to wake Puffy up from his nap, or whatever he's doing, and start putting those toys back on their shelves. Oh, and also, tell Mommy you're sorry for opening that paint and ask her how you can help clean it up."

Jess wails more loudly and utters unintelligible words. Dave steps into her nook and starts directing her.

I recall vaguely that Dave and I were discussing something in the kitchen before all this happened, but, whatever it was, it went out of my head along with the hundred things a day that I forget or misplace somewhere in my addled brain.

Chapter 35 Tom

"I testify that there is good and right and wrong on both sides of the fence. And even more shocking – we have far more in common with the 'other' side than we might imagine... I was loved from one side onto the other." – Abby Johnson on her conversion from director of a Planned Parenthood clinic to pro-life activist

"Tom, what're you, crazy!" Emma shrieks at me. "This is getting dangerous! We gotta get our kids out of here!"

I come to my senses.

"Of course. You're right."

I help my wife pack up the children and walk them to the car.

"Thank God," Emma breathes. The baby is still unhappy, but his bawling has reduced itself to more tolerable moaning, which can easily be corrected now that a diaper change is on the way.

"I've gotta go back," I announce.

Emma eyes me with disbelief.

"You're kidding, right?"

There's no time to explain, even if I understood why myself, which I don't. It's just a gut feeling that I have something to add to the mayhem. Something good.

"I'll see you at home."

"Tom, why are you trying to be a hero?! This is crazy! Things are getting wild over there! Besides, we only brought the one car!"

"Emma, I *have* to go back there. You can pick me up later. Or I'll grab an Uber."

I raise my voice to silence the objections she's starting to utter.

"Please, Em. Just take the kids home. I'll be OK."

Before she can continue, and over the pleas of my older boy who cringes at arguments, I return to the fray. I size up the situation, as I've learned to do quickly when a classroom brawl breaks out. Over on the other side of the square, the priest appears to be holding his own with the angry couple. Over here, where I am, a large woman in a plaid jacket is arguing with Sarah, the music lady.

"Don't you see, when you bring your trashy music here while we're trying to pray, it's like you're dancing on the graves of the thousands of babies this place has killed? This place takes the womb, which is supposed to be the safest place anywhere, and turns it into a tomb!"

Sarah is having none of the pro-lifer's melodrama.

"First of all, I happen to like my music, and don't appreciate you calling it trashy. The cops have been called more than once, and I've been assured I'm not breaking any noise ordinances. If your group has freedom of speech to pray out loud, I have the same right to play music at a reasonable volume. Secondly, think before you call this a graveyard. This is a medical facility that provides much more than abortion services. My gynecologists are here, serving me and other low-income women. This place saves lives."

The pro-lifer must have decided to take Sarah's music off the table and focus on the bigger issue.

"Well, what do you call it when they go into a woman's womb and *dismember* her living child? They usually go in blindly because many abortionists don't use ultrasound to locate the baby inside. No, they're just hoping they can find their 'target,' which is the baby they're trying to destroy!"

I wonder if I should step in and try to bring a more level tone to this discussion. I agree with plaid jacket lady, and she just made a good point, but her tone is so strident. If she could hear herself, she might reconsider her approach. While I'm considering my options, Sarah starts with the "glob of tissue" argument.

"We are not talking about a child. We're talking about a pregnancy which is not yet a living being. We're talking about –"

"Well, let me tell you something, young lady," the older woman cuts her off. Then, as if reading my mind about toning down her rhetoric, plaid jacket lady suddenly does a 180.

"No, I'd rather call you by name, you deserve that respect. It's Sarah, isn't it?"

The music lady lets loose an exasperated sigh.

"Yes. Fine. It's Sarah."

"Thank you, Sarah. I'm Helen, and I started out pro-choice. I actually volunteered in a clinic like this one for several years. I believed the same things you believe, that I was doing good for society. I believed them when they told me their main concern was to prevent unwanted pregnancy and disease, that they wanted abortion to be 'safe, legal and rare.'

"'Safe, legal and rare!' That used to be the rallying cry of abortion providers. You know what I found out? These places claim

202

only a tiny percentage of their services are abortions, but do you know what that translates to? When you add up all the numbers country-wide, you'll find they're aborting hundreds of thousands of babies each year! Sarah, do you realize something like 60 million babies have been killed since our country legalized abortion?"

Unfazed, Sarah replies, "Helen, I appreciate those statistics, but children need to be loved if they're gonna be brought into this world! Society can't afford to care for all the unwanted children that are being born every year. And if you're gonna talk statistics, how 'bout the fact that countless kids are abused every year in this country by their own parents! Something like 700,000! Can you imagine how much higher those numbers would be if we didn't have safe, legal abortions? Wouldn't you rather see a fetus painlessly removed from a uterus than let it be born into a life of abuse or poverty?"

Helen sighs.

"If only it *were* painless," she laments. "Have you heard of Abby Johnson? She was a director at a Planned Parenthood clinic. Defended the pro-choice cause for years. She had to assist in an abortion one day. On that particular day, the doctor was using ultrasound to see what he was doing. For the first time, she got to see with her own eyes what was actually being done. She watched that baby flinch and try to move away when the probe touched him. She saw those body parts being sucked out. They're called 'products of conception,' in the industry – I've heard Abby speak, and she said they nicknamed them 'pieces of children,' which is more accurate. She says she's seen those body parts get sealed up in plastic bags, then incinerated. *Burned up*! That's what the Nazis did after they killed Jews! Just burned them up like trash. Didn't even give them a funeral 'cause they considered them sub-human."

I try to disengage from the ultra-agitated tone Helen's still using and focus on the facts she's sharing, because what she's saying really is shocking. I always knew abortion was murder, but I had no idea how cold-hearted the abortion industry could be. I look to Sarah, to see if Helen's making any headway. Sarah's still tapping her foot to the tune blaring from her phone. I guess that's my answer.

"You want to hear a little-known fact, Sarah? Something the mainstream media really hasn't reported on, but it's a fact, you can look it up. Now we're learning it's not bad enough aborted children get thrown away like trash. Now sometimes their little body parts are being sold, as if they were baseball cards or, I don't know, French fries. Just a cheap commodity to be bought and sold, consumed for somebody else's purposes. Don't you see how wrong this is, Sarah? How can you be a part of it?"

"Just a minute. I'm not part of it, but I do support a woman's right to choose. And yeah, I saw those videos that supposedly prove clinics are selling tissue. First of all, they were taken out of context. Remember, there's a huge need for medical research, stem cells, things like that. Wouldn't you rather they made use of that tissue instead of just discarding it? For God's sake, my own mother donated her body to medical science when she died so she'd have a purpose, maybe help others by her death. Surely you can't find anything wrong with that."

"Yes, but Sarah, you said it yourself. She *donated* her body to science. She made a *choice* to share her organs that way. What choice do little unborn babies have? Besides, no one was making a profit from your mother's sacrifice. In fact, from what I understand, donating to medical science actually costs the family money. Do I have that right?"

"Oh, I don't know. It was a long time ago. I'd have to ask my father, and I'm not going there with him. It was bad enough when we got her remains back after two years – oh, never mind, that's a whole 'nother subject. The point is, we're talking about utilizing tissue for scientific research. Now, that's a worthy cause. You can't dispute that."

I stick a piece of gum in my mouth. I'm beginning to feel a bit weird standing here not saying anything, but I'm also starting to realize how little I actually know about this whole issue. I vaguely recall hearing about Planned Parenthood doctors haggling over the price of fetal body parts when they didn't realize they were being filmed by some brave undercover reporters. But what I remember wouldn't even fit on this gum wrapper.

"I'm not disagreeing with the cause, just the means and the motivation," Helen responds. "No one disagrees that we need to learn how the human body works and be able to harvest things for transplants. I carry an organ donor card myself, Sarah. The issue is how and why is this being done? It's being done on the backs of helpless infants and uninformed moms who don't realize what they're getting themselves into. I've talked to some of them. And to some of their partners, the dads of these babies.

"Here's the thing, Sarah. After I realized what was really going on, I couldn't work at that abortion mill anymore. I got out and now I volunteer for a crisis pregnancy center, and I hear stories you wouldn't believe. A lot of people can't forgive themselves for choosing abortion. It's literally wrecking their lives. And the relationships between couples take a terrible beating. Understandably. They've ended the life of their child, and paid dearly in dollars and regret. After that, many of them can't live with themselves or each other! I personally know two married couples who aborted a child because 'it wasn't the right timing.' They both ended up divorced, and both still have terrible guilt that ruined their marriages."

Sarah sighs and rolls her eyes.

"Sarah, I'm sorry, I'm not trying to be dramatic. But you see, this is why I feel so strongly about this subject. I see the effects on the parents, not to mention what's being done to the babies. These poor children aren't choosing to participate in medical research like your mother did, bless her heart – what a lovely thing to do. They're being victimized. The other thing that's different is, your mother got to die a natural death and *then* have her organs harvested –"

"No, I didn't say her organs were harvested. I said she gave her body for research, so medical students could study the human body. Oh, never mind, I'm getting upset talking about this. I'm sorry I brought it up."

"Oh, I'm sorry, too, Sarah. I apologize for getting that wrong."

"It's fine. Can we just get off this topic?"

"Can I say just one more thing, or will that be too upsetting for you?"

Sarah shrugs.

"Fine, but then let's drop it. Please."

"No problem. I said my concern was the means and the motivation. We've already talked about the means. Helpless, innocent children and, in many cases, naïve parents who, if they had a chance to see their baby on ultrasound before making their final decision, I guarantee you, many of them would change their minds. That's the means. Now, what's the motivation? If this were being done altruistically, with no cost attached, that might be one thing. But it's not. We've seen the footage. These places are making money off of killing these poor kids. Who's getting compensated? Not the babies, obviously. Not their parents – no, they're paying dearly for their legal right to end their child's life, and perhaps ruin their own. No, it's the providers who are making money. And, Sarah, please don't believe it when you hear they want to keep abortion 'safe, legal and rare.' If that were the case, Abby Johnson wouldn't have gotten up in arms when her higher ups told her she had to increase her abortion numbers. It's a fact. She writes about it in her book."

"Yes, I've heard of it. She wrote about how she had a good career and was well treated by Planned Parenthood, then one day just up and quit. Left everybody in the lurch, then started trash talking the organization she made a living off of for I don't know how many years. She's a real fine character, that one."

"Well, I don't know her personally, but I do know they tried to take her to court and lost. That should tell us something. In any case, she claims in her book that when funds got tight, the directors were told to increase their volume of abortions. Even though they promised her when she came on board that their mission was to make birth control available so there would be fewer abortions. When Abby pointed that out, she got in trouble. Got a formal reprimand, I think. What does that tell you?"

Sarah's not buying it.

"It tells me I don't know the whole story and shouldn't make a judgment about somebody else's work life."

"Fair enough. But the bottom line is, they wanted her to start pushing the abortion option in her clinic and she wouldn't do it. Because she believed in their purpose to reduce unwanted pregnancy, but now they were asking her to increase her clinic's death rate so they could make money! Doesn't that seem to go along with what we're finding out about the sale of body parts?"

Sarah rallies.

"Well, what would you suggest? Adoption is available, but I don't see people like you lining up to take in any of the thousands of kids who get beaten up in their homes every year. Or am I wrong about that? Are you offering to step up and adopt some of the desperate kids being passed around in foster care because their parents beat them up? Or because they're deformed or disabled, and nobody wants them?"

I shudder at that last statement. Too close to home?

Sarah pauses, waiting for a response. Helen, caught off guard, is rendered momentarily speechless. Sarah presses her advantage.

"I didn't think so. Well, maybe when the religious right starts coming up with homes and money for abused and unwanted children, instead of inflicting its patriarchal value system on women, maybe then I'll think about changing camps."

I wish desperately that I could think of some way to extricate Helen from the wall Sarah's backed her up against, but I've got nothing. Fortunately, Helen finds her voice.

"Well, Sarah, just because I may not be in a position to adopt doesn't make it a bad option. From what I understand, many couples want to adopt, but it's a very costly and difficult process. That's why people like me, who truly aren't in a position to adopt, can help by donating funds to make it possible for people who do want to, but can't afford it.

"Have you ever thought, too, that there are other ways to support children whose parents choose life when an unplanned pregnancy comes along? For instance, many, like me, support crisis pregnancy centers with both money and service. Also, lots of people – again, I'm one of them – work in church nurseries and donate their time in other ways so parents can get a break.

"I'm not saying this to brag, but since it seems relevant to what we're discussing, I belong to a group in my church that provides free babysitting for single parents so they can get out and do things they have to do, like go on job interviews, go shopping, stuff like that. And we do that regardless of what kind of needs the child has. One mom at our church – Francesca – her little girl's in a wheelchair and wears diapers. She always will. So, we set up a time when Francesca could show us how to change Penny if she needed it – we use this thing called a Hoyer lift to get her out of the chair and onto the bed – those of us who are strong enough, that is – and the other basics about Penny's care.

"A few members in the group work in the medical field. They say it makes them feel great to be able to use their skills to support parents who choose life. They're earning big bucks when they go to work, but they do this for free because it's a way for them to help in a concrete way, even though they're raising their own families and wouldn't be able to adopt.

"Do you see what I mean, Sarah?"

For a moment Sarah stands wordlessly, apparently taking great interest in a candy wrapper someone tossed into the gutter. Then she rallies.

"Well, that is lovely. Truly. But suppose a woman's been raped? Or worse – suppose a young girl's the victim of incest. Some low-life father or uncle robs the poor kid of her innocence, and now you want to force her to carry that baby to term? You're not even gonna make an exception for that?"

"You know, I'm glad you brought that up, Sarah," Helen responds. "I've done some reading on that subject. I struggle with that same question because you're right, it doesn't seem fair. Here's what I've learned. In cases of incest, when a young girl gets pregnant after having been molested by a family member, often she wants to keep the child. She's been horribly mistreated and is somewhat comforted by the thought of having someone of her own to love and be loved by. Oftentimes, it's the abuser – and sometimes, shamefully, the girl's own mother, to whom she may have confided the abuse – who insist on an abortion, so no one will know what's been going on. That goes directly against what the victim wants, because she knows her pregnancy will expose what's been happening to her. See, Sarah? The abortion is actually a second victimization, forced on her by those who don't want the truth to come out."

"Well, what about other rape victims? You're going to impose a nine-month sentence on them for a violent crime they'd like to move on from? Hardly seems fair."

"What isn't fair, Sarah, is inflicting a lifetime of regret on someone who was already victimized. The reading I've done suggests that many rape victims feel almost secondarily raped when they undergo an abortion. The first crime they had no say over; a man brutally invaded their bodies. But when they allow an abortionist to invade them a second time, they have no one to blame but themselves. Studies show these women have physical and psychological effects – PTSD, pretty much – that plague them years after they would have delivered the rapist's child.

"Is it fair to have to give birth to an unplanned child conceived through violence? Perhaps not. Is it hard? You bet. But many women who've been in this position say they're glad they chose to continue their pregnancy, whether they decided to parent their child or seek an adoptive family. Others express huge regret after choosing abortion."

Sarah looks ready to open her mouth, but gets beaten to the punch by an older woman who jumps into the conversation. She appears to be in her 60's, with hair that looks like it wants to turn white, but got stuck in the same in-between shade my mother ended up with. Mom refers disparagingly to her undecided hair color as "iron gray."

"Excuse me, ladies," the third woman begins. "Would you mind if I added my two cents?"

Chapter 36 David

"Your greatest danger is letting the urgent things crowd out the important." – Charles E. Hummel, "Tyranny of the Urgent"

"Hey, Mar, have you had a chance to read Tanya's research paper yet?" I ask after we finally get Jess to bed.

The look on her face tells me all I need to know.

"Look, Hon, there's no need to feel guilty. I don't know anybody who gets as much done in a day as you do. Still, though, you may wanna make time for this. This is some wild subject matter. And your Tanya's arguing the pro side of the issue. Do you even know what the issue is?"

As soon as the words leave my mouth, I wanna cut my tongue out. Why did I say it that way? Mary's face takes on the look of a wounded bird – an overworked, overwhelmed, overtired, wounded bird.

Before she can start to cry, I go into evasive maneuvers. I'm no starship captain, but I know when I'm hurtling towards disaster.

"Dumb question," I backpedal. "Tell you what. Lemme give you the highlights. You're obviously well aware of abortion, right?"

She looks at me like I just asked her if babies poop. OK. I'll take it. Anything but tears.

"Duh! Another dumb question. Auto-correct time!"

She smiles. Now we're getting somewhere.

"OK, well, there's this other type of abortion called 'something reduction.' I can't think of the exact term, but we can look it up later. It's when there's a big pregnancy – no, scratch that – it actually can even be with twins. Anyway, there's this pregnancy with more than one baby, and for whatever reason, the woman wants to, what they call, 'reduce' it. 'Reduce' is just a polite word for abort."

Mary's nodding.

"Yeah, Sweetie, I'm familiar with it. It's not something we come up against at the pregnancy center because we're usually dealing with people who, for whatever reason, feel unprepared for a child. What you're talking about is a large pregnancy, often resulting from fertility treatment, and then the medical providers feel it's a high-risk situation, so they do away with some of the babies. Right?"

This is great! Not only does she know what I'm talking about, but she's totally forgotten that I just more or less called her a neglectful mother.

"Exactly," I say. "And do you know how they 'do away with' those babies, as you say? They shoot their hearts full of a lethal drug, then leave the dead carcasses to rot next to the ones they let live."

"I think I did know that," she says somberly. "And yes, it's tragic. And merciless."

I take her hand.

"Well, apparently Tanya had to pick which side of the issue she came down on, and she chose the pro side. I figured you'd want to know about that."

Mary takes a sip of her coffee and sighs.

"You know what, Dave? The longer I live, the more I realize I'm raising my kids in a toilet. A real sewer. I mean, really, when you get down to it, there's no innocence for our kids anymore.

"Think about it. Abortion's been legal since the 70's. That's all these kids have ever known. A country that cares for its animals – and criminals – better than it cares for its own children.

"I mean, look at the influence Planned Parenthood has. A lot of the girls who come into our office have been heavily influenced by their website. It would be sickening if it weren't so sad.

"They're promoting a lot more than family planning, let me tell you. You should see some of the 'advice' they offer on their website. Mind you, I'm not saying there isn't some valid stuff on there. In a way, that's what makes it so insidious. On the one hand, they talk about healthy relationships and how to prevent pregnancy, but on the other, they turn around and encourage risky behavior. They get kids all gung-ho about having sex, then tell them to be sure and get tested for STD's, as though getting an STD were as normal and expected as getting a cold."

I'm about to respond, but she's really on a roll.

"Oh, and here's the best thing. They make sure to tell kids that, even though most states require a parent's permission or at least notification to get an abortion, a judge can waive that requirement. Isn't that lovely? I'm liable for everything my child does up until the age of 18, and God forbid I should spank her delicate, little behind to get her to comply with reasonable behavior standards, but if she gets pregnant after taking all the 'good advice' they offer about 'healthy, satisfying sex,' some guy in a long robe

215

gets to decide whether or not I have the right to even know she's pregnant!"

Mary's glorious face – the face that could've launched ten times as many ships as the thousand Helen of Troy inspired – takes on a frightening look.

"You know, Dave, our kids' hearts have been stabbed, too, but with something maybe even worse than poison: irresponsibility and indifference."

My wife has a flair for the dramatic at times, but this is one overstatement I simply can't argue with.

Still, I do want to weigh in. I don't know nearly as much about the abortion industry as Mary does, but I do know they get funding from our government every year. She's always signing petitions to our state's senators and representatives, asking them to pull the plug on those gimmies. I open my mouth to praise her for her good citizenship, but I'm a split second too late. She scurries on like a scattergun, aiming her contempt at a new target – one that's a bit closer to home.

"And have you seen some of the cartoons Jessica's watching? The characters are obnoxious and nasty to each other, and some of the themes are – well, they're sure not for children! I make her turn them off when I catch her, but in all honesty, I have no idea what she's watching when she's at the babysitter's."

She's probably right, but I'm not sure I want to go down this rabbit trail just now. If I'm not careful, she's gonna start in on the idea of ditching cable, and I'm not ready for that. I circle back to the original subject, hoping she'll forget about her TV vendetta.

"Well, the question is, how do we wanna handle this? I mean, I've told you the gist of the paper, but if you really wanna get inside Tanya's head, you'd better read it for yourself."

"I must make time for it. Y'know what? I'm tired, but there's no time like the present. Where'd you put it, Dave?"

"Ah, Hon, now's not the time. You're exhausted. You've looked beat ever since dinner, even though we've been discussing a heavy subject. It'll keep one more day."

"Oh, I look beat, huh? Thanks for the compliment!" she teases.

Uh oh.

"Hey, Hon, you know what I mean," I stammer. "I mean, you're always beautiful, even when you're tired. I mean, uh –"

"Dave, you're fine. And you're right," she concedes with a weak smile. "But if I don't do it now, who knows when I'll get to it? Tomorrow…"

She starts rattling off a list of obligations that sound like they'll require a lot more than 24 hours to complete.

"Well, how 'bout this? You tell her you haven't had time, so you had me read it, and –"

"Oh, no, Dave, that'll crush her! She was so proud that she'd gotten an 'A' on it."

She looks down at her gnarly hands.

"But in all honesty, I do have to ask myself how she could take such a position, knowing what I stand for. I mean, does she want me to debate it with her, convince her she's wrong? Or has she become so warped by the society she's grown up in that she truly

217

can't see the horror of what she's defending? Oh, Dave, what should I do?"

Great. Now that she's finally invited me into her diatribe, I can't think of a thing to say. I go for the stall.

"Hmmm. Yeah, I see what you're saying. If you try to make her see how awful this reduction thing is, she'll probably take it as a criticism of her, since she argued it's OK. It's a tough call."

My exhausted wife yawns and buries her head in my shoulder.

"Better pray about it," she says through another yawn.

Part of me wants to say, "OK, pray, but don't wait too long." I mean, who knows what's going on in Tanya's head? This may be just the tip of the iceberg.

Besides which, Mary's right. The world's getting slimier all the time. In some ways, I don't know how we're gonna protect Jess when it comes time for a cell phone and all that. Our pastor once said that giving a kid a smart phone is like giving her an adult bookstore in her pocket. You can't argue with that, but what's a parent to do? You can't *not* give her one, because then she'd be the laughingstock of her friends, who all have them, plus, then she couldn't call for help when some deranged nut job tries to mow her down with a semi-automatic in broad daylight.

You can't win.

Chapter 37 Tom

"This daughter is sacred of God. This child is destined for great good." – Cindy Speltz, pro-life activist, who kept her child after conceiving through rape

I like a good debate; in fact, I encourage them among my social studies students, so they'll know how to handle themselves when life makes them take a stand on things. But I'm also glad I sent Emma and the boys home. This conversational thread is getting heavy, even for me.

When the third woman asks if she can join in, I don't know what to expect. Part of me wants to throw support to the pro-lifer, especially if this new lady is gonna jump on Sarah's bandwagon. On the other hand, Helen's doing a pretty good job making her case, and I'm not sure I have any better arguments to offer. So, like a mannequin in a store window, I stay silent.

Helen doesn't seem to be thrown off balance by the newcomer. On the contrary, she smiles and says, "Sure. Of course. I'm Helen and this is Sarah. What are your thoughts on what we've been talking about?"

"Well, hi. Thanks. My name is Kathy," she begins in a voice that's soft but carries conviction. "I've been listening to your conversation and felt I had something to add because, well, you see, I have first-hand information about what you're talking about. Have you ever heard of Cindy Speltz?"

Sarah and Helen shake their heads. I'm not familiar with the name, either.

"OK, well, this is a woman who was raped in the '70's, shortly after the Supreme Court legalized abortion. She became pregnant as a result of the rape. I just heard her and her daughter speak on…"

At this point, Kathy mentions the name of a faith-based television network that I've never listened to. I make a mental note to later check out their website and see if I can verify her story.

I've been trying to stay just far enough away that it doesn't seem like I'm eavesdropping – although that's pretty much what I am doing. I hope my face doesn't register my reaction to Kathy's words. I'm a mix of skeptical and outrageously curious. It's like a car wreck that I can't help craning my neck to see.

I look at the faces of the two women she's speaking to. That's a little trick I've picked up from my years in the classroom. I do face checks once in a while as I'm teaching, to see if I'm losing my audience. Helen's holds rapt attention. Sarah's mirrors mine.

Kathy pays no attention to any of our expressions. She merely continues.

"As I said, this was a couple years after abortion became legal, and Cindy's family and friends strongly believed she should have one. Just about everyone thought she'd be better off going that route because she was young and had no money, and her family sounds like it was very dysfunctional. It sounds like poor Cindy was more or less expected to raise her younger siblings. Her mother had died, and her dad was a heavy drinker. When he found out she was pregnant, he made her leave home, even though she swore it wasn't her fault.

"So, there she was, out on the streets with no job, barely a high school education, and nowhere to turn. The saddest thing was, it sounds like poor Cindy had no frame of reference for how a man should treat a woman, since her father had been abusive and neglectful her whole life. I guess she was so mixed up about unacceptable behavior that she didn't even realize she could press charges against the man who raped her! So, she never even reported it. Can you believe that?"

It seems like a rhetorical question, so no one answers. Still, Kathy waits a few seconds, then charges ahead.

"Well, OK. I don't want to belabor the story with every little detail. What I really want to get at is the decision Cindy made, which was to keep her baby, and why she's glad she did."

I glance at Sarah to see if this has turned her off. To her credit, she's still politely listening, and even looks interested.

"Well, anyway, Cindy had a friend whose parents let her sleep on their couch while she tried to come up with a plan. She didn't want to abort her baby, but there didn't seem to be any other options. No one wanted to help her raise this inconvenient, *un-asked for* child. She was on the couch one night, crying, trying not to be overheard by the other people in the house. It was an apartment, I think, so there wasn't much privacy. Oh, well, I guess those details don't matter. Sorry, I'm terrible at telling stories.

"Suddenly, while the moonlight spilled into the room, Cindy swore she could hear a voice, not of anyone she knew, just a voice."

A siren sounds in the distance, causing Kathy to interrupt her reverie. Helen wears a spellbound expression, while Sarah's face is now a harder read. Being the only guy in this picture, I somehow feel apologetic. I continue trying to stay invisible.

When the screeching of the siren dims, Helen prods Kathy.

"What did the voice say?"

"Well, let me see if I can get this right," Kathy answers, hesitating. She appears to be searching her memory for the right quote. After a brief pause, she resumes.

"It said something like, 'This daughter is sacred and of God. This child is destined for great good!'"

She pauses again to let this sink in.

"Wow!" Helen says with amazement.

"Wow," Sarah echoes, but in a much different way.

"'Wow' is right!" Kathy gushes. "Well, Cindy didn't know much about religion or have much of a faith background, but she couldn't ignore that experience. The long and the short of it is, she followed what the voice seemed to be telling her, and kept the baby. Her daughter's name is, lemme see, oh, what was it?"

Sarah picks up her sign and says, "Never mind. That's a lovely story, but –"

"Oh, it was Jenni!" Kathy squeals, like a kid who just found a prize at the bottom of a cereal box. "That's right! Jennifer! And this is the part where the daughter starts weighing in on the program. Do you have just another couple of minutes for me to finish the story? I promise, I'll make it brief."

Sarah puts down her sign and nods. Good for her. I gotta give credit where credit is due. She may not be buying Kathy's spiel, but at least she's got the courtesy to listen.

Kathy continues.

"So, Jenni says, 'Things weren't easy for Mom and me, but somehow, we always had a roof over our heads and enough to eat. There were a lot of hard times, but somehow, we made it. And you know what? I like to think that that voice Mom heard was right: that I *did* come from God, and that I *do* have the potential to do great good. That's why she and I have told our story so many times to so many people!'"

Kathy looks expectantly at her audience.

"Well, that's really wonderful," Sarah says with sincerity, "and I'm truly glad their situation worked out so well. But we do have to realize that not every woman in that position would have that same kind of experience. Many rape victims really want to put the past behind them and –"

Kathy interrupts Sarah with an enthusiastic barrage of words.

"You're so right, Sarah!" she chirps. "Thank you so much for reminding me! There's one last, important piece I forgot to mention. See, this is why I don't tell stories! Cindy went on to work at a pregnancy center for many years. And here's what she told every expectant mom – and a few of them had been raped – who came into that place. Now, let me get this right. Oh, if I had a brain, I'd be dangerous. I think she'd say with a gentle look and a hand on their shoulder, she'd say, 'The worst is behind you. How can I help you now?'

"You see, Sarah, that's what so many women in crisis need to hear. Whether they've been thrown out of their homes, or abandoned by their baby's father, or raped like this poor woman was. Even if they're just considering an abortion because they don't feel ready for the responsibility of having a child. They need to hear that ending their child's life won't end their pain. It'll make it worse. They need to hear that carrying a baby for nine months is nothing compared to living the rest of their lives with the knowledge that they destroyed the greatest gift they ever received. And they need to hear they have other choices besides ending the pregnancy, and that there's help to be had. Do you see what I'm saying?"

Helen nods vigorously and chimes in with, "They need to hear it's not OK to criminalize their innocent babies!"

Kathy locks eyes with Helen and says with compassion, "Careful, dear. We're in agreement, but how we say things is almost as important as what we say. These poor women and girls aren't trying to treat their unborn children like criminals. They're just trying to find a quick solution. Isn't that really one of the major problems of modern life? We all have such trouble living with discomfort; we're uncomfortable just being uncomfortable! So, we look for the fastest way to get rid of our discomfort, and sometimes the escape we choose ends up, sort of, owning us."

She looks straight at Sarah.

"May I say one more thing to you, dear?"

Without waiting for Sarah to answer, she forges ahead.

"You've been so gracious with your time and attention. The daughter, Jenni, said when she was in high school, she got into a conversation with a classmate about abortion. Her friend took the position that abortion is unpleasant but has to be kept legal for cases of rape and incest. This girl didn't know the circumstances of Jenni's birth. Jenni was able to say, 'I *am* the reason you're talking about! If my mom had followed your logic, I wouldn't be here!'

"Well, you can imagine her friend didn't know what to say. It's one thing to hold an opinion, but, you know, it's something else when you're looking right into the eyes of someone whose very existence was threatened by that opinion.

"Alright, enough of my rambling. My goal in speaking with you today – and I thank you both for letting me join your conversation – was simply to dispel the notion that victims get better by victimizing others. I hope I've made sense, and that you'll consider the possibility that other unplanned babies, not just Cindy Speltz's baby, may be 'destined for great good' also."

Without another word, Kathy picks up her sign and melts back into the crowd.

Chapter 38 Tanya

"The average dog is a nicer person than the average person." –
Andy Rooney

I miss Ralph. I miss his fat, plodding poochiness. I miss his coarse fur. I miss being able to nuzzle into that ugly, unruly coat and just feel better.

Tanya, you have to get over it. Just take your walk and try not to think about it.

Walking is the only kind of exercise I don't detest, and today's an oddly nice day. We've had so much snow this winter, but all of a sudden, the weather gods decide to shoot temperatures up to the high 60's. It's crazy.

I have to be careful where I walk because there are so many puddles from all the melting snow. I sidestep one of them, which lies catty-corner to a green sign with white letters announcing, "Rock Face: Population 10,350."

Pretty soon they'll have to change that to 10,351.

I know Ralphie couldn't help me decide what to do about the baby, but maybe I could think more clearly if he was here to comfort me.

I guess I'm lucky to live in Rock Face. It really is a pretty town, despite the fact that there's nothing to do and nowhere to go. There are these crazy, giant rocks that jut out over the highway, which is why they call it "Rock Face." You always feel like one's gonna come tumbling down at you when you drive underneath, but somehow, they always manage to stay secured to whatever it is that's suspending them there.

It's almost like going through a car wash when you're still in the car. Everything's happening around you – the suds, the whooshing water, the cloth paddles that do the actual washing – but somehow, you always come out of it just fine. Better than ever, in fact, with a squeaky, clean car and a feeling of just having dodged the bullet.

If only my life could be like that.

The lady at the family planning clinic didn't come right out and say so, but it was pretty obvious she thought I should've gotten an abortion. She spent a lot of time telling me how easy it would be, but it didn't sound that easy to me. Sounded pretty painful, if you want to know the truth, with them sticking tubes and God knows what else up inside me to remove what she called "pregnancy tissue."

Who's she kidding? I'm no doctor, but even I know it isn't just tissue. I never knew tissue to kick me in the stomach and give me heartburn.

Anyway, it doesn't matter now, because it's too late. I don't remember exactly what the cutoff is in Pennsylvania, but she said I'm past it. There would have to be a really good reason to do it at this point, and it would be a much bigger deal than if I'd done it in the earlier stages.

I feel almost jealous of girls who find out they're pregnant soon enough that they can make the choice in time. The woman at the clinic and their website make it sound like a piece of cake, despite the discomfort. The procedure itself only takes about ten

227

minutes, and when all's said and done, I'd be in and out in a couple of hours, with nothing but cramps and bleeding to show for it.

I could explain away cramps a lot better than a baby.

She talked to me about adoption a little bit, but there are so many choices involved. I would have to read people's bios and stuff. I'm overwhelmed enough as it is. Plus, Chuck made it pretty clear he's against that.

Oh, Ralphie, what should I do?

Chapter 39 Tom

"I had been pregnant in the sixties, and at nineteen years old had an illegal abortion that probably influenced the messy state of my reproductive organs… Now I couldn't take my fate: You'll never have a baby. That was the sentence handed to me. I began to beat my fists against a door that maybe I had locked on the other side." – Gilda Radner, It's Always Something

Once Kathy leaves, there doesn't seem to be anything left for Helen and Sarah to talk about. Each returns to her respective post. I head over to see how the priest is making out with the irate couple. They're still going at it.

Between expletives, the male partner shouts, "My wife and I have been trying to get pregnant for a year and a half, and you have the audacity to stand out here and protest a woman's choice?"

More profanity, followed by, "Go home!"

The wife joins in with vulgar epithets and accusations, to which the priest, clearly thrown by the breadth of their anger, quietly responds, "But we're praying *for* babies, not *against* people. Any and all babies. Yours included."

A pro-lifer in ragged jeans steps in to help the rattled clergyman.

"Man, we're tryin' to help. Besides, what does your trying to *have* a baby have to do with us trying to *save* babies? We're on the same side!"

"That's bull!" the husband erupts. "You're only trying to get rid of people's freedom! You're not here to help anybody! You only want to judge other people's choices! Go home!"

More pro-life voices – some conciliatory, others harsh and judgmental (as if to prove the veracity of the charge which was just leveled against them) – enter into the debate. My feet propel me towards the couple.

OK, Coughlin, I urge myself, *are you ever gonna say something, or do you plan to just keep standing here like a statue while other people take all the flak? Why didn't you just leave with Emma and the boys if all you're gonna do is stand around and watch? Come on, man! It's now or never.*

"We *are* home!" one pro-lifer hisses. "This is the land of the free and the home of the brave. And last time I checked, we had freedom of speech and assembly in this country!"

Keep out of their personal space, I warn myself. *They're angry enough to be dangerous.*

As if I were approaching a rabid animal, I keep my distance. I want to be heard, not disemboweled.

"Folks, can I have a word alone with these people?" I begin cautiously.

The man looks suspicious and takes his wife's arm.

"Hey, man," I say, "all I wanna do is talk to you without everyone else hearing. Really, folks, do you mind?"

The priest looks wary, as do the rest of the pro-lifers within earshot. Everyone seems to think I'm out of my mind. They're probably right.

Still, something in my voice seems to command compliance when these types of situations arise in the classroom, just like that day in the locker room all those years ago. Slowly, the crowd around us disperses, and I find myself alone with the two enraged dissenters.

"Listen, man," the husband snarls, "I don't know what you want, but –"

"Nothing," I say emphatically. "I don't want anything, except to find out what's got you so upset."

I pause to gauge their reaction. So far, so good. I wade in a little further.

"Do you mind if I ask why a peaceful prayer vigil is affecting you both so personally? I mean, what's it got to do with you folks trying to have a baby?"

The wife starts to tear up and her husband flares again.

"Stop tryin' to psychoanalyze us! You're upsetting my wife!"

"I'm sorry. That's not my intent. I'm just asking questions. I'm really sorry you guys are having a hard time getting pregnant, but these people are just trying to defend the unborn. They're not out to get you."

"You don't have a clue!" the wife screeches. "You think this is some sort of a punishment, don't you! Well, it's not!"

"Punishment? For what?" I ask quietly.

"You think you're so smart! I was just a kid myself! I had no way to take care of a kid! What was I supposed to do? I didn't know it could cause problems later."

The light dawns. My mind flashes back to the day Macie Shaw asked if she could go to the nurse, and I tried to stall her because she's always looking for a reason to get out of class. It was only when her eyes started to well up that I noticed she had tied her jacket around her waist and was clutching her stomach. I couldn't write the pass fast enough.

I felt like as much of a fool then as I do now.

Still, the waters have parted in front of me, and I see no choice but to forge ahead.

"So, you're wondering if God's punishing you for the 'choice' you made way back when by not giving you a child now?" I press softly.

The wife bursts into tears, and her husband tenderly puts his arm around her. In a strange juxtaposition, he glares death at me. If he had a knife, it would probably be wedged in my jugular by now.

"Nice goin', man," he spits out acidly. "Now she'll be a wreck for the rest of the day. Thanks a lot."

He steers his crumpled wife away from the crowd.

I can't let them leave that way.

"Hey, wait! Please! There's gotta be help for what you're feeling. You don't have to carry this pain alone."

I take a deep breath, praying furiously for some hopeful words to come to me. The only thing that leaps to mind is Matthew. I decide to go for it.

"Look, my wife and I, we're having our third son, and he's gonna have some problems. Serious problems. We weren't sure what to do, how to handle it, but we found this place that helps people like us. It's a pregnancy center downtown. Maybe –"

The man turns abruptly from his wife's shaking shoulders.

"Leave us alone!" he fumes. "You don't have a clue what we're going through!"

"Please, hear me out!" I beg. "I'm trying to tell you about the services this place offers."

I fumble with my phone to look up the contact information for the pregnancy center where that nice woman, Mary, works.

"They have a sign there saying they help people who've gone through what you guys have. I think they have some sort of support group. You don't have to live in bondage to this – this one choice. You can move past it."

It's no use. I'm talking to their backs and praying the guy doesn't turn around and deck me. In a last-ditch effort, I shout to them, "It's free!"

They get into their car and speed off.

With slumped shoulders, I call Em to ask for a ride home.

Chapter 40 Emma

"If you feel you have never completely healed or recovered from an abortion experience, or that a past abortion may be affecting your current quality of life, then Surrendering the Secret is for you...Our mission is to provide a supportive and confidential environment that facilitates healing and restoration from a past abortion and [bring] a sense of hope and purpose for the future." –
www.surrenderingthesecret.com

"Well, Tom, did you accomplish what you set out to do?" I ask, trying to keep the annoyance out of my voice.

He tosses his coat over the chair. I hate when he does that. I open my mouth to correct him, but then remember *he* hates when I do *that*. This isn't starting out well.

"Listen, Em, could we talk about this later? This whole thing has me pretty wrung out."

I review the facts in my mind, trying to decide whether I'll feel better if I beat him over the head with them.

1) Tom insists on staying at the abortion clinic, even though I beg him to leave with us.
2) Kyle frets during the whole car ride home, worrying that "the bad people might do something to Daddy!"
3) I have to explain half a dozen times that they aren't bad people, they just hold a different opinion than Daddy and I do.
4) I have to explain half a dozen times what an opinion is.

5) Kevin's diaper doesn't make it through the ride home. He leaks all over himself and the car seat. That isn't Tom's fault, but his not being here to help doesn't make my life any easier.

6) Neither kid will go down for a nap. See #5.

7) Just when the boys finally exhaust themselves and are ready to sleep, Tom calls to be picked up.

8) When I complain that his timing is terrible, he offers to take an Uber, even though he knows that whole idea makes me nervous. On a rational level, I know it's not much different than taking a cab, but since when are pregnant women supposed to be rational?

9) Scratch the last part of #8. I was perfectly rational when I was expecting my first two. This pregnancy is a whole different ballgame. I can manage *competent*. I can even pull off *cooperative*, if he catches me in the right mood. *Rational*'s a bit too much to ask.

10) I throw both kids back in the car. We meet up with Tom, who answers our questions with one-word answers and quite obviously wants to be left alone.

I try to decide whether I'm more tired or upset. I mentally flip a coin, and *tired* wins.

I opt for sarcasm instead of belaboring the subject of Tom's inconsiderate behavior.

"Oh, I see. We couldn't discuss it when we were there, because whatever you had to do was more important than your safety and helping me get the kids home. Now we can't discuss it because you're – how did you put it? – oh, yeah, 'wrung out.' Tell me, Thomas, when *can* we discuss it?"

He hates when I use his full name. His mother used to do that when she was aggravated with him. I guess everyone's mother does that. I should have considered that when we were naming Kyle and Kevin. When I get mad, I have to throw in their middle names, since their first names don't lend themselves terribly well to diminutives.

Emma, why don't you just go lie down while the boys are napping, and let this go till later? This isn't helping anything.

Because I want to argue almost as much as I want to rest!

"OK, Emma, fine. If you wanna talk, we'll talk. Whaddaya wanna know?" Tom says with exasperation.

"How 'bout everything, for starters?" I say, just to rankle him.

"Look, Emma, I'm not trying to fight with you. I'm not even trying to argue with you," he says with resignation. "It's just, I don't know what I thought I could do by staying. I guess I just thought I could bring some semblance of reason to what was going on. Like I do when things get out of hand in the classroom. Y'know?"

His conciliatory tone brings me up short. Maybe the rational part of my brain hasn't completely taken a hike.

"Yeah, Babe, I know," I answer, this time without any edge to my voice. "So, go on."

He launches into a brief but somewhat detailed description of what went on while we were gone. It sounds like a lot of things

236

that aren't meant for young ears. I'm glad he made me take the boys home.

When he gets to the part about the rape victim, I'm agape. How could anyone make such a choice and not be bitter about it? But this woman sounds like, not only isn't she bitter, she's downright grateful for this child born of violence.

I can't fathom it.

"I don't know, Em. I was so sure at the beginning that I had some, I don't know, grand purpose in being there. I mean, I sort of felt *called*, almost. Know what I mean?"

I nod my head.

"But then, when I finally opened my mouth, which wasn't till the very end, I felt like I really blew it. I mean, those people really needed help, y'know? And I couldn't even remember the name of the stupid program I was trying to tell them about! They're walking around with a wound the size of the Grand Canyon, and maybe those people at the pregnancy center could help them heal from it, but I couldn't even come up with the name of the center, let alone the program! I felt... useless."

I search my brain for the name of the support group Tom's referring to. I've been to see Mary more often than he has, and my mind's eye can see the poster in her office. It has a picture of a sprig of purple flowers on it. It's right on the tip of my tongue. But pregnancy brain strikes again.

"Aaaah!" I groan to show him I'm frustrated, too. "I can't think of it, either! But I know what you're talking about. Well, let me ask you this, Babe: did you at least tell them what it was about?"

237

"Yeah. As much as they would listen, I mean. They were walking away at that point. But, yeah, I guess I gave them the gist of it. I at least mentioned that there's a support group in a pregnancy center downtown. Oh, and that it's free! So – that's a start. Right?"

"Right," I smile, and fold myself into his arms. As he strokes my hair, it comes to me.

"Surrendering the Secret!" I yell, then quickly lower my voice so I don't wake the kids. "That's the name of the group!"

Tom slaps his hand on his forehead.

"Duh! Where was that when I needed it?" he chides himself.

"I dunno, Babe, but you gave them enough to work with. If it means enough to them, hopefully they'll pursue it."

"You're right," he says, then pulls me up off the couch. Not an easy trick, with Matthew weighing me down.

"Yeah, you're right. Well, I'd better start thinking about dinner," I say, heading for the kitchen.

"It's not dinner I'm thinking of," Tom says, grinning. "How 'bout we start with dessert?"

At times like this, I notice how really handsome he is. Not in a traditional way, but he has just enough stubble on his chubby Irish face to make him irresistible. I follow where he leads.

Chapter 41 Emma and Tom

"The ultimate measure of a man is not where he stands in moments of comfort and convenience, but where he stands at times of challenge and controversy." – Martin Luther King, Jr.

The pains start after dinner. I figure it's indigestion because I overdid it on Tom's bacon and eggs, his specialty whenever it's his night to cook. Probably stress eating over what could've happened to him at the prayer vigil. My Tom doesn't always know when to stop being a knight in shining armor. It's one of the things I love and hate about him at the same time.

I'm often starving these days. Half the time, I can barely force down part of an apple, then the rest of the time I'm gorging.

I'm sure it's partly the weather. This winter's been brutal, with some form of precipitation almost weekly. Schools have been closing left and right, which causes problems for Tom and me, because our day care calls snow days whenever the school district does. Most of the time, Tom's school closings line up with Kyle and Kevin's, but a couple of times, we had to scramble to find someone to sit with the boys while we dug out our cars and trekked to work. All this shoveling and schlepping makes me ravenous.

Lie down, Emma, I tell myself when the gymnastics in my belly start again. *It'll pass.*

But it doesn't. By 11:30, Tom's snoring softly next to me and I feel like a building's being bulldozed in my gut. I know this feeling, and it terrifies me this time.

I know how to *do* childbirth. It's no picnic, but I can get through it. It's what comes afterwards in this case that makes fear tug at my heart the way Kyle tugs my pantleg when he's sick.

I don't feel ready for this baby's entrance.

The doctors have me scheduled for a C-section, but that's a week away. The winds of late March screech outside, and I join them with a bloodcurdling shriek that wakes Tom and scares the daylights out of poor Kyle.

"Mommy, somebody's yelling!" he wails as his chubby feet tromp into our bedroom. Jumping between us on our queen-sized bed, Kyle lands on my left arm, which sends new pain signals into my already contraction-racked body.

"Aaaah! Kevin – er, Kyle, you're on Mommy's arm! You gotta move!" I howl, causing him to burst into tears.

****

I wake up when Emma screams, and quickly size up the situation. This isn't so different from two years ago when Kevin made his arrival. Same thing: middle of the night, freezing cold, Emma panting and screaming. The problem solver in me takes charge.

"Move over, Ky-Guy, you're hurting Mommy," I order while manually shifting him. "How far apart are the contractions, Em?"

"How should I know! I thought it was indigestion!"

I wince at Em's sharpness, suddenly remembering how much fun it is going through labor with a woman who's blaming you for every spasm.

Steady, Tom. She's just scared. You gotta handle this.

"OK, Em, I'm gonna call the doctor. Everything's gonna be OK."

I pick up Kyle, realizing everyone will be better off if Em has the bed to herself. Slinging him over my shoulder like a duffel bag, I inch my way through the dark and promptly stub my toe on the dresser. Resisting the urge to let loose with a four-letter word, I stumble out into the hallway and pull up the doctor's number on my phone.

My next call is to Emma's sister. I wish there was somebody else, what with Ted and Linda losing out on adopting yet again, but there really isn't. Emma's folks live in Florida, and her dad has dementia. It's all Em's mom can do to look after him, let alone pinch hit for us. My parents are in the Midwest, and we're not what you would call close.

Linda puts on a brave face, but I know it's killing her to take care of our two kids when she can't even have one. I think Ted would be OK just having Lin, but she really has the baby bug. It was a cruel blow when the system, in all its wisdom, placed little Danny back with his biological father last month. They let Ted and Linda do all the grunt work of training the kid, finally getting him onto somewhat of a schedule, and completely giving their hearts to him – and then some idiot judge who's just following a set of antiquated guidelines puts him back into harm's way. Not only would he have been much better off with them, but he'd have learned a thing or two about living a clean, decent life. Fat lot he'll learn from a drug-dealing dad and a strung-out mother.

241

Bureaucracy at its finest.

But I can't think about that now. Ted and Linda have to deal with their problems, and I have to deal with mine.

"Hey, Lin? Sorry to wake you. She's ready to go. Can you guys come over?"

Chapter 42 Linda and Ted

"Children with special needs inspire a special love." – Sarah Palin

Ted and I jump into the car after throwing a few things into a bag, then beat a path to Emma and Tom's after we get his call. Well, we can't exactly beat a path. The wind-whipped night and wet roads force us to go a lot more slowly than Emma probably needs.

"Honey, are you OK to drive?" I ask my disoriented husband. It's all I can do not to make a joke about his hair, which is matted down on one side and jutting out on the other. He's so meticulous about his undercut, and I kid him because he takes much longer with the blow dryer than I do. My blonde Adonis.

"Course I am," he answers indignantly.

"It's just, you look so exhausted. Maybe I should drive."

"Linda, I'm fine. Just hand me the coffee, will ya?"

I pass the travel mug into his cold hands. Ted never wears gloves, even when the temperature's in the teens.

"That's better. Thanks, Hon," he says, handing it back to me.

I take a sip myself, then almost spill the whole cup when we skid around a curve. Thank God for streetlights that brighten the hazy roads, because we might as well be driving on buttered asphalt. The wheels on the car ahead of us keep kicking up spray from the wet pavement. Even though Ted has the wipers going, it's hard to see.

I decide to bring up a subject that's been on my mind. Maybe if I keep him engaged, we'll get there in one piece.

"Sweetie, can I ask you something?"

"Course. What's up?"

"Well, it's actually more of a comment than a question."

"Shoot," he replies through a yawn. "I'm listening."

"Well – hey, watch it, there's the turn!"

I can almost see his hackles go up. Men and their egos.

"I saw it!" he barks.

"OK, well, what I've been thinking about is Emma's baby. They think he's gonna be pretty disabled. Spinal cord problems. May never walk. Poor little baby."

"Yeah. Such a shame."

"I think Emma's pretty upset about it."

****

Here it comes, I think to myself. *Oh, Linda, why'd you have to pick tonight to have this discussion? There's not enough coffee in the world to make me ready to talk about fertility problems and disabilities in the middle of the night.*

I will myself to listen to my wife, even though this conversation doesn't bode well for taking care of our two nephews for the next couple of days.

If she gets herself all worked up, we're gonna have an awful few days with those kids.

I yawn again, partly because it's the middle of the night, and partly out of adoption exhaustion. That's the term Linda and I made up to describe all the crazy emotions we've gone through since this whole process began.

244

"Course she's upset," I reply. "Anyone would be with that diagnosis."

"Well, I was thinking, I don't know, maybe this is too weird, but, well, here goes. Since they're not happy about this third baby, at least Emma's not, it occurred to me maybe we should offer to adopt him."

If she wants to have an accident, this is one sure-fire way to increase the odds. After I pick my jaw up from the floor, I grab the coffee from her again. If we're gonna discuss insane, graveyard shift adoption plans, I'm gonna need more caffeine.

"Lin, can we talk about this when we get there? I better concentrate on these roads."

"Oh, sure. You're right, Babe. Hey, are those snow flurries?"

Chapter 43 Tom

"Waiting for the spark from heaven to fall." – Matthew Arnold

With the adrenaline of Hercules, I maneuver Emma and Ky-Guy down the steps and through the living room. I reassure my son that Aunt Linda and Uncle Teddy will arrive soon to take care of him and Kev, and that very soon their new brother will be born. I help Em on with her coat, which she can't button around her oversized belly.

I take my focus off Emma for a minute to look down at the miniature version of myself. Kyle's tousled brown hair is sticking up the same way mine does right before a haircut.

I wonder what the new baby will look like. Will I be able to do any of the things my other boys and I do with this poor kid? Will anything ever be right again?

I turn back to Emma, who must be having another contraction and is trying hard to control the pain with deep breathing.

"Atta girl, Em, you're doin' great. Your sister'll be here any minute."

The waiting seems endless but, in reality, I think only twenty minutes go by before we hear the squeal of brakes outside the house.

Chapter 44 Linda and Ted

"Finally married to a wonderful man in my mid-thirties and desperate to start a family, I endured letdown after letdown as our hopes of conceiving a child were dashed, one blow at a time." – Christine Rhyner, *How Much Did You Pay for Her? Forgiving the Words that Hurt Adoptive Families*

"We'll be fine!" I call after my sister and brother-in-law as I watch Tom help Emma into the car. Emma looks back helplessly at Kyle, who's begging his mommy not to go.

"We'll be back as soon as we can, Ky-Guy," Tom reassures his crying son.

"Aw, shhh, it's OK, Bud," I soothe Kyle while holding him and smoothing his hair.

More crying.

"They'll be back, I promise, Sweetheart. Meantime, Uncle Teddy and I are here. What should we have for breakfast when we wake up?"

Food is a popular topic with my nephew. I picture menu choices scrolling through his little mind. Finally, he squeals the name of a sugary cereal that I'll certainly regret giving him.

"You got it, Bud! Now let's try to get some sleep so breakfast'll come quicker, OK?"

"'Kay," he sniffles, then, "Aunt Linda, can I sleep with you guys?"

I glance at Ted to get his take on Kyle's request. In a way, I hope he'll find some reason to protest. Everything's so weird these days, I'm not sure this is a good idea. What a crime that an innocent appeal from a scared little boy has to be viewed through the lens of a crooked world.

But Ted looks blearily at me and nods. OK, away with the doubts. What's right is right.

"That's a big 10-4, Kyle!" I say, finding that I'm happy about it. It'll be sweet to curl up with this little cherub.

Noting the confused look on Ky's face, I add, "That means Y-E-S! Do you know what that spells?"

"Yes! That spells 'yes!'" Kyle exclaims.

"OK, now Uncle Teddy's gonna take you into your mommy and daddy's room to lay down with you. I'm gonna go check on Kevie, then we'll all snuggle together. Do you have to go potty first?"

"No, I'm fine," Kyle responds confidently.

"I wouldn't bet on that," Ted smiles as he escorts Kyle up the stairs. "Come on, dude, let's check out the potty once before we call it a night, 'kay?"

"'Kay, Uncle Teddy."

After using the bathroom myself and peeking at Kev, I creep quietly into the master bedroom. By the glow of a night light, I can see Kyle's pajama-clad posterior poking its way into poor Ted's nasal passages. I clap a hand over my mouth to keep from laughing. If I wake him now, all bets are off.

Linda, get a grip. Those kids are gonna be up at sunrise. You only have a couple of hours to sleep, so you'd better make it count.

Still, I have trouble drifting off. I'm not used to Tom and Emma's bed, and I'm definitely not used to sharing my husband with a squirmy preschooler. Also, my heart still aches over Danny and the other two babies we didn't get in the end.

It's so unfair.

Criminal, theft, screwed up, rotten, asinine, lame – sometimes when I can't sleep, I come up with descriptors like these for a system that's so inherently flawed it sucks money, time and joy out of honest people like Ted and me, whose only wish is to give a child a forever family.

Finally, though, fatigue takes over, and restless dreams fill my mind.

On a hillside, a well-built, bronze-helmeted male is carrying a bundle. A scarlet plume on the crown of his head gear sprouts out like bristles on a well-used paintbrush. He trudges along on thonged sandals.

Besides his bundle, which is resting on a round, metal tray, the man grasps a spear bigger than himself. Veins stand out like taut cords on his muscular arms.

Wading through the fogginess of my dream, I begin to realize that what I've mistaken for a metal platter is actually a shield with grooved edge work around its border. Without warning, the man tips the shield, revealing an upside-down letter "V" on its steel gray exterior. The oblong item which had previously rested on the shield drops to the ground.

Whatever that thing is, it begins flailing and wailing.

The camera lens in my dream zooms in on the package the soldier so casually abandoned. Drawing closer, I hear human cries. Unwrapping what I now see is a piece of filthy swaddle, I discover a naked infant not more than a few days old. Instinct kicks in, and I scoop up the baby and clutch him to my breast. Only then do I notice his head is swollen and there's a gaping hole in his back, out of which spills syrupy blood and bulging spinal cord.

Without thinking, I drop the poor child. Now the tiny cries, which had eased with my touch, intensify. I have a decision to make: do the right thing, or walk away and let horror carry the day.

Terror jolts me awake.

"Ted, wake up!" I whisper frantically after moving Kyle's bare foot away from my husband's ear.

Ted's rhythmic snoring gives way to panic.

"What! What's the matter?"

"I had a terrible dream."

"Oh, Honey, try to go back to sleep. It's just stress. You'll feel better in the morning."

"No, Ted, I'll have forgotten it by then! Please!"

After surrounding Kyle with a fortress of pillows so he won't roll out of bed, we take ourselves into the adjacent bedroom.

"OK, Lin, what's the matter?"

I explain the dream, to which he replies, "OK, Hon, you had a bad dream. It's that series we watched about ancient Rome. It's probably that part about how they left messed up babies in the wilderness. Whole thing freaked you out, and you're still thinkin' about it."

"Sparta," I correct him. "The documentary was about Sparta. And they weren't all 'messed up.' Don't you remember what it said? Any baby they considered imperfect they just left to die! Well, Rome did it, too, now that you mention it. And remember they said something about how Greek fathers had about a week to decide to either keep their kids or to throw them out like trash? I don't understand how those people could be so cavalier about –"

I let my sentence dangle because I can see Ted's eyes glazing over. He doesn't share my interest in ancient cultures, and only watched the show because I asked him to. I need to make this relevant to us, to our situation, to today.

"No, Ted, I think it's more than me thinking about the show. Do you believe in signs?"

"Signs? Whaddaya mean?"

"You know, signs. Like premonitions or warnings. I think that's what this was."

"Come on, Lin, it's four in the morning. I'm beat. Can't we do this some other time?"

Although I know it isn't fair, I quietly begin to cry. Soft, quiet sobs, but loud enough for him to hear. Ted reaches for me and puts his arms around me, as I knew he would.

"OK, Hon," he concedes, "what's the sign?"

"Don't you see, Ted? We can't have a baby. Emma and Tom are having a disabled baby that they don't want. At least, Emma's having a real hard time accepting him. That baby doesn't have to be left out in the cold like those ones in Sparta. *We* can rescue that baby. *We –*"

251

I pull her closer. Her hair smells like honeysuckle. If we weren't doing the family bed thing with Kyle, and I weren't so exhausted, I might even put the moves on her.

I love her for the instinct in her that wants to raise a child, anybody's child, no holds barred. I've tried desperately to give her a baby, but all our efforts have only frustrated us and ripped through our savings. We'll have to go into debt to try any of the fertility techniques we've been considering. Besides, the more I think about them, those so-called "alternatives" seem more like lab experiments than actual reproduction.

"OK, Lin, I can see you're serious about this. Let me give it some thought. Do you think you can get back to sleep?"

Chapter 45 Linda

"Everyone dreams of having a baby. Nobody dreams of having a two-year-old."– Thea Williams

"Aunt Linda, get up!"

I wake to Kyle's excited screams. Kevin wails in the other room. Ted snores quietly beside me.

"What, Hon? Are you OK?" I ask my nephew.

"Yeah, I'm OK," he answers. "But me and Kevie wanna go find our Easter baskets!"

Oh, no. He's right. It's Easter and I have no idea where or even if Emma has any candy, let alone Easter grass and baskets. That was the last thing on anybody's mind in the middle of the night.

"Oh, OK, Honey. Yeah, your baskets."

I sit up reluctantly and shake Ted.

"Uh, wake up, Uncle Teddy. It's Easter morning, and the kids wanna check out their baskets. Where do you suppose the Easter bunny would've hidden their candy, Uncle Ted?"

If I'm looking for support, I've come to the wrong man. Ted's neither a dad nor a morning person. He sleeps heavy to begin with, and last night we slept with a fidgety four-year-old.

He grunts and rolls over.

"Come on, Uncle Teddy. The boys are excited about Easter. We need to figure out where the bunny left their candy!" I say with greater urgency.

My husband's a sweet man, but when he's sleep-deprived, he's less pliable than Mount Rushmore.

In the meantime, Kevin climbs out of his crib. He comes screaming into our room with a diaper practically down to his knees. When he realizes his parents aren't here, he goes into hysterics. I pick him up and try to soothe him, telling him Mommy and Daddy are at the hospital getting ready to meet his new baby brother.

He's having none of it.

I take him over to the rocking chair in the corner of Em's room and try to calm him with a song. He not only doesn't take to my voice, but promptly demonstrates his disappointment by letting loose a warm, yellow liquid all over my lap.

I decide then and there that Ted needs to accept his share of the misery.

"Ted Genovese, I need you up and I need you up now!" I shriek, sounding as self-controlled as a drunk at a wine tasting.

"Huh? I'm up, I'm up!" he cries apologetically. "Whaddaya need me to do?"

"OK, find me a diaper for Kev. Oh, and don't forget wipes. He peed all over me. Then try to text Tom and see if he knows anything about the Easter bunny's plans," I say in a conspiring whisper. Then I buy us some time.

"Kyle, I know you wanna get downstairs, but first we have to get Kevie cleaned up and both of you have to get dressed. And the bunny says you have to eat breakfast before you have any candy."

Remembering I promised him Cocoa Puffs for breakfast, I realize we're in for the sugar high of the century. Oh, well. I give up on any semblance of sanity for the day and prepare for the chaos.

When all is said and done, we have two dressed children but no return text from Tom. I put Ted to work scrounging through cabinets to see if he can find a candy stash and try to delay the inevitable.

How could they forget to do Easter for their kids? Are they that obsessed with the new baby's problems? How 'bout taking care of the ones they already have?

I mentally yell at myself, realizing I have no clue what they're going through. Still, if it were me…

"Hey, guys, look outside. Look at all those branches that came down last night! How 'bout we go outside and pick up the biggest sticks we can find?"

The guys think this is a great idea, and it keeps them busy until Kevin decides it's fun to stab his brother in the neck with a saber-shaped stick. His giggles come close to drowning out Kyle's squalls of pain. I'm about ready to cry myself, when Ted comes outside and declares he's going to the store "on bunny business." This announcement prompts pleas from both kids to go along. I have to think fast to come up with a plan that will keep them distracted and home.

It's a funny thing. I've always intended to parent without letting my kids get sucked into the vortex of some video screen. I revise my thinking while popping the disk into the DVD player, heaving a sigh of relief.

Chapter 46 Tanya

"The pains of childbirth were altogether different from the enveloping effects of other kinds of pain. These were pains one could follow with one's mind." – Margaret Mead

My hands are shaking so much I can barely text.

Cn u com right now i think its time

No response. I wait a few minutes, then fire off another urgent message.

Nothing.

Don't tell me Chuck has his phone turned off – not now! Just because of one near-accident when he was checking a text, he's been paranoid about it ever since.

Chuck, this is not the time to be careful!

That's right, Tanya. The time to be careful was last summer.

You're a little late, girl.

The pun strikes me funny, and I laugh out loud. Seconds later, I go into outright bawling.

What's wrong with me? How can I be making myself laugh and cry at the same time?

I want Mom.

Get a grip, Tanya. They won't be home for hours.

The place where David's aunt lives is having an Easter egg hunt. They took Dolly over to visit and grab some eggs. Afterwards, she's getting her picture taken with the Easter bunny.

That line won't be long on the day before Easter.

Knock it off, Tanya. Sarcasm isn't helping.

Freakin' cold day to be outside scooping up eggs. Yeah, but at least she's only grabbing eggs. I'm about to lay one!

More crazy laughter, even though there's nothing to laugh about.

The wind pummels against the windowpanes.

Wait, is it starting to hail?

Good. Maybe they'll call everything off and come home.

No. Not David. He'd rather miss Jess's wedding than skip visiting that old aunt of his for one week.

Should I call them? After all, they are my parents.

Wait, did I just refer to David as my parent?

I bag the thought immediately. What would I say – *Hope you're having fun and by the way, come on home 'cause I think I'm in labor?*

There's only one problem with that. They don't know I'm pregnant.

Baggy sweats sure hide a multitude of sins!

Mom sure would agree with the sin part.

Yeah, but she'd also understand. It's not like she hasn't been there herself.

Forget it, Tanya! It's too late to tell her. Not when you're on the brink of giving b –

I hear myself scream.

The videos didn't come close to showing how much this hurts!

My mind flashes to Grandma. She adjusts her thick, old lady glasses on the bridge of her nose, then gets down on the floor, in spite of her arthritic knees, to do a seek and find book with six-year-old me.

"Oh, look, Tiny Tanya, you found another one!" she coos. "You are really good at this!"

Of course, I was good at it. We did the same books a hundred times.

I try to pretend she and Granddad are with me, telling me what to do.

They'd say to call the doctor, you idiot!

That would be a great idea, except I'm stuck in the bathroom because I can't stop peeing. Besides, I don't have the doctor's number saved in my phone.

If only I had a smart phone to look it up!

God only knows where Mom keeps all the important phone numbers. I think she still uses an address book, as if we weren't living in the digital age.

Who cares, Tanya? You couldn't go look for it anyway.

Thanks a lot, Mom.

Why are you blaming her? She didn't get you into this mess.

A killer pain rocks me to my core. It doubles me over so that I'm staring down at the bathroom floor. Sharp, animal-like sounds let loose from somewhere deep within my trembling body.

I feel sick.

I hear the tinkling sound that signals a text. I instinctively look down at the phone, shocked to find I still have it in my hand.

Way to go, Tanya. Don't worry about those labor pains. Just make sure you stay chained to technology.

Another contraction rips through me, and the phone goes flying. It spins off at a 45-degree angle and lands under the closed linen closet door. I'd need octopus arms to reach it from the position I'm in.

Panic grips me, followed quickly by hopelessness.

Another jolt of wrenching pain.

The phone lies uselessly out of reach.

Chapter 47 Mary

"Parenthood: The only place where you can experience heaven and hell at the same time." – Unknown

"OK, Ms. Gullickson, can you explain it to me again? I want to make sure I have the details accurate for my report."

I sigh. I can barely wrap my mind around the fact that I'm a grandmother, and now I have to tell and retell a story I'm not really even a part of.

Why do the police always have to show up with ambulances anyway?

"Officer," I say, trying to compose myself, "I know almost as little as you do. All I can tell you is my husband and I got home, I don't know, 40 minutes ago, I guess, and our little girl had to go potty. I mean, to the bathroom. When I brought her upstairs, we found my older daughter on the bathroom rug and everything covered in blood. The baby was –"

I choke on the rest of my sentence. Dave comes to the rescue, putting his arm around me and finishing the grisly story.

God bless that man! How does he always manage to stay calm under pressure?

"What my wife and daughter found was that our older daughter, who we didn't realize was, um, pregnant, had apparently given birth in the bathroom and cut the umbilical cord with those scissors."

He points to the shears I keep in the medicine cabinet above the toilet.

"Go on," the officer insists.

"Well, Tanya – our daughter – she was on the floor, as my wife said, and the baby was, uh –"

He gestures towards the toilet. I guess he can't bring himself to say it out loud. I can't blame him. It's so...

Horrifying. Disgusting.

I'm sure it's not intentional, but Dave shudders when he reports these facts. Before he can catch himself, his face scrunches up in an awful mask.

My face probably looks the same.

"And that's when you called the ambulance?"

Dave nods.

"And when did you pull the baby's face out of the toilet bowl?"

How can he say it so nonchalantly? Like he's asking if we'd like whole wheat or rye for our toast.

"Immediately!" I scream. "I mean, Dave, my husband, he came running when I screamed. He grabbed the baby right away, then called 911. I had to take Jessica, my little girl, out of the room – she was frightened, of course. But David grabbed the baby right away. Oh, Lord, will she be alright? Will my Tanya be alright? There was so much blood!"

"The team'll get them to the hospital fast. And they got the infant breathing before they left. So that's a good thing."

It's the first sign of compassion this man has shown.

It must be awful to have to always keep a professional distance.

261

Like being a voyeur. A peeping Tom, spying on other people's misery.

"And when did the child's father arrive?"

Dave again takes the lead.

"Chuck? He must've pulled up shortly after we got home because we started hearing pounding on the door right after we found Tanya," he answers.

"They're good kids, Officer. They really are," he adds.

The cop continues with his questions, then calls for Chuck, probably to see if his story matches ours.

None of my years working with women in crisis pregnancies prepared me for today. I hold onto Dave for dear life. My nails dig into his hand.

Stop squeezing so hard, Mary. You're probably leaving little half-moons on his knuckles.

When will this interrogation end so I can go see my daughter?

Chapter 48 Emma

"Babies are the future… What could be more compelling than a baby?" – N. Scott Adzick, M.D., Director of Center for Fetal Diagnosis and Treatment, Children's Hospital of Philadelphia, https://www.pbs.org/show/twice-born/

Pain. I expected it after the C-section, but there's pain and then there's *pain.*

The nurse comes in and says they'll be removing the catheter soon, so at least I'll be able to feel my legs again. Then I can get up and go to the bathroom myself and maybe feel a little bit like a grownup again. Maybe they'll give me some real food, too, instead of all this liquid garbage. I know they have to let my stomach rest after the surgery, but this is getting old.

I can't stand having a cold, let alone this feeling of helplessness.

The doctor's been in. He says they're optimistic that the baby's first surgery will go well. They have to do spinal surgery and put in a shunt, so the fluid won't build up around his brain. I've read that shunts fail and have to be replaced every so often. More to look forward to.

With everything that's going on, it's just as well he's not nursing. Let the poor child deal with healing instead of trying to learn how to latch on and all that stuff. Plus, I can have stronger painkillers since I'm not breastfeeding. Does leave me feeling full and sore, though, until I dry up. Can't come soon enough.

Tom comes in with Kyle. They wheel me and my bag full of pee down to the hallway outside the neonatal intensive care unit to see Matthew. He looks so vulnerable with all the equipment he's hooked up to, poor baby. What a way to start life.

A chatty nurse who's just coming on duty pauses in the hall to talk to us.

"Oh, hi, Mrs. Coughlin! And you must be Mr. Coughlin! I'm Katie, I was Matt's nurse last night. There's your little boy. He's a real cutie. We're all in love with him."

I try to come up with a smile, but feel my mouth settle into a contorted frown.

I can't take my eyes off Matthew's head. Although covered with a blue cap, it's noticeably larger than Kyle and Kevin's were when they were first born.

I'm afraid to imagine what his back looks like. If I saw it last night, the anesthesia must have blocked it out. The pictures I found online of spina bifida were gruesome and frightening.

There's a bank of windows in the rear part of the NICU, which are visible from the hall. I force my eyes off Matt and onto a fluffy clump of cotton-ish clouds nestled between otherwise dark, thundery ones. The sun can't decide whether to break through or hide.

Kyle's excited and doesn't understand why he can't touch, feel, experience the baby. Tom lifts him up to the nursery window and guides his plump, mischievous hands to the glass.

"There'll be time for real touching later, Ky-Guy. For now, we look at him this way. And when he gets home, you gotta be careful, Bud," Tom explains. "He's real small, even smaller than Kev, and he's very delicate."

"What's 'delicate'?" Kyle wonders.

"That means he's not strong yet. He's not a playmate yet." He looks at me.

"But someday he'll be both those things. We just gotta wait awhile."

I look away from Tom's hopeful eyes.

"Hi, Maffew," Kyle coos. The baby's eyes remain closed, but a fleeting smile crosses his lips.

Probably gas.

Then he rouses with a gentle cry.

"OK, time for us to go, big guy," Tom says to Kyle. "Mama's tired and the nurses have to take care of Matt. He's cryin' 'cause he needs something."

"I wanna feed Maffew!" cries Kyle.

"No, Kyle, the nurses have to do that. For now, at least."

Turning to me, he adds, "I'm gonna bring Kev in next, after I drop this one home with Linda and Ted. Didn't wanna overwhelm you. Sound good, Sweetie?"

He really is a dear man. And he's trying so hard. I give him a weak smile.

"Sounds good. See ya soon."

Tom kisses me on the cheek and wheels me back to my room. I give Kyle a squeeze and tell him I'll see him soon.

After they leave, I return to my private anguish.

****

265

When I sneeze, a whole gymnastics squad starts doing somersaults on top of my incision. I groan. With my stomach muscles clenched, the pain gets worse; I make a mental note to hold in any future sneezes or die trying.

My roommate hears my agony and offers comfort.

"Hey, is there anything I can do? I couldn't help overhearing. Want me to call for the nurse?"

Talking isn't on my top ten list of activities at the moment, but I don't want to be rude.

"That's OK. She'll be in soon enough. Thanks."

My neighbor is undeterred by my brevity.

"I'm Margaret Clauser. I guess we're stuck in here together for the foreseeable future!"

Oh, no. She wants to make friends, or at the very least, chat. I'm in no mood for banter.

"Emma Coughlin," I offer with what little enthusiasm I can summon.

"Boy or girl?" she asks.

"Boy. You?"

"I have a beautiful little girl. Her name's Serena. That means 'serene,' just like it sounds. And she really is. She's just a joy. What's your son's name?"

"Matthew."

"I love that name. What does it mean? Did you look it up?"

"Yeah. It means 'gift of God.'"

"Oh, wow. To me, every baby is a gift of God, don't you think?"

This is the wrong time to ask. Between incision pain and the conflicting emotions swirling inside me, I can't make that call.

"Uh huh," I mutter.

"Do you have any other children?" she probes. This woman isn't going to let up.

"Yeah. Two boys. You?"

"Serena's our first. We've been trying for a long time. Hopefully we'll be able to give her a brother or sister in the future."

"I'm sure you will," I reply out of politeness rather than interest.

"What are your other kids' names? I love discussing names, don't you?"

No. No, I don't, not at this moment. At this moment, what I want and need is rest and time to myself. Since I can't have either, I give in to self-pity. An involuntary tear rolls down my cheek. It's not lost on Margaret.

"Oh, Emma, have I upset you? You're crying!" my new BFF exclaims. She gives new meaning to the word "relentless."

"No, I'm fine. Just a little emotional, I guess."

"I know what you mean. We've waited so long – three years – and she's finally here!"

Just then a dark-haired man with glasses pushes open the door. He comes in quietly carrying a large bouquet, which he sets down on Margaret's nightstand. He bends down and kisses her, then asks, "How are you, Hon?"

"Roger! They're beautiful!" she cries, throwing her arms around his neck. "You shouldn't have! But I'm glad you did!"

267

She remembers her manners and introduces me.

"Oh, Emma, this is my husband, Roger. Roger, this is Emma."

I drag myself away from my pity party long enough to say, "Hello."

"Oh, hey," he replies, then turns back to his wife. Lowering his voice, he says, "Margie, they wanna know if you wanna see her."

"Of course, I want to see her! What a question! It's probably time to feed her! Poor baby's probably starving! Tell them to bring her right in!"

Roger takes on a deer-in-the-headlights look. He touches his wife's hand.

"Margie," he begins, "Honey, don't you remember?"

"Remember? Of course, I remember! I remember that I have a blonde-haired little girl who's ready to gobble up some of this milk that's making me so top-heavy! Come on, let's get her in here!"

"Honey, don't you remember what the doctor told us? Don't you remember about Serena?"

"Roger Clauser, you'd better stop all this silliness! Bring my daughter in here now! I need to feed her!"

All of a sudden, Roger seems to remember he has an audience. I'm not trying to overhear, but these hospital rooms aren't exactly spacious.

"Listen, I don't mean to be rude, but would you mind if I pulled the curtain?" he asks apologetically. "I need to talk to my wife alone. You understand."

"Oh, sure," I fumble. "Of course. No problem."

It doesn't make much difference. I can still hear everything, despite how hard I try not to.

"Margie, Honey, remember what's going on? Do you remember about Serena, Sweetheart?"

"Roger, what are you talking about? Where's my baby? I want to see her!"

"And you will, Sweetheart, but not the way you expect to. Oh, God, why does this have to be so hard? Why didn't they give you a private room in this God-forsaken hospital? I told them not to give you a roommate, but they said they couldn't help it, they were booked solid. Margie, please try to remember!"

Suddenly, Margaret lets loose with a hair-raising scream, followed by the sound of loud sobs. I can hear Roger soothing her, telling her it'll be alright. His voice has a catch in it.

After a while the crying subsides, and Roger says, "OK, Honey, do you think you're ready to see her now? It's OK if you're not."

Margaret mumbles something unintelligible. A few minutes later I hear footsteps, followed by hushed voices. From the sound of things, more than one person has come in. Someone must have brought in her baby, because I hear Margaret singing in a broken voice. It's a lullaby, not one I know, and she's singing through tears.

269

After Margaret finishes the song, I hear the voice of a different woman, someone with rehearsed but sincere sounding sympathy.

"OK, Sweetie, what would be good now? Would you like to take some pictures so you can remember her? Would that be good?"

A muffled answer comes from Margaret. Then her husband's voice: "I think we should, Margie. It'll be good, y'know, later."

The sound of cell phones snapping photographs.

All in all, I guess the people stay for about an hour. Margaret cries on and off, and different voices chime in to comfort her.

I feel like an intruder.

****

It's about 9:00 and our room is silent. Tom and Kev have come and gone. How I wish I had thought to tell him to hold off. The last thing Margaret needs is toddler noises. Thankfully, Kevin was fussy, and Tom took him home early.

This time I'm the one who initiates conversation.

"Margaret, um, are you OK?"

No answer.

"Margaret, um, Margie, I'm sorry about the noise earlier. I hope it didn't disturb you."

After a pause, she answers, "No, that was fine. You have a nice family."

"Thanks. So do you."

Am I going to leave it like that, with unspoken knowledge hanging between us like rotting fruit?

I have no obligation to this woman. I'm not a grief counselor or a therapist. I'm not even really in my own right mind, I'm pretty sure, what with all that's going on. Still, you don't just gape at the scene of a car wreck without at least offering a blanket. I screw up my courage and every ounce of caring I have for someone other than myself.

"Margie, do ya wanna talk about it?"

No answer.

I forge ahead, praying these are the right words.

"You were so sweet to me earlier. I wasn't very talkative then. I'm sorry. But people do tell me I'm a good listener when I'm not in raging pain!"

Nothing.

"Well, listen, I'm here if you need me."

Something I said must've gotten to her because after a few minutes she starts telling me some of what she and Roger are going through. The voice I heard earlier asking about taking pictures was one of the perinatal hospice nurses. They had been preparing her and Roger for this.

That lullaby was the first and last song she would ever sing to her daughter – both a welcome and a farewell.

Margaret has a sweetness about her that draws me out. I find myself telling her about Matthew's problems. They sound small, compared to what's on her plate.

It's only a matter of time before we cry together.

Two mothers, both aching, for different reasons.

"Oh, Emma, I'm so sorry you have so much to deal with!" she says, as if she's not stuck at the other end of the grotesque continuum some heartless power dumped us on.

Emma, you don't really believe that. Where's your faith in God?

It's still here, flickering. But it's being sorely tested.

"Oh, listen, me too, but, hey, look what you're going through! I feel terrible about how abrupt I was earlier. If I had only known –"

"Emma, let's not go there. You didn't know. You were trying to take care of yourself, your pain."

I can't believe I felt so irritated with this dear woman a few hours ago. She really is a treasure.

I decide to take a risk.

"Margaret – wait, do you prefer Margie?"

"It doesn't matter. Roger calls me that. He thinks it's softer. Most other people call me Margaret."

"OK, I'll go with Margie, if that's OK. He's right, it does have a softness about it. Margie, how long have you known? I mean, when did you find out about, y'know? I mean, if it's not too hard to talk about."

She dabs at tears and blows her nose. She's one of those loud blowers, which surprises me. I almost laugh at the irony of this slight little woman letting out a noise like a foghorn. I force myself to refrain.

Laughing would probably hurt too much anyway.

"No, it's OK. I don't mind. Maybe I should. The first ultrasound showed serious problems. They tried to get me – us – to abort little Serena. They used a lot of nice words for it, but I knew what they were talking about."

I nod. I know those euphemisms.

"Rog and I talked and prayed about it. We decided God had sent this baby to us, and only God was allowed to take her away. We prayed and prayed that she'd be OK."

She blows her nose again, this time not as loud.

"Then, when she stopped moving at 29 weeks, I prayed to feel something. Anything. Just to know she was, y'know, OK. A couple times I thought I felt something, but it wasn't the same."

Margie pauses for a full minute or so before continuing.

"It wasn't – right.

"Sure enough, when I went in to be checked, they said all they could get was an 'agonized heartbeat.' Let me tell you, those words, 'agonized heartbeat' – you want to talk about agony? I thought my heart would jump right out of my body."

I'm not sure I should have opened up this subject. My own heart is aching in a big way, and I'm not sure I can handle anymore.

It's too late. The die has been cast. I nod, trying to show sympathy for this woman whose cross seems so much greater than my own.

"They said it wouldn't be long," Margie says between nose blows. "After a while, there was nothing. They delivered her and – and –"

Loud, wrenching sobs rock her small frame. I wish I could get up to hold her, but my own pain is breaking through. Why isn't it time for our medication!

"Oh, Margie, I'm so sorry!" is the best I can muster. For some stupid reason, I feel compelled to add, "My arms are around you!"

Why did I say that? It's a ridiculous phrase my mother uses because we live so far apart. We rarely get to hug in person.

I wish Mom could be with me now. I wish Dad didn't need her so much. I wish…

Who knows when I'll get to see my parents again? Between Dad's dementia and Matthew's problems, neither of us is in any position to travel.

This is no good, Emma. Keep your mind where your feet are.

Right now, your feet happen to be propped up in a hospital bed that feels like a rack.

That's your reality, girl. So be it.

I feel the tears starting to come again. I stifle them by making a follow-up joke.

"I mean, my arms would be around you if I could get out of this stupid bed without my whole body screaming in agony! Oh, curse pain anyway!"

She laughs at that. I laugh with her, in spite of the torment it wreaks in my poor body.

*No, Emma. Don't laugh **in spite of** it. Laugh **to** spite it!*

Her next words catch me off guard.

"Emma, would you like to come to Serena's funeral?"

I sit there like an idiot, trying to think of something to say. My silence must have answered her question.

"Oh, what was I thinking? You have two little boys at home and a sick baby who needs you!" she says through tears.

I find my voice and my conscience.

"Of course, I'll come!" I blurt out. "Of course, I will, Margie!"

"No, Emma. Your place is with your family," she says without any trace of resentment. "But listen, I do hope you'll do me one favor. As you're raising Matthew, I want you to think of me and Rog. Maybe you'll pray for us."

She pauses, collecting herself. My mind flashes to a movie I once saw where an elderly mother was on her death bed, clutching at some unseen strength in order to give final instructions to her adult daughter. Between gasps, the mom was uttering pieces of recipes and childrearing advice, knowing this would be her last chance to impart wisdom that would impact the living.

Like that heroic character, Margie appears to be digging deep, trying to counter her grief, so she can get past it long enough to share something greater than her pain.

"And think of the gift you've been given, even though that gift is gonna take a lot of maintenance. Thumb your nose at the people who told you – told both of us – that our children's lives wouldn't be worth living. Think of other lives that didn't measure up to society's standards. Joni Eareckson – oh, what's her married name? Anyway, have you heard of her?"

I haven't.

"She's a quadriplegic. Lost all her mobility, arms and legs both, in a diving accident as a teenager. Tada, that's her name, Joni Eareckson Tada. Do you know what she does now? She writes books and paints with her mouth! Her *mouth*, Emma! She holds the brush with her *teeth*! Some of the most gorgeous artwork you ever saw! She runs an organization called 'Joni and Friends' to help families cope with disability. She's received awards and degrees for all the work she's done from a wheelchair!"

She blows her nose while I marvel at the bravery of such a person. Many would have written off their lives after becoming so disabled. What tenacity!

"Then there's Andrea Bocelli, the singer. His voice is – well, it's outstanding! Did you know his mom was advised to abort him back in the day? What if she had?"

Another pause.

"And don't forget Helen Keller. She couldn't see or hear – it took her years just to learn to talk so people could understand her! Still, she graduated with honors from Radcliffe, I think, and then wrote books and gave lectures about disability."

I feel compelled to add something to Margie's monologue.

"Yes. Yeah, I know. They're all amazing people."

She stares at me, apparently in disbelief. What did I say? Didn't I show enough admiration for this heroic bunch?

"Emma, they're more than amazing. They're God's vessels. What do they all have in common?"

I'm not sure if it's a rhetorical question or if I'm supposed to answer. I wait and, sure enough, she goes on.

"They all have a voice, Emma! Whether it's slurred speeches, or songs, or – or a paintbrush clenched between teeth – whatever means they have, they all raise their voices and say, 'We're here! We exist and have something the world desperately needs!' Don't you see, Emma?"

Where's the nurse with my pain meds? Where's Tom when I need him to come strolling in?

As if she can read my mind, Margie cries out, "Emma, I know you're in pain, but look at me! Look at my smile!"

The ferocity of her ludicrous command startles me. I obey. For the first time, I notice a demure little overbite, almost cute.

I guess my face must register "so what?" because she continues with fierce determination.

"See that, Emma? See that overbite? I always wanted to have that corrected, but my parents didn't have money for braces. So, I live with it.

"It messes up the way I eat a hamburger. I always eat the bun unevenly. There's always less of the bottom roll left when I get to the last bite – it's ridiculous!"

What is she talking about?

"So, it makes me a little different than the 30 million people in the world with perfect smiles, but I don't feel any less full than they do when I eat a burger.

"Don't you see, Emma? My silly mouth gets the job done. It might look funny to some people, but at the end of the day, I've still gotten fed and I can still go about my business."

"Margie, you have a very nice smile, regardless of the –"

"Emma, I'm not talking about my overbite! I'm talking about life! I'm talking about messiness and inconvenience, which is what life is, and even more so when you add disability to the mix! Welcome to the world! Welcome to life in an imperfect, upside down world!"

She blows her nose, loud and hard.

"We'd all be a lot better off if we learned to live with the beauty of imperfection! I can't change the craziness of life, and neither can you by choosing to raise your precious, imperfect child, but…"

Pause.

"But will you do the best you can with what you've got? Will you give Matthew all you've got?"

Big, wet tears roll down her cheeks and onto her blue hospital gown. Her nose is running again, but this time she doesn't bother to blow it.

"Look, Emma, I'm just gonna say one more thing and then I'll shut up. Lord knows, we both need rest and painkillers.

"I can't promise you anything except that, for right now, your son is alive. He has a chance. Whether he's productive for society depends on his God-given abilities and how you raise him. What I can promise is that when you walk into eternity, you'll be able to say, 'I did the best I could with what I was given.'

"What do you say, Emma? Is that enough for you?"

Chapter 49 Mary

"The best way out is always through." – Robert Frost

There are times when sadness settles deep within a person's heart, and no amount of cheerful thoughts can chase it away. When I go in to see Tanya, I summon up every positive image I can think of, but no happy place in my mind's eye can dispel the grisly scene I witnessed in the last hour and a half.

In the end, sheer will is the only thing that drags my feet into forward motion. Maternal instinct drives me towards my daughter, but guilt and shame conspire to keep me away.

Guilt for what? I wonder. *And what do I have to be ashamed of?*

This must be how mothers of criminals feel, I answer myself dully. *Guilty for acts they didn't commit because they must've done something terribly, terribly wrong to have raised someone who did.*

That's great, Mary. Just assume the worst of your own daughter. Don't bother to get her side of the story.

An overly calm nurse gives me permission to see her in the emergency room.

"OK, Mrs. Ritter, you can go right through to room 11," she announces.

"That's 'Gullickson,'" I reply out of habit, then wonder why it matters. I follow the signs to a tiny cubicle passing for an exam room. Tanya's lying on a gurney. Her face is the color of drained pasta, and her cheeks are streaked with dried tears.

I force words to come out of my mouth.

"Tanya, Honey. Are you alright?"

She doesn't answer.

The sight of her bloated belly under the hospital gown gives me chills.

How could I not have known?

Concern wins out over chagrin. My next words are, "Tanya, why didn't you tell us? Honey, we would've helped you! We wouldn't have let you go through this alone. Oh, Sweetheart."

No reply.

"Tanya, can you speak to me, Sweetheart? Mama needs to hear your voice."

I know I sound too motherly, but suddenly I can't help myself.

"Tanya, please. Your father and I want to help."

"He's not my father," Tanya says weakly.

That sting is worse than the 24 I once got after accidentally disturbing a wasp's nest. But I persevere.

"Well, anyway, Dave wants you to know he loves you and is here for you. He'd have come, but someone had to stay and take care of Jessica."

No response.

"Tanya, they think the baby's gonna be OK. You have a beautiful daughter. She may have some brain damage, though."

The minute I say it, I regret it. I realize with a sick feeling that my child is fighting for her own life.

I reach out to take her hand. Tanya stiffens and turns towards the wall.

Chapter 50 David

"Tomorrow will be more hopeful than this awful piece of time we call today." – Suzanne Collins, The Hunger Games

"The whole thing is just nuts," Mary says. "I mean, if I read it in the newspaper, it'd be hard not to laugh. It's – it's – ridiculous, that's what it is! And horrible! And my Tanya is in the middle of it! Oh, Dave, how can this be?"

I take her hand and squeeze it. We're sitting in the lobby of the detention center where the powers that be have brought Tanya now that she's been discharged from the hospital. The cop had warned us she might be taken into custody pending an investigation to determine if she was in her right mind when she left the baby underwater after cutting the cord.

Mary buries her head in my shoulder. I smooth her hair and whisper, "It's gonna be OK, Hon."

She pulls away.

"How? How is it gonna be OK? Our daughter's a mother, we're grandparents, Jessica's an *aunt*, for heaven's sake! And the police want to bring charges against my Tanya, my baby, and maybe she'll go to prison, and what'll happen to *her* baby, and –"

I put my arm around her and shush her softly. She seems to be taking an absurd pleasure in belaboring the situation and berating herself.

"Oh, Dave, how could this have happened? How could I have missed it? My own daughter and I was clueless! If I had an ounce of integrity, I'd quit my job and start taking care of my own family's unplanned pregnancies!"

"Mar, what's the point in doing this to yourself?" I reply. "What's important is what we do now. Can't you see that?"

"I know you're right, Dave, but I'm so *angry*. I'm *enraged*. You wanna know why? I'll tell you why. Because the world did this to her. I tried. You *know* I tried. *God* knows I tried to show and model for her what was right. But you saw that paper she wrote for school. She defended that horrible reduction thing, killing unwanted babies inside the womb! They should call it 'abortion with a twist.'

"Do you know, as a nation, we've killed more babies since abortion became legal than all the people the Nazis killed during World War Two? It's true. Look it up. I'm talking Jews, gays, the disabled, you name it. Our nation has slaughtered around 60 million babies in the name of reproductive freedom in less than 50 years. The Nazis murdered around 20 million. But if we were to compare abortionists to the Gestapo, oh, boy, would there be hell to pay!"

I've never seen her like this. She gets agitated sometimes, yeah, but right now she looks ready to bust a blood vessel. Her voice has risen to the point where she sounds like a mating cat. I'm about to jump in, but she barrels ahead.

"Dear Lord, you read that paper of hers! I – her mother, who supposedly loves her more than life itself – you know how far I got on that paper? To page three! You heard me! I fell asleep after three pages!"

OK, apparently, we've left Nazi Germany and returned to Rock Face, Pennsylvania, and Tanya's term paper.

"And now look where we are! If only I'd been able to stay awake and finish reading it, she and I could have talked about it, and maybe she would've told me what was going on. You've seen how she's been changing. But, oh, Dave, these last few weeks, I felt like she was getting back to the Tanya I used to know. She was becoming human again. Warm. Caring. Like giving Puffy to Jessica.

"She's still there, Dave. Under everything this world's tried to make her believe, all the cesspool of nonsense she's internalized about babies being nothing more than tissue – easily created and easily destroyed. *She's still there.* I can sense it, even though she's not talking right now. *She's still there.* She can be reached if we don't give up. I know it."

My mouth is open to agree, but Mary's not finished whipping herself yet.

"But, oh, Dave, how much of this am I responsible for? I, who've been her role model, the poster parent for pro-life, director of a pregnancy center, and I missed the fact that my own daughter was pregnant! And not only that, what kind of example have I been? My track record for waiting till marriage isn't exactly stellar, now, is it?

"I mean, really, Dave, when you get right down to it, how can this surprise me? Between my example and the garbage the world's been spewing as truth for the last 40 plus years, how can I be surprised? How *dare* I be surprised!"

In all honesty, I can't disagree with a lot of what she's saying.

I mean, there used to be a little something called restraint in our society. And decency. Now what have we got? Click a button on the internet, which is readily available on phones we put into the hands of young kids, and boom! Instant gratification. Porn, gambling, you name it.

A lot of talking heads defend to the death freedom of speech regarding the internet and "entertainment," but what they fail to mention is how quickly the proverbial book will get thrown at people for crossing some thin, arbitrary line into the very areas to which those same voices demand unlimited access. Just ask any porn consumer who goes a step too far into some part of the web the cops are monitoring. They slap cuffs on him faster than you can say, "freedom of information," and his life is turned upside down for years on end. Not that I'm defending porn viewing; I think it's a nasty habit that leads to unrealistic expectations and warped thinking. But I also think our society is completely inconsistent in the way it screams for free access on one hand while, on the other, issuing Draconian punishments for the poor fool who some lawmaker decides went too far. We can't have it both ways.

And let's not forget how inconsistent our government can be about other things. Take car seats, for example. They have expiration dates on them, for crying out loud! Mary picked one up at a yard sale when Jess was on the way, then realized it was past its expiration date. We had to shell out a lot of cash for two brand new ones (one for each car), even though the one she bought looked like it was right out of the box. Just because of some arbitrary date. But, on the other hand, Mary says she hears rumblings that some states are thinking of allowing abortions all the way up through the point of delivery. She's really worried about it!

Seems pretty ghoulish to me to abort a full-term baby, and it really doesn't track with all the laws parents have to abide by once the kid is here. It's like the state will sanction any atrocity you want to inflict on a kid before it's born, but heaven forbid parents try to save a few bucks on a used car seat. That's way too dangerous.

I reel myself in from this internal dialogue. I'm getting almost as mental as Mary is right now. She's on the verge of hysteria, and I need to calm her down. But how?

"Let's take it one day at a time, Hon. That's the only way we're gonna get through this. One day at a time. I'm here. You're here. Most of all, God's here. He'll show us the way one step at a time. He's done it for us before."

Don't ask me why, but right here in the lobby, I bow my head and begin to pray. Out loud. I speak quietly so if anyone comes in, I won't look like a crazy person. I pray for my wife, my daughters, and the newest member of our family – a nameless child who less than a week ago was non-existent for us.

****

Author's note: The statistics Mary references about death tolls from abortion and Nazi activities can be found at https://nrlc.org/uploads/factsheets/FS01AbortionintheUS.pdf and https://www.ushmm.org/wlc/en/article.php?ModuleId=10008193.

Author's note: The concerns Mary expressed to Dave about expanding abortion legislation were not unfounded. On January 22, 2019 (the 46th anniversary of Roe v. Wade), New York's Governor Andrew Cuomo passed the Reproductive Health Act, allowing abortions at any point up through birth. The governor celebrated his "progressive" legislation by illuminating the One World Trade Center, site of the September 11 terrorist attacks, in pink. See https://www.foxnews.com/politics/new-york-celebrates-legalizing-abortion-until-birth-as-catholic-bishops-question-cuomos-faith.

Chapter 51 Trish

"Strong minds discuss ideas, average minds discuss events, weak minds discuss people." — *Socrates*

"Hey, Trish, did you see the headline in today's paper?" my colleague, Pam, asks as we both diaper infants in Rock Face University Hospital's NICU. It's been a heavy morning – one of our little guys even coded – but we have a brief respite from all the excitement. It's actually a nice break to turn my mind off for a few minutes and just do a mundane diaper change.

I look up from the child I'm changing. My gloved hands are covered in nature's finest.

"The paper? No, why?" I ask, hoping she's not going to drag me into a discussion of current events. We're on opposite ends of the political spectrum, and I find it's best to keep my distance.

"It's so sad," she replies, shaking her red mane out of her eyes. She likes to toss her hair up into "messy buns," which always start falling apart by the end of her shift.

"The Ritter baby's mom's probably gonna go to jail," she continues, gesturing to a silent little girl hooked up to tubes and machines in a corner of the nursery. The infant lies motionless most of the time, as if the effort of crying would be too much trouble for her frail lungs to handle.

I take Pam with a grain of salt. She loves to carry tales, with no thought as to whether or not she's upholding professional standards.

"Wait, I thought they discharged her already. Didn't they send her home?" I wonder out loud.

Trish, you fool. Just look up the story and read it for yourself. Why encourage her?

Too late. She launches into a detailed explanation of everything I do and don't need to know. Good thing our patients can't understand English yet.

"I'm not sure. I think they sent her to some sort of holding cell or place like that while they decide whether or not to bring charges. The full story's starting to come out. Apparently, she tried to drown the poor little thing. In the toilet, of all places! They had a picture of the mom. She looked even more pathetic than when they brought her up from the ER the other night. So lost. Reminds me of how I was at that age. No clue what I wanted to do, no way ready to be somebody's mother. She probably just didn't know what else to do."

Pam's attempts to feign sympathy don't fool me. I've known her for too long. She's a good nurse, but I wouldn't choose her for a friend.

Why do people like Pam get so such pleasure from gawking at other people's mistakes?

Apparently, I need to take my own advice. Before I can stop myself, I wade in deeper.

"Oh, man, that's terrible! What happened?"

Pam relates all the horrific details that the media reported about the Ritter girl's birth experience. I suspect it's quickly becoming common knowledge to the poor kid's classmates and the

288

entire community of Rock Face. I wouldn't be surprised it the story's gone viral already.

"Didn't she know she could've dropped the baby off here instead of trying to drown the poor thing?" I exclaim. "It would've been so easy to just hand her off to our Safe Haven."

I'm referring to the program our state and many others participate in, which offers impunity and anonymity to mothers who drop off unharmed babies under a certain age to hospitals and police stations. The moms can go on with their lives, and the state finds homes for their children.

"I know. But, you know, I don't think too many people realize it's here. It's sort of a well-kept secret. It could've saved this girl's life, in a way. Not to mention the baby's. God knows how long that poor kid was under water after she cut the cord. Can't be good."

Tiny lungs from a nearby incubator utter tiny cries.

"Oh, now, who's that? Oh, it's little Matt. Now, there's a real sweetie, even if he does have a long road ahead of him," I say, thankful for an excuse to change the subject. The Coughlin baby is quickly becoming a favorite with the staff; even with all he has going on, he's easy to soothe and responds sweetly to the human touch. His parents may not know it yet, but I have a feeling he's going to bring as much joy as he does complication to their lives. I've been a nurse for a long time, and I sort of have an instinct about these things.

On the heels of that thought, I wonder for the thousandth time why on earth Matt's mom is sharing a room with Mrs. Clauser.

I realize our beds are maxxed out, but couldn't they have found a better pairing than two heartbroken moms? One's baby didn't make it, bless her heart, and the other's facing a lifetime of raising a disabled child.

Then again, maybe in some odd way they can comfort each other. After all, grief may have different sources and take different forms, but it's still grief.

All these sad stories are starting to get to me. The Ritter baby and her troubled mother, the heartache of the Clausers, Matt Coughlin's uncertain future. Nursing is always a mixed bag of satisfaction and sorrow, especially in a unit like the NICU. Why aren't I used to this by now?

I hope the small-minded Pams of this world stay out of their way.

Chapter 52 Emma

"When I've been tempted to do something wrong, I ask myself, 'What would my children think of me?'" – David Parrish

"I'm holding up," I respond to Linda's question about how I'm feeling. We have the visitors' lounge to ourselves, and Linda and Ted have brought me the first real food I've eaten since the C-section. Things are looking brighter with every bite.

"I guess it's just gonna take time for us to get used to everything," I add, wiping ketchup from the corner of my mouth. "I'm sure once my incision starts to really heal, everything will seem better."

Linda has a funny look on her face, like she's trying to make up her mind about something. She shoots a questioning glance to Ted, who, if I'm not mistaken, shakes his head almost imperceptibly.

I may be doped up, but I'm with it enough to detect the obvious.

"Hey, you two, what's up?" I ask.

Linda clears her throat. Ted cracks his knuckles.

I hate when men do that.

"Well, Em, Ted and I have been talking about something. Got a minute?"

I laugh.

"Where am I gonna go?" I joke. "They tell me I have at least another day in these palatial surroundings! So, what's up?"

Ted looks awkwardly at the floor. Despite his lack of support for whatever she wants to talk about, my sister perseveres.

"Well, Em, here's what we were thinking," she begins. She tries a few more openings before giving up and blurting out the most offensive ten words I've ever heard anyone speak: 'We'll adopt Matthew if you and Tom can't raise him.'"

For a second, I want to hit her. How can she think so little of me? Am I wearing some kind of sign that makes people like Margaret and Linda think I'd be capable of disowning my own child?

The look on my face must speak volumes because she starts apologizing profusely and chastising herself through tears for upsetting me. Ted alternates between comforting her and saying things like, "I knew this wasn't a good idea, Lin! I told you we shouldn't do this!"

If it were anyone else, I would just let her cry. But this is Linda, my only sister, who has twice put aside her broken heartedness to come and help my expanding family, while waiting for her turn to come.

"Come here," I say, holding out my arms. She enters them gratefully, wetting my hospital gown with her tears. I motion for Ted to come, too, and we do a big, unbalanced group hug that almost topples my IV pole. If anyone walked in at this moment, we'd probably all be whisked off to the psych ward.

"Lin, Ted, I don't know what to say. I think it's beautiful that you guys would wanna do this. Y'know –"

My cell phone goes off, and we all jump. I look down to see Tom's number. Now, here's a divine interruption, because I have absolutely no idea what to say next.

"Tom!" I jabber into the phone. "Honey, it's so good to hear your voice! Linda and Ted just got here, and they brought me a wonderful cheese steak! How are you and the boys?"

"Everyone's fine, Hon!" he answers with a sort of surprised sounding glow in his voice. I guess he doesn't have much reason to expect peppiness from me these days.

Either I or the pain meds decide he should be in on this conversation.

"Tom, you'll never guess what Linda and Ted just brought up."

Linda takes on a stricken look, shakes her head, and waves her hands while mouthing "no" over and over again. I ignore her because I need help with this discussion.

"Tom, what would you say if I told you they just offered to adopt Matthew?"

For a minute there's silence, and I wonder if my phone dropped the call. Then I hear Tom's impossibly calm voice, the one he reserves for classroom situations that demand nerves of steel.

"Well, how interesting is that?" he says without emotion, and I know it's safe to put him on speaker.

"Tom, I've got you on speaker now. Don't you think we should discuss this together?"

Again, with practiced composure, he replies, "That's fine."

293

"OK, we can all hear you now," I say, suddenly realizing the awkward absurdity of what's happening. People have group chats to discuss party plans, not in-family adoptions of disabled children.

Ted starts to babble.

"Listen, guys, this was a crazy idea. I should've said 'no' the minute Lin suggested it. No, wait, I don't mean to blame her. I mean, we're both a little sleep deprived. I mean, not because of Kyle and Kevin, it's just –"

Tom laughs. One of my favorite things about him is that he knows when something's too ridiculous to argue about. When he speaks next, his everyday voice comes out.

"Look, you guys, back it up. No harm done. You meant well, and Emma and I both know that. But guys, I just could never give up my own son. No matter what. I mean, what would my other kids think of me? And what would Matt think of me when he found out later? That he was too much trouble for his dad to bother with? I mean, my kids' opinion of me matters almost more than my opinion of myself. I just couldn't do it."

Ted's so busy being relieved that Tom and I aren't furious that he doesn't notice the crestfallen look on Linda's face.

"You know, Bro, you're not as dense as I always thought you were!" Ted jokes, breaking the tension. "You're actually pretty deep!"

Tom laughs again. I hug Linda, whose shoulders are softly shaking.

"Lin, I'm sorry," I say. "It's God awful unfair, I know. I don't understand any of this, and the last thing I'd ever wanna do is hurt you guys. But Tom's right. As hard as this is, we just couldn't give up our own flesh and blood. Y'know?"

"Linda, can you hear me?" Tom asks.

"Yes, she's right here, Hon," I answer because all she can do is nod.

"Listen, Linda. Even if I could bring myself to do it, I couldn't live with my kids thinking I bailed just because something was tough. Can you understand that?"

After a pause, he adds, "But you know something? If I were gonna pick anyone to raise my kids if I couldn't do it – it would be you guys. OK? In fact, Emma and I should really think about writing a will, y'know, for guardianship and all that. What if –"

Ted interrupts my husband. He can see where this is going, and it isn't the time.

"Yeah, Tom. She knows. We know. We can discuss a will and stuff later. Listen, I better get her home," he adds, steering my crumpled sister out of the room.

Chapter 53 Tanya and David

"The meaning of life. The wasted years of life. The poor choices of life. God answers the mess of life with one word: 'grace.'" – Max Lucado

I sit frozen on a hard chair while I wait for my visitor. My eyes are practically swollen shut from the barrels of tears I've cried over the past few – what? Hours? Days? Months? I don't even know what day it is, let alone how long this has been going on.

My chest and belly ache from racking sobs. Though my stomach's empty, I fight against perpetual nausea. It even hurts when I go to the bathroom. I wonder if this is the start of a UTI.

He comes in. His dark, wavy hair is tamed back in its usual unfashionable way. My grief fog lifts for a minute, and I think for the thousandth time how someone needs to take him aside and bring him up to date on current trends.

He's gained weight since I last saw him. His head looks precarious topping off that pear-shaped build, like somehow it might just topple off those skinny shoulders and land on the floor next to those gargantuan, smelly feet of his.

His clothes, as always, reflect a tight budget and even narrower fashion sense. At times I've been embarrassed by his lack of style. Yet, today he carries with him a strong presence that, somehow, I never noticed before.

He sits down across from me and leans forward.

I don't look at him, but instead keep my eyes on the paint-chipped floor. Slowly, he raises my face and offers me his handkerchief.

Who carries a handkerchief these days? I find myself thinking ironically, followed by, *What am I, crazy? Who worries about nonsense like that at a time like this?*

"How ya doin'?" he asks.

"What do you want?" I choke out.

I pick at a piece of loose skin around what used to be one of my fingernails. It's gnawed and swollen and starts to bleed. I hear Mom's voice in my head.

Oh, Tanya, honey, you've bitten it down to the quick again! Oh, Sweetheart, you have such pretty hands, if only you wouldn't bite your poor little nails!

Without thinking, I wrap his clean, white hankie around my bleeding finger. I wonder if he'll recoil or say something cute like, "Just keep it." But if he noticed, he doesn't let on.

"I came to talk to you," he replies softly.

I sneer.

"There's nothing to talk about. My life's ruined."

His voice doesn't waver as he responds, "Oh, no. Your life's just beginning. And I still want to be a part of it."

"Yeah, right!" I smirk. "Well, that's not funny. It's – it's – it's cruel!"

"Tanya, don't you get it? I know what you've done, and I still want you in my life.

"He pauses, then adds, "Whaddaya say?"

297

As soon as the words leave my mouth, I wish I could take them back. I sound like a trailer from a chick flick. Tanya's in no mood to let me get away with it.

After Mary finished her visit with Tanya, I asked if I could go in for a few minutes. Don't ask me why, but after praying with my wife in the lobby of this God-forsaken place, I knew this was the time I should again offer to adopt Tanya.

"What do you mean, 'I want you in my life?'" Tanya retorts. "What, are you asking me to marry you or something? You're already married to my mother, in case you've forgotten! How can you make such a sick statement at a time like this!"

I take a deep breath and think about how to respond to her hostility. I figured it wouldn't be easy seeing her under the circumstances, but I didn't think she would make it this hard.

This detention center is a real hell hole. I'd prefer to be anywhere but here. But here is where Tanya is, so it's where I need to be.

What was it my brother, Len, used to say?

"It's not about what you want; it's about what's needed."

He said that when I asked him if he liked his job. Looking back, I'm sure he hated it. This was shortly after my dad died, and before he and Al set up their own business. At the time, he was working the cash register in my uncle's drug store, probably getting paid less than high schoolers make now to flip burgers. Uncle Harry may not have been able to pay Lenny much, but he did come up with the money to bury Dad. Maybe he was the guy who taught Len about sucking it up and doing what's needed.

Now it's my turn.

I mentally steel myself and continue.

"Tanya, of course I'm not asking to marry you. What I do want is to be more than your stepfather. I'm asking again if you'd allow me to legally adopt you, so we can go through this thing together. Whatever that means. Whatever comes. We'll take the legal stuff one piece at a time.

"I want to be there for you as your father, your dad. I don't care what you've done. I care about you. I mean, I love you. I've loved you since I first started to love your mom, and I'll always love you, even if you don't want me to adopt you."

I feel mighty awkward, and also like the proverbial sitting duck. If she lets me have it, I'm not sure I'll ever have the guts to ask again.

I pause and hand the results over to God.

"Whaddaya think?"

She blinks her red, puffy eyes several times. The sight would be comical if it weren't so tragic.

"Are you kidding me, David? Do you have any idea what you're saying? Look around you. I'm in jail, for God's sake!"

"It's for God's sake I'm asking, Sweetheart. Because He loves *me*, with all my faults, how can I turn my back on *you* at a time like this? God forbid I should do anything less than embrace you as my own child, which is what I've wanted to do since the day I said 'I do' to your mom. I've always thought of you as my own daughter, and I want the world to know that nothing you could do could ever change that. I'd still be proud to have you take my name – God-awful as it is – but it's OK if you keep your own, too. Names don't matter. *You* matter."

I've never before seen Tanya speechless. She twists my handkerchief and wipes her eyes. I read skepticism, then cautious trust, in those red-rimmed eyes.

"But… I always thought you loved Jess and sort of, y'know, *tolerated* me. And now – with everything that's happened…"

How could she think that? Haven't I always treated her like my own?

Take it easy, Dave. It is what it is.

"Tanya, with everything that's happened, you need a father more than ever. Don't you think? And as far as loving Jess and just 'tolerating' you – well, nothing could be further from the truth. I mean, yeah, Jess is my flesh and blood, but you're Mary's flesh and blood, and Mary's what makes my heart keep beating. She's, I mean, she's pretty much the reason I wake up every day.

"So, Tanya, you're part of Mary, and I want you to be as much a part of me as she and Jessica are. So, whaddaya say?"

She starts to cry.

"I mean, how can you want this? How can you want *me*? Don't you even wanna know what happened? Aren't you afraid I might hurt Dolly? The cops think I tried to – tried to –"

She puts her head in her hands and sobs quietly.

Oh, God, what do I do now?

"Tanya," I say, hoping words will find their way into my mouth, "Tanya, the person who gave the toy she loved most in the world to her baby sister is not someone I'd be afraid might hurt her."

That wasn't bad. Thanks, God.

"And that's the same person who loved her dog more than anything. The girl – no, the young woman – who cried so hard over losing her pet could never have tried to harm her child.

"I know you'll tell me and your mom the whole thing when you're ready. But, for now, could ya use a hug?"

Watch it, Gullickson. You might be pushing your luck.

She nods almost imperceptibly. I go over and put my arms around her shaking shoulders.

"Look, we don't have to rush this. I mean, if you need time to think about it –"

"OK," she blurts out. "Yes, David! The answer is YES!"

Chapter 54 Ted

"Hope springs eternal in the human breast." – Alexander Pope

"Ted, come look at this!" Linda calls from the bathroom where she's bathing Emma's kids. I'll say this for Linda: she knows how to compartmentalize disappointment and go on with everyday activities.

When I get there, she motions that I should look at the article she has up on her phone.

"Lin, you amaze me!" I chuckle. "How can you be giving two kids a bath and checking your phone at the same time?"

"Oh, Hon, you know me. Always multi-tasking. No, I just stole a peek while the guys were splashing around. But really, take a look at this."

A headline in the news feed caught her eye: "Charges Considered for Teen Mom Whose Newborn Almost Drowns." It's a sad item about an 18-year-old girl right here in Rock Face. The kid delivered a baby in the bathroom of her house, then left it to drown in the toilet, of all things.

After showing me the article, Lin links over to a late-night talk show host's spoof on the sordid mess. As usual, the comic's making light of someone else's tragedy the way road ragers vent their spleens on people they figure they'll never meet. Never ceases to amaze me how easy it is for onlookers to make judgments without accountability.

"Wow, that's sad, Babe. And this jerk's just making it harder for all concerned."

"Ted, do you realize what this means? It says they're going to put the baby in foster care unless a relative's willing to take her while the cops decide if the mom has to face charges. Ted, this is our chance!"

Maybe it's fatigue, but I think I just heard my wife suggest we adopt a child whose first view of life was the inside of a toilet.

"Lin, you can't be serious. You're not, are you?"

"Oh, Ted, of course I am! The article says it's a little girl, and nobody can take her – neither set of grandparents, and not the dad. The poor baby probably has health problems, they don't know to what extent, they're still doing tests. But, oh, Ted, this is our baby! I know it's meant to be!"

This isn't exactly good news to me. I love my wife more than anything on earth, but in all honesty, I always pictured us parenting a "normal" child. When Tom and Emma rejected our offer to adopt Matthew, it actually came as a huge relief. Don't get me wrong; I'm not lazy – no one who takes on the grueling process of adoption could ever get away with being lazy – but I could use a break from all the stress we've been dealing with for years. What Linda's suggesting would likely involve just the opposite. Here's a child who was so unwanted that its mother may have tried to end its life, probably causing brain damage and lifelong special needs.

This isn't for me.

But how can I break her heart again?

I decide to bide my time. This will probably fall through just like every other door we've knocked on.

303

Chapter 55 Emma

"For after all, the best thing one can do when it is raining, is to let it rain." — Henry Wadsworth Longfellow, "The Poet's Tale; The Birds of Killingworth" cited in <u>Tales of a Wayside Inn</u>

The skies are in a bad mood the day of my homecoming. Unlike the day we peeked at Matt in the NICU, this time there are no white clouds to offset the angry, gray ones. But I don't care. I just want to be in my own home, hugging my kids, sleeping with my husband.

Matthew's being well cared for at the hospital as he awaits his next surgery. Church friends have set up a schedule to bring us dinners. Things are looking up.

Kyle holds my hand, insisting I close my eyes as I step over the threshold.

"'Kay, now open 'em!" he orders.

Turns out he enlisted Kev, and the two of them stacked all the toys that wouldn't fit into their toy box into a big mound, one on top of the other.

"See, Mommy? We cleaned up the whole house!"

I forget my wound for a second and try to bend down and pick him up. When my stitches scream that this is a bad idea, I pat his head instead.

"Kyle and Kevin, you guys are Mommy's big boys, and I'm so proud of you! You did such a great job of cleaning up! Thank you so much for helping Daddy and Aunt Linda and Uncle Ted!"

The next thing that hits me – besides Kevin, who practically knocks me down, nearly unleashing a variety of words I haven't used since college – is the plate collection hanging in the dining room. There it is in all its fractured glory. Strange, though; I must have gotten so used to the mended one that it no longer bothers me. In fact, it looks almost as if it belongs there.

I smile to myself.

Emma, you'd better get some sleep. That plate's an eyesore, no mistake about it.

It looks silly, sporting a long, jagged crack and missing some fragments. The fall caused a chip that was already there to expand into an uneven, diamond-shaped fissure, and now the whole thing looks like it's waiting for a transplant.

I've reminded myself a hundred times to find something new to put up there. Now, in an unsightly way, it strikes me as absurdly beautiful.

Tom catches me staring at it and looks sheepish.

"Yeah, I know, Em. I did a lousy job fixing that, huh? I just threw it up there with some glue and a prayer, mostly 'cause it seemed to mean so much to Ky. Thing is, it was just so messed up, I couldn't do much with it. Guess we're gonna have to get a new one."

I squeeze his hand and smile.

"No, Honey. That's not gonna be necessary. It's good just the way it is."

Kyle breaks into our moment.

"Mommy, Kevie and me wrote a song for Maffew. Wanna hear it?"

He cups his hands around his mouth in a conspiratorial whisper.

"Acshully, Mommy, just I wrote it. But don't tell Kevie 'cause he thinks he helped. It goes like this:

> Go to sleep, little Maffew, and you will be alright.
>
> Close your eyes, little Maffew, and you will be OK.
>
> If the sun doesn't dawn in your dreams tonight,
>
> Be sure to wake me with the sound of your fright.

Well, do ya like it, Mommy?"

His simple, off-key melody makes the breath catch in my throat. When I can finally speak, I brush away tears and say, "Yeah, Kyle, I like it. I like it just fine."

****

Author's note: the song that Kevin sings to Matthew was actually composed by my then five-year-old son for his newborn brother.

Chapter 56 Tanya

"There is no terror in the bang, only in the anticipation of it." – Alfred Hitchcock

Two of my fingers are bleeding. The thumb on my left hand and the pinky on my right.

I can't help it. Whenever there's a loose piece of skin anywhere around them, it drives me crazy.

Tanya, when are you gonna stop making excuses? You have a gross habit. That's all there is to it.

David hands me a tissue with a smile. I get ready to say something snotty, but then I realize his face shows concern, not scorn.

Why do I always want to think the worst of him?

You could try being nicer to him, now that he's sticking his neck out for you. He offered you his name, for crying out loud, not to mention his full trust and support.

A man in a too tight suit opens a door across the hall from where we're sitting and says, "Miss Ritter, we're ready for you now."

My stomach lurches the way it does after the roller coaster car lugs its way up to the top of the track and you're waiting for all hell to break loose, and you realize there's no getting off, and the only way you'll ever see solid ground again is to let the ride do its worst and pray you survive whatever torture comes with each next set of drops and curves.

Mom, David and the lawyer all stand up.

I can't move.

"Tanya, Honey, it's alright. We're all here," Mom says with unnatural sweetness, like the sicky sweet icing you squeeze out of a tube to decorate cakes. Our health teacher told us diabetics sometimes carry those for when their blood sugar drops too low.

Tanya, what is wrong with you! Think of why you're here!

No, thanks. I'd rather think about sickening cake icing.

Mom offers me a hand. To my surprise, I accept it.

I feel my feet moving me towards the door, despite the fact that my brain is ordering them to take off in the opposite direction.

Maybe the county should ask the taxpayers for more money, because the walls in this courthouse sure could use a coat of paint.

Tanya, you idiot, forget about the walls!

Mom practically has to drag me over the threshold into a large area with lots of offices. We follow the guy into a conference room with ash gray walls.

That figures.

The guy who's bulging out of his suit, which I'm now noticing is the color of Jess's vomit after she got into Mom's chocolate chip stash, motions us to sit down.

Mom helps me into a chair and stations herself next to me.

I hope they let you come to jail with me, Mom, because apparently my days of seating and unseating myself are gone forever.

"OK, Miss Ritter, Mr. Allenbury, the assistant DA, will be in shortly," he says, as casually as if he's telling us the server will be right over to take our order.

308

Thanks. I'll have a burger, fries, and my freedom, please.

"How you doing, Sweetheart?" David asks.

Just great. Never better.

I stifle the sarcastic impulses, and mutter, "OK."

Dawn, the lawyer who's here to represent me, finally gives us a sign that she's alive.

"OK, now, Tanya, when this man comes in, it's very important that you follow my lead. Remember, this meeting is to determine whether or not the DA is going to bring charges against you. So, if they ask you anything that I feel may jeopardize your chances of being fully exonerated, I'm not going to allow you to answer.

"If you aren't sure what to say, or if you think something you're about to say will get you into trouble, just look over at me and I'll help you out. Got it?"

I nod.

Her words are reassuring, but the way she says them isn't. She's… mechanical. Like she's said the same thing 100 times before and is just repeating it out of habit.

Reminds me of the one and only airplane flight I've ever been on, when Mom, David and I went to his brother's funeral in Texas, a few months before Dolly was born. The flight attendant spouted off tons of instructions about what to do, "should the cabin lose pressure," and they all sounded really urgent and important, but her tone was almost robotic. We all laughed later about the irony of her giving us life and death information in such a lifeless way.

Now that I think about it, that was the only time David smiled during the whole trip. I guess he really loved his brother.

It wouldn't have killed you to be a little nice to him that weekend.

"Ms. Ritter, I'm Peter Allenbury. I work for the District Attorney's office. I'll be taking your statement," the man in the storm cloud gray suit announces as he struts in.

I want to bolt, but Mom's hand closes in on mine like a hug.

Chapter 57 Mary

"Every generation needs regeneration." – Charles Spurgeon

When I squeeze my daughter's hand, two thoughts collide in my head at the same time:

1) Why does the DA have to dress like an undertaker? and

2) Why does one little squeeze leave me feeling like an arthritic cripple?

I shake them both off and try to focus on what he's saying.

"OK, now, folks, I'm going to ask one of our admins, Jackie, to come in as a witness and record our conversation. This is for everyone's protection, so we're all on the same page legally. Any questions so far?"

We shake our heads and murmur that we understand.

Dawn Shuller, the attorney David's sister-in-law recommended, says nothing. Kate works as a paralegal, so she should know who's a good lawyer in our area. I sure hope she didn't steer us wrong.

I look over at Tanya while they're getting things set up. She looks small to me in this setting. Small and fragile.

"OK, let's begin," Allenbury begins. "Please state your full name and address for the record, Ms. Ritter."

Tanya responds in a shaky voice.

"And what is your date of birth?"

After she answers, he makes her identify each of us and give permission for us to be there.

"OK, and for the record, please state the name of the attorney you've retained to represent you."

Someone who'd better be worth the college funds she's depleting.

"Mr. Allenbury, would it be possible to move on to more substantive questions?" Dawn pipes up as if she heard what I was thinking. "My clients' parents are here to support their daughter, but they have another small child at home, and this office has already kept us waiting for over an hour."

OK, this was probably either very smart or very stupid, according to the education I've gotten from old lawyer shows. Based on the credentials I picked up from the aforementioned dramas, I deduce that she's either shown the DA how confident she is of Tanya's innocence (inferring that it shouldn't take long to get this "trivial" matter sorted out) or ticked him off royally.

"All in good time, Ms. Shuller," he answers coolly.

Strike one.

He continues peppering Tanya with a few other incidental questions, such as how long she's lived at her current address, and if she's ever lived anywhere else.

Get on with it!

"OK, now, Ms. Ritter, please state your whereabouts on the afternoon of March 31, 2018."

No, wait! Go back to the non-essentials. I'm not ready for this.

Too bad, Mary. The game's afoot.

Why do I think of stupid things like that at a time like this?

"Um, I was home."

"OK, so you were at the address you identified as your primary residence when we first began the interview?"

"Yeah, er, *yes*. I mean, it's my only residence."

You go, girl.

"And please tell me how you were occupied on that afternoon."

She squeezes my hand. Hard. It hurts.

I involuntarily squeeze Dave's hand with my other one. He squeezes back. It doesn't hurt.

Maybe some of Dave's energy and strength can transfer from his hand to mine and into Tanya's, like a lightning rod.

"I was, um, having a baby."

It's not that I'm surprised at this news. Lord knows, I've had plenty of time to get used to it. It's just shocking to hear the words finally coming out of my daughter's mouth.

"Can you give me an idea of the timetable? I mean, what time did labor commence, and when did it end?"

What difference does that make? He's just nitpicking.

It's his party, Mary.

"I, um, I'm not really sure. The whole thing's pretty fuzzy."

She looks at Dawn, who nods at her.

"OK, the police report puts them at your residence at…"

I allow my mind to turn off briefly. I can feel myself getting fatigued, and I want to be alert for what's important.

He tries to pin her down about some other minutiae, and she continues to answer vaguely. Good. She's following the advice Dawn gave us when we signed on with her.

You know, Mary Ann, your attitude is pretty lousy. Do you or don't you want to know the truth? Do you or don't you want justice to be served?

I don't know about justice anymore. I just want my baby back.

Your baby hasn't been a baby for a long time, and the sooner you realize that, the better off you'll be.

He takes her through the labor in excruciating detail. The fact that she was on the toilet. Alone in the house. Couldn't reach Chuck. Afraid to call us.

Why don't you ask her if she can catalogue each contraction for you, Mr. Assistant DA?

When she gets to the part about dropping her phone, Dawn lights up like a firefly and makes a great point.

"Mr. Allenbury, for the record, since my client had no access to a phone and was unable to leave the bathroom, she was in no way able to seek help for herself or her child. For this reason…"

She rambles on in some "legal-ese" that confuses me, but I think the gist is that there's no case against Tanya.

Hope flutters briefly in my heart.

"Your concerns are noted, Ms. Shuller," he replies, undaunted. "That is precisely what we're seeking to determine, as you're well aware. Now, let's proceed."

Come back at him, you dope! That's what we're paying you for!

But I guess Dawn feels she's made her point, so she lets him move on.

Strike two.

It's odd, but listening to her relate the details of giving birth, I'm back reliving my own birth story with Jessica. I momentarily replace the DA's questions with the music I had looping in the delivery room – my two favorites, a classical piece and another one about prayer.

Good suggestion, Mary. Why not try praying?

Lord, here I am again. Thank you so much for allowing us to reconnect with our daughter, despite these terrible circumstances. Thank you that Tanya has finally made peace with Dave. He's always been her dad. She just had to figure that out.

Still, though, I'm terribly upset and confused about what comes next. Could you lead the way and stay behind, before, and most of all, beside all of us as we travel this unknown, difficult path?

Allenbury's next question jolts me back to the present world.

"Now, tell me, Ms. Ritter, what did you do after you cut the umbilical cord?"

Here it is. It's time to face up to whatever the truth is.

Tanya's voice trembles as she answers.

"Well, um, it's a little hard to explain because so many thoughts were going through my mind, and I was also really, really tired. And, see, the thing is, there were a whole bunch of thoughts going around in my head, all at once, sort of. I mean, it's probably gonna sound like it took a long time, but I think it was really only a few seconds, or a minute or two."

"Just tell us what you remember, the way you remember it," the DA prods.

"Well, like I said, I took the scissors Mom keeps in the bathroom – I could reach them from where I was sitting on the, y'know, the, the ..."

"The toilet, Ms. Ritter?"

"Um, yeah," she admits, and immediately reddens. "Well, I guess I already told you that. Anyway, I had them in my hand. They had blood on them from cutting the, y'know, cord. I guess the first thing that happened was, as I'm holding them, I think of this talk my classmate, Zara, gave for our senior project. It was this debate project we had to do, and she talked about assisted suicide, which is where doctors are allowed to help patients, y'know, end their own lives if they want to. And, according to Zara, it's legal for doctors to do that in a bunch of states. So, I thought, 'If doctors are allowed to help people, y'know, basically kill themselves, why wouldn't it be OK for me to, y'know, help this baby, y'know, in that way?'"

I gasp. I pray no one else heard. Apparently, at least one person did, though, because Dave squeezes my hand, and I think I hear him say, "Shhh," under his breath.

"Uh, Mr. Allenbury, does this pertain to the subject at hand?" my beloved husband interjects.

Thank God.

The DA rebukes Dave for interrupting, but his disturbance has had the desired effect. It derails Tanya's narrative momentarily and forces that useless Dawn to take a position. She and Allenbury bicker for a few minutes, but in the end, she agrees to let Tanya continue.

Strike three.

Lord, I've known you to put more time in my morning when I'm running impossibly behind. Won't you please give us one more strike before you call this game for the other team?

"And then I remembered learning about some guy at one of the big colleges who thinks the world's overpopulated, so if a baby's parents ask a doctor to kill it, the doctor should just do it. Oh, and he thinks they're maybe not even people yet, till they get to a certain age. Wait, was that the same guy? See, I found out about this stuff when I was doing my own senior project, and there were all these people who had all these different opinions. I had to do all this research about this thing called, um, uh, oh, what was it called? Sorry, I'm kinda nervous."

She picks at her thumb and wriggles in her seat, the way she used to when I was potty training her. I could always tell when she hadn't cleaned herself well enough. She would squirm around in her seat the way she's doing now.

Mary, that's just weird!

Dave puts a hand on her shoulder. She settles in her chair and seems to rally.

"Oh, yeah, it was called reduction. Selective reduction. That's when people are having a lot of babies and they think there

317

are too many, so they sort of, um, cancel part of the pregnancy. Well, I guess that's a different topic."

Allenbury is looking impatient. He looks like he's about to say something, but then Tanya seems to collect her thoughts and return to her original point.

"So, anyway, I'm thinking about this guy who believes babies aren't really human and I thought, 'Well, maybe he's got a point.' So, all this was going through my mind, kind of like the way ingredients get all mixed up in a blender. And then, for a second, I thought of this guy, I forget his name, but he was an abortion doctor in Philly who went to jail 'cause he gave out drugs illegally and kept his clinic really gross and hired people who weren't really trained to help him with the abortions and kept babies' feet in jars and –"

"Do you mean Kermit Gosnell, Ms. Ritter?" the DA asks.

Gosnell! That monster! Why would Tanya think of him right after giving birth?

Doesn't it even faze her that he kept the severed feet of murdered children in jars! She just threw it in casually with his other atrocities in a disgusting laundry list of horrors.

"Yeah! That's him. Well, I came across this Gosnell guy in my research for the reduction paper I told you about. And he, well, he would give women abortions when they were pretty far along in their pregnancies. And sometimes – I mean, I guess it wasn't too often, but sometimes the baby would come out, y'know, alive, even though they tried to um, abort it. So, Mr., I mean, *Dr.* Gosnell, he would – I know this sounds gross – but he would take a pair of

318

scissors and, y'know, do something to the baby's neck, I mean, the *fetus's* neck, to, y'know, finish killing, I mean, *aborting* the baby– well, is it a baby once it comes out, or is it still a fetus, since they were trying to abort it –"

Don't say it, Tanya! You couldn't! You didn't!

"Well, anyway, I'm sitting there, thinking, 'Would it be so wrong? I mean, if a doctor could do it? I know he went to jail and all, but still, he is a doctor. I mean, they have to promise not to hurt anyone, right? So, he must think, er, *know*, um, whether or not it's a real baby, right?'

"But then, while I'm trying to decide if it's OK to do something with the scissors, like, abort my own baby, kind of, even though it's already come out, then I realize the baby's not crying or anything, like they always do right after they're born. So, then I wonder if it's even alive at all. And then I think, 'Tanya, you're so stupid. You're sitting on the reason this baby's not crying. Its head is in the, y'know, the water from the toilet, 'cause that's where it landed, sort of, when it came out. I mean, I hadn't held it or anything."

As I continue to listen to my daughter relate her thought processes on that terrible afternoon, I shudder. Practicality intervenes, though, and I realize this isn't looking good at all for Tanya. Why is her lawyer allowing her to give all this grisly detail? Is she trying to make her a scapegoat?

Welcome to reality, champion of life. You're pretty quick to want leniency when it's your own child on the other side of the issue you thought was so clear cut.

319

Oh, Lord. Why does she keep referring to the baby as "it"?
I don't know how much more of this I can take.

"But I'm getting pretty lightheaded at this point, and I feel like I'm gonna throw up. And there's nowhere to throw up until I get the baby out of the, y'know, toilet, unless I want to puke, er, *vomit* all over the floor, so I'm trying to figure all that out, then suddenly, like a miracle, I don't have to puke, I mean, *vomit*, anymore. It was amazing! So, I thought, *thank God!*

"But then, I still have to figure out what to do about everything, and it occurs to me, if I leave her in there, maybe the decision will be made for me, sort of. Y'know? And I wonder to myself, 'Would it really be drowning, or would it just be assisted suicide, since, y'know, the baby's not really a person yet, like that guy from the university said, and since the world's overpopulated anyway, maybe it's, I dunno, OK to help nature along –"

Thank you, Lord! She said, "her" instead of "it"!

Mary, you fool! Listen to the rest of what she's saying!

"Um, sorry to interrupt again," my darling Dave jumps onto the dangerous precipice Tanya's dangling on, "and I really wouldn't expect to have to point something like this out to the attorney my wife and I are *paying* with our kids' college funds, but shouldn't you be suggesting to my daughter that she's maybe providing more information than is wise under the circumstances? I mean, I didn't go to law school, but isn't it obvious?"

Bless you, David. This may be strike four, but I'll always love you for it.

"Mr. Ritter, er, Gullickson, I must caution you that if you make one more outburst, you'll be instructed to leave. Is that clear?"

"Fine, it won't happen again, Mr. Allenbury, and I am sorry. But honestly, I've never been so sure of anything in my life. I mean, the things my daughter is telling you – wouldn't any decent attorney representing her object, or do whatever you call it in a meeting like this, to stop her?"

Allenbury is rendered speechless. So am I. So, apparently, is Dawn. She sits there with a scowl on her face for a few seconds, then appears to find her voice. As she's about to open her mouth, Tanya beats her to the punch.

"Listen, Mom, David, everybody. I think it's gonna be OK. I mean, if you guys let me finish my story, I really think it'll be OK. Another kind of miracle happened at the end that made it, I don't know, sort of amazing. At least for me. Can I please finish?"

"By all means, Ms. Ritter," the DA answers before anyone else can jump in.

"Well, um, I was really upset and nervous about all this, 'cause I'm in so much trouble, and my whole life's a mess – well, not everything, I mean, my stepdad, David, he wants to adopt me – well, that's a whole 'nother story. But, I mean, I really was terrified when I came in here about what was going to happen to me.

"But as I'm telling you what happened, I realize, I mean, I *know* I really didn't do anything wrong. And I kind of have *faith*, I guess, that you guys'll see that, too."

Oh, Tanya! Did you just say 'faith?'

"So, as I'm wondering whether to leave her in or pull her out, the face of my little sister, Jessica, jumps into my mind. I don't know why. I was remembering her on this one afternoon my boyfriend and I – well, he's my ex-boyfriend now – Chuck. Actually, he's the baby's father. Well, I guess you know that. Anyway, he and I had taken Dolly – that's what I sometimes call her – to the park.

"Matter of fact, Mom," she says, looking directly at me, "it was the day we lost the baby bottle with the money in it for the pregnancy center. I still feel bad about that. It really was just an accident. Well –"

"Ms. Ritter, please keep to the facts," Allenbury insists, to which Tanya replies, "Oh, sorry. Well, that was a real nice day, and Dolly has this really pretty blonde hair like mine used to be, I guess, and the sun kind of beat down on it while she was on the swing. And it made her hair sort of look like it had these gold streaks in it. And I remember thinking when I was sitting there in the bathroom after having the baby that it's a shame Dolly's hair will probably get darker like mine did, and what a shame that is, 'cause hers is still so pretty, just like she is.

"It's funny how light hair always seems to turn dark, doesn't it?

"And then I remembered how she always calls me 'Tonna' because she can't say my name right, although she's getting closer. And how she always wants me to read to her and snuggle with her and all. And how she loves hugging my Puffy – that's this toy I gave her."

I blink back tears.

"And it suddenly dawned on me that whatever this was in the toilet," Tanya's voice rises in pitch and volume, "it looked exactly the way my baby sister did when she came out! In fact, it *is* the same thing – a person!

"And I suddenly realized that, no matter what the doctors and all the people who think selective reduction and abortion are OK – no matter what they all say - well, they're not staring down at this little tiny girl that looks just like my baby sister did the first time I saw her! I mean, when Dolly was born, she didn't even weigh as much as some of the books I carry for school. She was lighter than my science book! Can you believe that?

"And I thought, 'Tanya, what are you doing? You can't be thinking about using scissors to hurt your own child or leaving her in the toilet to drown! You might as well be doing that to your own sister!'

"I know it sounds like this took a long time, but really, all this stuff kind of hit me all at once. So, I thought, 'Tanya Elizabeth, you have got to help your baby!'

"So, I sort of wiggled myself down from the toilet, but as I said, I felt dizzy, and there was all this blood coming out like it does each month, y'know? Oh, sorry, I don't mean to be gross. So, what happened, I sort of slid away from the toilet, and I was feeling really weak and horrible, but I thought, 'Tanya, come on! You can do this!'

"But then things started to get white like strobe lights, and I could hear footsteps on the stairs and then voices in the hall. I think it was Mom talking to Dolly, maybe. And I tried to call them, but I just felt so horrible. And I tried to get closer to get the poor baby and to call Mom, but the white lights got brighter, and –"

"Tanya, that must have been when you passed out!" I blurt out with a force that scares me. "Oh, I'm sorry, Mr. Allenbury. It won't happen again."

"Please see that it doesn't, Mrs. Gullickson. Proceed, Ms. Ritter."

"Well, that's really all I can remember. Oh, except that one more thing went through my mind. I had this image of my dog, Ralph – he passed away recently – go through my mind. And for some crazy reason, I had this thought, 'I bet if Ralph were here, he could help me get to Dolly – I mean, to the baby.' It's crazy, I know. The next thing I knew, I was in the ambulance. And then, well, you know the rest."

Pause.

"Mr. Allenbury, do you believe me?"

Chapter 58 Tanya

"There is the great lesson of 'Beauty and the Beast,' that a thing must be loved before it is lovable." — *G.K. Chesterton*

I'm free. At least, as far as the law's concerned.

When I finished giving my statement, Mr. Allenbury presented his report to the District Attorney with a recommendation that no charges be brought against me. The DA agreed. So, now I'm on my way home with Mom and David.

It all seems like a weird, horrible, surreal dream.

As we pull into the driveway, Dolly comes running out with David's sister-in-law, Sharona, dogging her heels.

"Sorry, guys, there was no stopping her!" Sharona laughs in the merry way she has. You'd never know she was widowed in her 40's when a heart attack took David's brother without warning. She's as sweet as pie and loves kids more than anything.

Now, there's a woman who deserved children.

"No worries, Sis," David smiles, scooping Dolly up in his arms and landing a big, sloppy kiss on her messy curls. "We can't thank you enough for watching this little lady. I don't know what we would have done if –"

"Now, none of that, Davey. I'm right where I wanted and needed to be. That's what family's for, isn't it? She even made a sign to welcome her big sister home."

She turns to me.

"I welcome you home, too, Tanya," she says awkwardly. Still, I think she means it.

Dolly breaks the tension.

"Tonna! Tonna! I missed you! Where *were* you?" she demands in a guilt-inducing tone. As if I don't feel guilty enough.

What should I say to her?

"Hey, little lady, let's give Tanya a chance to get settled," David answers for me. "Remember, she had some business to take care of. We're all glad to see you, though!"

So that's what they told her.

"But, Tonna," Dolly complains, "you were gone *so* long!"

She stretches out the "so" to make sure I know just how desperately she's been waiting.

"Oh, Dolly, I'm sorry," I choke out, not knowing what else to say. How can I ever explain this in a way she can understand?

It would help if I understood it myself.

Mom rescues me.

"Jessica, you made a sign for your sister? How sweet of you! Let's all go inside and see it right now!"

****

"Tanya, Honey, we're going to have to discuss your little daughter's future," Mom announces as we walk down the hall after putting Dolly to bed. She got a Bible story, a fairy tale, and two songs out of us tonight.

I'm not ready for this.

As if reading my mind, Mom says, "None of us feels quite ready to face it, but it's time, isn't it?"

She puts an arm around my shoulder. I turn and melt into her arms. The tears that have been dammed up all day burst forth.

326

"Mom, I'm s- s- sorry!" I stutter. "I shouldn't have... I mean, I wish I... I mean –"

"Now, none of that, Sweetheart," she says, sounding just like Sharona. She must be thinking the same thing, because she says, "Remember what Sharona said? That's what family's for."

I sob right here in the hallway until my chest hurts.

"Better?" Mom asks when I'm all cried out.

"I guess. A little. Not really," I reply. My voice sounds almost as hollow as I feel.

"OK, now, it's your choice. Do you want to have this conversation tonight, or wait till tomorrow? One more day isn't going to hurt."

Maybe one more day will hurt. I'm not sure I want to sleep with this on my conscience for one more night.

Tanya, you're gonna sleep with this on your conscience for the rest of your life.

"Let's do it now," I mutter, picking my finger.

"OK, if you're sure. Come on. Let's go find Dave. He and I have been talking and praying about this. A lot. I think you may like some of our ideas."

Chapter 59 Tanya

"The birth moms took responsibility to bring their daughters life and to do all they could to place them in a loving family with two committed parents. They have earned our respect and undying gratitude. They did not give their children away. They never owned the children. No one 'owns' children. Every child in every family belongs to God. We're just doing the parenting until they figure out how to serve God themselves." – Adoptive parents Paul and Cheryl Wilkinson

"So, Sweetheart, your little girl seems to be doing well," Mom begins after settling herself on the sofa next to David. "Dave and I went in to see and hold her several times while she was in the hospital, and you were… away. She's a tiny, little thing, but all pink and adorable – just like you were."

"Yeah, Tanya, the docs have been pretty pleased overall with the progress she's made," David adds. "They say she's hitting most of her milestones. Maybe some slight developmental delays, but they don't even seem too sure about that. Like, it may not even be an issue. We basically have to wait and see."

"So, you see, Honey, despite everything, God has been watching out for this precious baby. Oh, sorry, I didn't mean anything by that. I just, you know, well –"

"It's fine, Mom. I know what you meant."

Mom breathes a sigh of relief.

Have I really been that much of a monster that my own mother has to watch every word that comes out of her mouth?

"Well, anyway, she's being very well cared for by a lovely couple – the Genoveses. It's really quite a coincidence (if one believes in coincidence – I prefer the idea of divine intervention, myself). Anyway, Dave works with Ted. He and his wife, Linda, have fostered at least one child before, and actually reached out to us, through the hospital social worker, about fostering your little one.

"It seemed like a wise idea. We didn't feel prepared to handle anything except your situation and taking care of little Jessica. And Chuck indicated that his family wasn't in a position to care for her either, so…"

It's not that I tune her out, but reality suddenly sinks in the way it must have hit the passengers on the Titanic.

I'm a mother. I have the stretch marks and leaky bladder to prove it.

The only thing I don't have is a baby.

I've never even held my own daughter.

"Tanya, what do you think about what we've just told you? I mean, we had to make some decisions while you were… away, so…"

I wish she'd stop saying 'away.' I was in a detention center! We aren't talking about summer camp.

I decide not to correct her. She's been through a lot, too. If it makes her feel better to put her own spin on it, why burst her bubble?

"So, what's next?" I wonder aloud. "I mean, do we bring her home? Does Dolly get a little 'sister?'"

Mom studies her hands. David says nothing.

I guess I have my answer.

It isn't that I feel strongly about raising her. That may sound weird, even unnatural, but I spent most of my pregnancy trying to hide it and pretend it wasn't real. Once she was born, my whole focus became, a) what's going to happen to me? and, b) how am I going to live in this town, now that my story's all over the news media and the late-night talk shows? And, like I said, I've never even held her.

David joins the conversation.

"Tanya, here's the thing. There is a couple – the Genoveses, who your mom mentioned. They've expressed interest – actually, a huge desire – to adopt your baby. What would be your reaction to that?"

For some reason, I feel tears come. Not full-out water works, just tiny springs threatening to well over. Mom notices.

"Oh, Sweetheart, I know how you must feel."

No, she doesn't. She may know what it feels like to have an unplanned pregnancy, but she doesn't know what this feels like. To be painted as a criminal in the press. To not know her own child. To have no good options.

To wish she were dead.

"Tanya, this doesn't have to be decided today. Or even tomorrow," David says. "It's OK to take some time to heal. The Genoveses are enjoying your little girl and taking good care of her."

"That's right, Honey," Mom adds. "This is a big decision. We get that. And we love you."

330

I can't hold the tears back. They spill over.

Mom gets up and hands me a box of tissues from the table next to the couch. She sits down next to me on the arm of the chair and puts her arms around me.

She must really feel sorry for me. Otherwise, she would never sit on the arm of the chair!

"Thanks," I manage to say.

Maybe if I had something else to pay attention to, I could stop this awful blubbering.

I fix my eyes on Dolly's toy area in the gated off area of our living room. It's pretty messy, as usual. Mom's always trying to train Jess to put things away where they belong, but by the end of the day, she usually gives up and leaves it a wreck. Somehow, it always gets put back in order by the next morning – by the toy fairy, I guess.

I wish that fairy could do something about the wreck that's my life.

How's Jess gonna learn to clean up her own messes if her parents always do it for her?

Tanya, that's the first maternal thing you've ever said.

"OK, let's talk to the Genoveses," I say with a decisiveness I don't really feel. "It can't hurt to talk."

Chapter 60 Chuck

"Fathers, do not provoke your children to anger, but bring them up in the discipline and instruction of the Lord." – Ephesians 6:4, the Bible, English Standard Version

"How could I have let this happen? I mean, I just can't believe this is actually *my* life!" I whine to my father on one of our rare visits. I would cry if I could find a way to justify it, but I feel emasculated enough as it is. I don't dare allow even the tiniest teardrop to fall from my eye. Especially not in front of him.

My parents' divorce is proceeding slowly and painfully. They're fighting over everything from child custody to whose turn it is to buy underwear for my little brothers.

I'm brutally aware that my mistakes are making it that much harder for everyone. There's a sickening sort of notoriety in my situation. Even though Tanya's been exonerated, it's been in the news. I can't go anywhere without being recognized. Reporters stalk me and stick microphones in my face for sound bites to raise their ratings. And God knows what poor Tanya's going through. I bet, like me, she wishes she could jump out of her skin and be somebody else. Anybody else.

"I know, Son," Dad answers, then seems at a loss for words.

We sit there for a minute in awkward silence. Then he comes out with, "Well, thank God, at least you're not responsible."

I stare at him, dumbfounded. A wave of anger washes over me. Is this not Charlie Hammerschmidt, the man who always modeled responsibility, to the point of working multiple jobs so he could sign all of us up for baseball and swim lessons? Isn't this the guy who made me take back the chocolate bar I stole from the drug store when I was four? The cashier tried to blow it off, make light of my "light fingers," but Dad wouldn't have it. He made me return the candy, apologize, and pick up trash from the store floor as a sort of penance.

And now here we stand, with him trying to absolve me from blame over a life and death issue that has my newborn daughter in the custody of strangers.

"Not responsible? I'm not *responsible*? Dad, I made a baby! Your son made a *baby*! And because it wasn't convenient and I felt overwhelmed, I left the mother of my daughter hangin' out to dry because I was too lame to make a decision! Not responsible? Are you kidding me!"

Charlie looks mortified. Good.

A couple times he opens his mouth, but nothing comes out. Finally, he says, "Look, Son, I'm sorry. Sorry for saying the wrong thing, and sorry for the divorce. I know it's been hard on you. I guess if anyone's responsible, it's me, 'cause I just haven't been there for you lately. I've been all mixed up in this mess with your mother."

I explode.

"You leave her out of this! How dare you bring her into this! She's not the one who wants this divorce! If you hadn't gotten 'tired of being married' – no, what was it you said? Oh, yeah, if you hadn't felt 'trapped,' we'd still be a family. She'd still be home taking care of your children instead of working herself to death to keep our house and pay a lawyer!

"Y'know what – I'm outta here!"

I storm out of Charlie's rented room and into my Monte Carlo, where my rage can have free reign, and no one can judge me for the sobs that make my shoulders shake and my lip quiver and my grief unbearable.

Chapter 61 Ted

"For this child I prayed, and the Lord has granted me my petition which I made to Him." – 1 Samuel 1:27, the Bible, English Standard Version

"Know what we're gonna call you?" Linda coos to the baby sleeping in her arms. "Serena René. Y'know why? 'Cause 'Serena' means 'serenity' and 'René' means 'reborn'. You've given us both of those things, and we're gonna try to give them to you."

Serena makes a little noise which I can just barely hear, but Linda hears it and presses the baby to her chest. She pats Serena's tiny back with the velvety fingers of a mother in love.

"You have a brand, new life with your daddy and me, Serena. Hey, maybe we'll nickname you 'Reenie.' What do you think of that?

"We've waited a really long time to become parents, Reenie. No, I'm not sure I like that. Serena's such a beautiful name, it's a shame to shorten it.

"I hope you like your name. My sister, Emma – she's your auntie – suggested it. She said she once knew a lady who called her daughter 'Serena,' and that lady had a lot of serenity. I hope the same can be said of your daddy and me."

Serena lets out a belch that could bring down the heavens. Linda laughs and continues cooing sweet syllables to her.

"This is new for us, Serena, so you'll have to be patient with us. Daddy's holding back a little piece of his heart, but don't you worry – I know what he looks like when he's in love, and it's starting to happen.

"Your birth mom's gonna be alright, too. I met her and your grandparents. They're all really nice people.

"And don't you worry about what you may hear later in life about your birth mommy. Some mean people may try to tell you she tried to hurt you, but I don't believe it. Your mama never meant to hurt you; she just didn't know what to do. She was young and scared and felt very alone. But she doesn't have to be alone anymore. She has a family who loves her, and that includes you, Daddy and me!"

The baby notices me over Linda's shoulder. A big, toothless smile crosses her fist-sized face.

My heart does a little dance before I can reign it in.

It's happening again – I can feel it. My wife's bonding with this baby, and the parents' rights haven't even been severed yet. We're doing what's known as an "at risk" placement, and we've been here before. The baby is placed in our home, awaiting the severing of parental rights. It takes about a year before the whole process is finalized, at which point the birth parents can no longer take back their kid.

They call it an "interruption" when the birth parents change their minds and yank their baby back from you. Hundreds of diapers and dollars later, and they call it an interruption. The term doesn't even make sense. When you get interrupted in a conversation, it's rude, but not final. I mean, you go back to what you were saying after the offender shuts up. When your adoption gets interrupted, it's over.

This is far from a sure thing.

The birth dad, Chuck, is on board with us adopting the baby, and all the grandparents are. The mother, Tanya, says she is, but I read a lot of ambivalence that Linda just doesn't want to see. Who's to say this won't go sour like the others did?

And let's not forget how things turned out with Danny. His dad said a few right words to the powers that be, kept a few appointments, and they sent that poor kid right back to the druggie family that left his broken body shaking off withdrawal symptoms before he was old enough to spit up.

Funny how you never hear about Hollywood couples getting their hearts broken like this. They never seem to have to go through this kind of nonsense trying to adopt. They can have 15 marriages behind them and 12 stints in rehab, but there are always plenty of newborn American babies to go around for them.

Yet, the agencies swear money and prestige have nothing to do with it.

I'm so torn this time. Yeah, the baby's adorable, and doing pretty well, despite how she started off life. She takes a bottle like a champ and isn't fussy like Danny was. The docs say it's amazing, given the fact that we're not sure how long she was underwater before the grandparents got there and pulled her out.

I want to want this baby, little Serena. I want so much to be on board with it, to feel the kind of tranquility the name implies and that Linda obviously feels. I want my wife to have her heart's

337

desire, and I do want to be a dad. But the "eyes wide open" part of me still realizes there could be an awfully long road and plenty of heartache with this one.

Linda's so in love, she doesn't even realize I'm standing in the doorway watching her. I pull myself away from my reservations and break into her moment.

"Serena, that's a good name for her, and so much better than Cassie!" I joke, referring to the name we always said we'd use for a daughter.

"Oh, Honey, isn't it beautiful? And the René part is so fitting, don't you think?"

I wrestle with myself. Should I shatter her fantasy and remind her what can and likely will happen? Or should I go along with her optimism even though I'm so torn?

I guess I'm a coward, because I wrap my arms around the two of them and say, "Yeah, Lin. That's what it is. Fitting."

Chapter 62 David

"I am only one, but I am one. I cannot do everything, but I can do something. And I will not let what I cannot do interfere with what I can do." – Edward Everett Hale

"Hey, Chuck?"

"Yeah?"

He sounds guarded. I guess the reporters haven't been leaving him alone, either.

"Hey, it's Dave. Dave Gullickson. Tanya's stepdad. Hope you don't mind me calling. Mary, er, Tanya's mom, gave me your number."

Chuck replies after a short silence.

"Nah, it's fine. How is she?"

"Well, I guess she's as well as can be expected. We're takin' it one day at a time, y'know?"

"Yeah. Well, that's good I guess."

After a short pause, he says, "What can I do for you?"

Good question, I think. *I wish I had a good answer.*

The weirdness is palpable. I can tell he's as uncomfortable as I am. The trouble is, I never really got to know Chuck. Most of the time Tanya was dating him, she was playing the independence card, refusing to bring him around. Small talk isn't my strong suit under the best of circumstances; in this situation, it's next to impossible.

I'm not even sure what I'm trying to accomplish. Tanya and Chuck's relationship is history. The baby's being taken care of by a

339

great couple that wants to adopt her. All the loose ends – for Chuck, at least – are tied up.

But Mary wanted me to contact him. Once things settled down after the initial shock, she started to worry about him as well as Tanya. It really surprised me, since he has to take **fifty percent** of the blame for all that's happened. Mary's career must have her wired to consider both parties in an unplanned pregnancy. Still, I admire the fact that she can be so objective.

Anyway, she just blurted out one day, "Dave, how would you feel about getting in touch with him? That young man needs someone like you to talk to."

I don't mind telling you I was taken aback. Mary sensed my hesitation but persisted.

"Dave, remember how he was the night everything happened? He seemed so alone. Remember how no one came to be with him? It was like he was all alone in the world."

I dug through my blurred memories of the night Tanya delivered, and realized Mary was right. I vaguely remember putting my hand on the kid's shoulder for a minute, but then had to quickly turn my attention to making things as normal as possible for Jess, not to mention supporting Mary. Chuck sort of got lost in the shuffle.

My wife was also right that no one came to help the poor kid through what had to be the worst moment of his life. When the cops finally finished questioning him, he went home alone.

"I hear you, Mar, but doesn't this kid have his own parents? I mean, wouldn't it be kind of strange if I just called him up out of the blue and said, 'Hey, let's do lunch'?"

"I don't know, Dave. I just know that boy needs a friend."

Leave it to Mary and her maternal instincts. She can't pass a stray cat without wanting to take it home, microchip it, and call it her own. I just can't believe her compassion extends to a guy who got our daughter pregnant and whose indecisiveness led to this whole mess. Still, this is typical Mary, and I trust her gut. I agreed to make the call.

"Well, uh, I was talking to my wife, uh, and we were wondering if …"

I wish I could erase the half sentence that just came out of my mouth and start over. I decide to try.

"What I mean is, could ya use a cup of coffee?"

Chapter 63 Tanya

"At a time like this, scorching irony, not convincing argument, is needed." – Frederick Douglass

I'm surprised to see Pastor Kaplan and his wife when I open the door.

"Oh, hi," I say without enthusiasm.

Where have you been the last few months when I could've used a friend?

"Hi, Tanya. Would it be OK if we came in for a few minutes?"

"Tanya, Honey, who's at the door?" Mom calls from the kitchen.

"Pastor Kaplan and Vicki!" I yell over the racket Dolly's making in her corner of the living room. "Hey, Jess, couldja keep it down?"

"OK, Tonna," she replies, then continues on at the same decibel level.

"Seriously, Dolly, lower the volume. We have company."

She smiles impishly, but things do get a bit quieter. Mom enters the room, drying her hands on her apron.

"Well, Seth, Vicki, to what do we owe the pleasure? How are you? Where are the kids?"

There's an edge to Mom's voice. She's annoyed with them, too, but trying not to show it.

"Oh, hi, Mary. Everyone's fine. Vicki's mom's with the kids. Thanks for asking."

Awkward silence.

"Well, Vicki and I were just talking the other day, weren't we, Hon, and we realized we haven't seen much of you guys lately, so we thought we'd drop by."

"Yes, that's right. We've missed you folks!" Vicki says.

Mom stares at them – hard. I know that look. It's the "I'm angry but trying to be a Christian" look. But she overcomes her meaner instincts and asks them to sit down.

I've gotta give Pastor K. credit. Once they're settled in chairs, he quits trying to avoid the obvious, and jumps in to face the music.

"Listen, both of you. Can we start over again? We all know I should've been here much sooner. So should our senior staff. I can't answer for them. I can only speak for myself."

Mom, sensing this isn't gonna be a conversation for young ears, calls to David.

"Excuse me for a minute, Seth. Dave, could you come in here for a minute?"

After a minute, David comes to the top of the stairs.

"What's up, Hon?"

"Sweetie, would you mind taking Jessica upstairs or outside for a bit?" she whispers conspiratorially.

Dolly moans about having to leave her play area, but in the end, David coaxes her away.

Pastor K. continues.

"Good idea. Thanks, Mary. I don't know where my head is!

"Anyway, as I was getting ready to say, quite honestly, I'm ashamed. I could give you lots of explanations about how busy I am and how hard it is trying to juggle ministerial duties with family responsibilities, but that's basically a crock. I mean, we're all busy. But, in all honesty, I feel like I've failed in my relationship with this family – with you, Tanya, in particular.

"All I can say is, I'm sorry. And I hope you can forgive me."

Vicki beams at her husband, then adds her two cents.

"Yes, and I'd like to apologize, too. I should've reached out to Tanya months ago. The fact that I've let it go this long isn't right."

I'm not sure what to say. Part of me is enjoying seeing them crawl, but another part of me feels bad that they feel bad.

Maybe there's hope for you after all, Tanya.

While I sit there picking at some skin on my thumb, Mom says warmly, "Well, that's awfully nice of both of you. We appreciate it."

One thing about her – she doesn't hold grudges.

Lucky for me.

"That said," Pastor K. adds, "we really would like to start over, in every way. I'd like to know how we as a church, and I, in particular, can be of help. I'll share our conversation with the other ministers, and maybe we can try to come alongside you and walk with you through… everything.

"And, Vicki, Honey, I think you had an idea, too, didn't you?"

Before she can answer, I find my voice.

344

"Pastor K., I really can't see myself coming back to youth group. First of all, I'm ready for college, and now –"

"Oh, listen, Tanya, no argument there!" he agrees. "Besides which, I know there's probably a lot of dust still to settle, and you may want to ease yourself back into things. That's totally fine, and very understandable.

"Actually, though, there's a reason Vicki's here. Besides the fact that we come as a set! No, seriously, go ahead, Hon."

Vicki has never been real talkative, but she takes a deep breath and dives in. I literally feel like I'm watching her drag herself out of her comfort zone.

"Well, you see, Tanya, Seth's right. This is hard for me, so bear with me. I know this has been a really hard time for you – for all of you. So, I thought, maybe my experience could be, I don't know, helpful, in some way."

She looks at her husband. He smiles and nods at her to continue.

"Well, you see, Mary, Tanya, I had an abortion when I was in college. Before I met Seth. I was a Christian, but I guess I let my faith take a back seat to… other things.

"Anyway, this isn't the time to go into the whole story, and I know your story's different from mine, but there are also some similarities. So, I thought maybe you and I, Tanya, could get together once a week or so, and talk. Seth gets home early on Tuesday nights, and he puts the kids to bed that night anyway, so you and I could meet after dinner. If that works for you, I mean."

Mom's doing a good job of not looking shocked, but I have to pick my jaw up off the floor.

Finally, I say, "OK. Yeah. I guess so."

****

"Hi, Tanya," Vicki says when she opens the door for me.

The sound of childish chatter floats down from the second floor.

"I'm glad you could come. Here, let's go into Seth's office so we won't hear him and the kids. Would you like something to drink?"

"Sure. What do you have?"

She gives me the drink options and returns with my soda. I seat myself in Pastor K.'s office, which is cramped but comfortable.

"Well, Tanya, you know conversation isn't my strong suit. But we're here for a reason. So, how 'bout we pray and see where God takes this?"

Without waiting for me to answer, she launches into a quick prayer asking God to bless our time together, care for us and our families, and give both of us guidance on our journeys.

She closes with, "In Jesus' name, amen," then looks at me expectantly. When I don't take the hint, she asks, "Well, what would you like to know?"

OK, I guess this is how this is gonna go.

"Well, I guess if you don't mind sharing some of your story with me, that would be great. I mean, I sort of thought I was the only person in church who, y'know, got pregnant, y'know, without being married. And then, to think about abortion, well, that went

346

against everything I was ever taught. I felt so, I don't know, torn, I guess. I mean, my mom was and is all about life, but in school and talking to the lady at the family planning clinic and looking at their website, I learned a lot of other things that sort of went against those beliefs. That's one of the reasons I couldn't bring myself to tell my mom when I, y'know, found out."

"Yeah, Tanya, I get that. Let me first say, there are more of us than you think. Sadly, there's a pretty large number of Christians who find themselves in this position. A lot more than you might expect.

"Well, like I said, I was in college, dating this guy. He and I were both Christians; in fact, we met at church. But somehow, we talked ourselves into thinking what we were doing was OK. We talked about marriage, and it just seemed alright.

"When I found out I was pregnant, I couldn't believe it. He and I talked, and it was obvious he hadn't really meant what he said about marriage, so…"

I nod. She speaks haltingly. I can tell this is painful for her, so I decide not to ask any more questions.

"Wow," I say. "That's, um, that's…"

What should I say?

"Well, Tanya, I could give you a lot more details, but I try not to delve too deeply into those memories anymore, if you know what I mean. What I did want to share, though, was how I got help for the tremendous guilt that came afterwards.

"You see, I was afraid to tell anyone I was close to. I kept it a big, dark secret for many years. My parents still don't know, and I

347

may never tell them. They would probably understand, as I imagine your parents do about your situation – you have such a great family – but I still carry a lot of shame about the whole thing, and it goes against everything they, *and I, for that matter,* believe in.

"Anyway, one day the guilt was so unbearable that I started looking for help on the computer. I came across a group called 'Surrendering the Secret.' Have you heard of it?"

I shake my head.

"That's OK. I hadn't, either. Well, it's an eight-week support group and Bible study to help women heal from past abortions."

But I didn't have an abortion. And I'm not really into the Bible anymore.

She reads my mind, or my face, or both.

"Tanya, I know your situation is different, but I thought this might speak somewhat to what you've been through or may go through.

"If it's not too difficult to discuss, do you mind if I ask, how is your baby doing, and what are your plans for his or her future?"

She doesn't even know I had a girl. She must not read the papers.

Tanya, this woman is trying to help you. Don't be so critical!

This is the first time I've put it into words with anyone except Mom and David. Who knew it would be this tough to say out loud?

"No, that's OK, I don't mind. It's just, I mean, it's a bit hard to, y'know, discuss."

"Take your time," she smiles. She has a small gap between her two front teeth, which suddenly makes me feel less awkward about the zits on my face and the way my thighs spread over the chair like an oil spill. "And only share what's comfortable for you."

"Well, uh, I have a daughter. Her name is Serena. Serena René. She's going to be adopted by a couple named Linda and Ted. They, I mean, the man, works with my stepdad. Well, I guess I can call him my dad now. He's gonna adopt me."

The irony hits me for the first time. Two adoptions in one family. Two completely different sets of circumstances, but both done out of love.

I know David's motivated by love, but will Serena believe I love her?

"Oh, that's wonderful, Tanya!"

"Yeah. He's a good guy. Anyway, with Serena, we're gonna do what's called an open adoption, so I can stay in touch with them and have visits, stuff like that."

Suddenly, I feel sad. A FOMO kind of sad. The way you feel at the end of the summer, when school's about to start, and you realize you didn't do half the things you wanted to with all your free time, and now it's too late. That time is gone forever.

I thought when I signed the papers that it was the right thing to do. Chuck and I talked with our parents, and we agreed this was the best way. He wasn't on board at first, but when he realized he

349

really couldn't raise Serena at this point in his life, he signed the consent forms, too.

If it's the right thing to do, why do I suddenly feel this aching loss?

"Tanya, can I get you a tissue?" Vicki asks gently. I realize tears are rolling down my cheeks.

I nod.

As she hands me the box, she says, "Tanya, I'm sorry to have stirred things up for you. Should we stop for tonight?"

Yes. No. I don't know.

After I blow my nose, I say, "I guess we can keep going. But I don't get this. I don't get why I feel so upset. And I don't see how your program could help me. I didn't, y'know, I mean, I don't really fit into that group, right? I didn't do what you did. Not trying to be mean. I'm just trying to understand."

Vicki smiles, revealing her gap again.

"No worries. I know what you mean. No, you don't fit the picture exactly, and thank goodness you don't! But perhaps what you're feeling is some of the same kind of loss. Perhaps you feel you'll be judged harshly for your decision, even though you're trying to do what's best for Serena."

"Yeah, I am worried about that! I mean, what if she hears stories down the road about the way she got born and thinks, y'know, I tried to hurt her? And what if she doesn't get why I'm giving her up?"

I taste salt as tears trickle into my mouth.

"Oh, Tanya, you aren't giving her up!" she sniffs. "You're placing her for adoption with a family who wants her very badly and is in a good position to raise her. You're sharing the best gift you have to offer!"

I can tell she needs the tissues because of the catch in her voice.

We're quite a pair.

"Thanks, Tanya. I'm getting emotional, I guess. But for all the right reasons.

"Look, our stories may be different, but I wonder if some of the materials from 'Surrendering the Secret' could help with some of the feelings you're expressing. I'm not talking about taking you to a group of people you don't know. I'm thinking one on one with me. And there's no obligation. The help is here *if* you want it, *when* you want it.

"What do you think?"

I take another tissue and say, "Yeah. I guess. Why not?"

****

Walking out to the car, I notice the humidity has backed off, and the storm that was threatening seems to have subsided. The gray clouds have parted and made way for a blanket of stars. I can smell fall in the air. It won't be long till I need a sweater.

Acknowledgement

I would like to gratefully acknowledge the following groups and individuals:

my parents, who fanned my interest as a writer, provided the inspiration for the marriages portrayed in *Belabored*, and supported my children and me during the most difficult period of our lives;

my siblings, both biological and through marriage, who served as unending sources of love, encouragement and constructive criticism in my life and the development of this book;

my children, who let me grow up with them into a mom I hope they can always be proud of;

my grandchildren; it is for them and their futures that I have written this book;

my church family, whose prayers, gentle reminders and inquiries about the progress of my book moved me out of inertia and into publication;

various friends and family members who trudged valiantly through early drafts of *Belabored*, offering loving feedback and suggestions which vastly improved subsequent drafts and helped me tie up loose ends;

several physicians who wish to remain anonymous; these practitioners graciously shared their medical expertise so the health conditions described in *Belabored* would be depicted accurately;

John Williamson, Esq., leader of the Pro-Life Union of Delaware County and founder and host of the Pro-Life America Radio podcast (prolifeamericaradio.com); John provided legal advice prior to the publication of *Belabored*;

the Pennsylvania Family Institute, to which I reached out for legal advice; they connected me with a legal expert who didn't wish to be acknowledged, deeming such recognition "an undeserved honor";

Karen Hess, former Executive Director of AlphaCare Pregnancy Center, Melanie Parks, Executive Director of Amnion Pregnancy Center, and Louann Rodgers, President of the Board of Directors of Amnion, who answered my questions about their work and allowed me to tour their facilities, so that the vital work of crisis pregnancy centers could be brought to light in *Belabored*;

Mary Kellett, Founder and Director of Prenatal Partners for Life, whose story inspired chapter 33 of *Belabored*, and whose input and website contributed vastly to the authenticity of Emma and Tom's journey towards acceptance;

Abby Johnson, whose story appears with permission in chapter 35;

Cindy Speltz and her daughter, Jennifer Maas, who kindly allowed me to share their story in chapter 37;

Joni Eareckson Tada, whose story appears with permission in chapter 48;

Becky Lazo, who shared her vast experience in the publishing industry with me, and also proofread my book proposal. Becky's knowledge of the publishing industry helped me navigate a world I don't understand (Becky cut through eight pages of fair use and copyrighting questions that had been worrying me for over a year – all in one 20-minute phone conversation);

Ed and Gina Brocklesby and Paul and Cheryl Wilkinson, who built their families through adoption; these couples shared the joys and heartaches of their stories with me, so that the adoption process could be realistically depicted in *Belabored*;

countless fellow authors, including Mary Dolan Flaherty, Rhonda B. Gaines, Dianne E. Butts, Jeanette Levellie, and Robert Cook, who offered gentle advice and wise suggestions about the manuscript and publishing process;

fellow author Megan Breedlove and her husband, Phil. Meg has been a cheerleader for me since I first met her at a writers' conference years ago; Phil (who has never even met me) gave me technical advice over the phone to try to retrieve a deleted version of *Belabored*;

various individuals who prefer not to be named publicly, but whose experiences have a direct bearing on the subject matter in *Belabored*; their stories provided crucial elements and quotations for the book;

and, above all, my Lord and Savior Jesus Christ, without whom neither this book nor this servant would amount to anything.

Praise For Author

"Real people with complicated lives are the ones who wrestle with abortion decisions. The challenges and victories and their ripple effects come alive through this compelling novel."

Karen Hess, Former Executive Director, AlphaCare Pregnancy Center, Philadelphia, PA

"Belabored unapologetically tackles controversial and sensitive topics relating to the sanctity of life in an informative, yet highly readable format. Williams' characters are steadfast and unwavering, yet relatable and authentic. The author's voice shines through each one. A must read for today's shifting times."

Mary Dolan Flaherty, Author,
Spectacles of Hope: Defeating Your Shouldas, Wouldas, and Couldas

"Simply put, Thea Williams is masterful in *Belabored* by weaving a realistic story of women facing the complexities and struggles of self-awareness in their Christian faith, while making life-changing decisions on abortion, adoption, and selective reduction. Their journey is complicated, challenging and heartwarming, while evoking an emotional connection from the reader of empathy, courage, and forgiveness. It is a 'must read' for those of us who need a reminder of the true purpose of life as we seek love, acceptance, and security within our faith, careers, and family. It touches the human spirit on so many levels! Well worth reading!"

Rhonda B. Gaines, Author,
Power of the Boardroom: Redefining Life's Priorities – One Woman's Memoir